Effective Consultation With The LIFO® Method

Effective Consultation With The LIFO® Method

Allan Katcher Ph.D.

Gerrit Knodt Ph.D.

Betty Forbis

With:

René Bergermaier
Reiner Czichos
Alfred V. DeLeo
Willie Donald
Roger Harris
Shirley Murray
Marijke Theunis
Linda Wiens
Gem Brion Zabala

ISBN: 1508925658
ISBN 13: 9781508925651
Library of Congress Control Number: 2015904320
CreateSpace Independent Publishing Platform
North Charleston, South Carolina

TABLE OF CONTENTS

ACKNOWLEDGEMENTS

I am deeply indebted to the Business Consultants, Inc. (BCon) organization members, especially two former CEOS, Yoshida-san and Saito-san. I am also appreciative of the support that the current CEO, Tetsuji Yokozeki, and members of BCon have provided, and for their permission to publish some of the content.

Stuart Atkins has been not only a founder of The LIFO® Method but also a source of inspiration and enlightenment as well. We owe him considerably for his contributions and publications.

Many additional valuable and enriching contributions have been made by the LIFO® agents and licensees around the world. You will find some of their contributions in this book. However, there are thousands more who are training and consulting every day. We regret that we couldn't have articles from all of them.

Gerrit's wife, Bernadette, and mine, Gloria, read some of the chapters and reviewed them, making suggestions. We acknowledge their efforts and inspiration.

The organization, editing and suggestions for new chapters was the result of outstanding editing done by Nancy Marriott of New Paradigm Writing and Editing Services, who added sensible suggestions as well as attending to the wording and phrasing that was originally written. We are especially thankful and proud to have enlisted her assistance in this effort.

Finally, we want to thank Ethan Schutz and his staff for their encouragement and review of this book. Marcia Johnson has been helpful with many stimulating remarks and luncheon discussions; Jerry Miller for help in checking legal issues.

FOREWORD

There are several key influences, both from people with diverse backgrounds and from fields of study, that have come together over the years to create The LIFO® Method.

My (Allan Katcher) background includes a mixture of undergraduate training in experimental physiological psychology, enrollment in a special master's program that featured exposure to organismic psychology, psychoanalytic and Rorschach theories, and practice in projective test usage. At the time, when I was studying for my master's degree, I had the experience of working as a psychology instructor at Brooklyn College. I later went on to earn a doctorate at the University of California at Berkeley, where I completed a study of children's perceptions of genital identity.

The contrast of thinking from my early training to the world of Gestalt psychology and clinical thinking was both challenging and stimulating. I was struggling to see how experts like Bruno Klopfer, Ruth Munroe, and Ernst Kris developed their insights, and translated them into comprehensive and valid descriptions of behavior. It took quite a few years of practice to develop some of the skills I had witnessed. This training that emphasized the use of clinical intuition influenced my ability to make valid LIFO® interpretations from score profiles.

After receiving my doctorate from UC Berkeley, I taught for five years at the University of Washington: introductory psychology, child and adolescent psychology, personality, and a graduate seminar on psychoanalytic theory. At the end of that time, I was approached by Elias Porter, concerning a position with The RAND Corporation's System Development Project. The project later became a non-profit company, called the System Development Corporation

Working at the System Development Corporation helped me to gain practice in dealing with all kinds of working groups—from those directed by lieutenants to those by generals. We were engaged in the unique task of simulating the air defense environment, conducting "battles" involving the defense by single radar site units to complete national defense situations. I was fortunate to be involved with developing the training programs for debriefing leaders to facilitate group problem solving. Using video feedback, we were able to develop behavior changes in leaders that led to measurable improvements in their behavior that facilitated group problem solving.

Later, when Stuart Atkins and I were developing The LIFO® Method, I began to see that what we were doing in our debriefing training made sense, considering the congruence measures involved in the LIFO® Life Orientation Survey. The basic training model in the defense work was to determine what the leader wanted to achieve in his meeting, measure what happened, and then see what needed to be changed to realize what was desired.

The next major influence after my work at the System Development Corporation came about when I met and became involved with Stuart Atkins in developing a consulting practice. Stuart had a lot of practical experience that sharpened my skills, and we enjoyed sharing our various skills in joint training and consulting projects.

Elias Porter, an old colleague from System Development Corporation, called one day to see if we would like to be involved with him in developing some training tools. He introduced us to the writings and ideas of Eric Fromm.

Atkins and Porter developed the basic framework for The LIFO® Method. I became more involved as we started to develop the LIFO® Life Orientations survey and began to interpret profiles, writing the first versions of the training program book and conducting training programs to license professionals to use the instrument. We became fascinated by the richness of descriptions that could be provided from LIFO® profiles and the applications of strategies that could be used in coaching to help people change their behavior.

After many experiences, shadings and nuances were observed that changed the interpretive meanings and therefore modified the original conceptions. However, as we became involved in international applications, the applicability and validity of the main concepts appeared to be universal.

As a result of examining people's descriptions of how behavior changed radically under different situations and roles, I began to develop other surveys that took these factors into account. Others in the growing agent network helped to broaden the inventory, so the original Life Orientation Survey (revised to sharpen the focus on the Intention-Behavior-Impact model) was complemented by surveys such as: learning styles, teaching styles, selling styles, customer styles, leadership styles, coaching styles, etc. Kenneth Finn and my son Andrew helped devise the first computer report program for LIFO® interpretations, further developed by Stuart Atkins, Inc. and Business Consultants, Inc.

Subsequently, Stuart and I decided to separate and divide the areas of responsibility so that he directed the U.S. market and I took the international one. Many years later, Business Consultants, Inc. purchased the international business, then the U.S. business, and also The Human Elements business. Finally, the management of the domestic and international LIFO® business was assumed by The Schutz Company.

CO-AUTHORS AND CONTRIBUTORS

Betty Forbis. It was more than 20 years ago that I met Betty and her colleague Greg Metzler. They had asked me to provide training in the LIFO® methodology for them. We spent considerable time, not only in the original training program but also in discussions and reviews over the next few years. In addition, Betty invited me to participate in her proprietary management course, The Experience Compression Laboratory. This particular session was held in Norway. I was utterly fascinated by the poignant experiences this program provided for me and admired the unique skills exhibited by Betty and her staff to achieve such outstanding changes in insights and performance. Subsequently, I was invited to join the training group, and the time spent in collaborating and training with them became peak learning experiences for me.

Betty's ability to write individual and group interpretations of LIFO® profiles is outstanding. I felt that she wrote the best ones I have ever seen, using her SG and AD styles to create "novels" about the person and group who had taken the survey. They provided a very unique description that went beyond the obvious to provide depth of understanding that was appreciated by the person who received the report, often accompanied by coaching. During the last few years, Betty wrote a Human Resources Guide for LIFO® trainers that had very rich material. When I read it, I felt it should be incorporated into this book and invited her to join us in our efforts. I was delighted when she accepted the invitation to join us in our efforts as one of the editors.

Gerrit Knodt was one of the professionals involved in a Citibank LIFO® Licensee certification program. In that program and in many subsequent meetings, I found his enthusiasm, energy and vision to be very stimulating. We fell easily into rich discussions of many topics concerning individual and organizational development. We shared not only ideas but personal experiences as well and became intimate friends. Fortunately, he also had a wife, Bernadette, who was equally brilliant and ideational, so it became a special treat to be able to visit them. We have become strong friends over the years. I was also delighted when he agreed to become one of the co-authors.

Our other contributors represent both LIFO® agencies and LIFO® licensees:

René Bergermaier has more than 30 years of human resource experience, mainly with IT utilities and automotive companies. Before LPC, he founded HRC together with Dr. Ingwer Borg, and has worked extensively with HRC in all aspects of organizational surveys, as well as having personally handled major accounts for the firm. Before that, he worked at Digital Equipment for seven years as head of the human resource department at Motorola. He has become a source for stimulation and a treasured friend.

Reiner Czichos' participation resulted from both experiences where he contributed a great deal to German conferences on LIFO® training and from co-authoring our book on *Learning Dynamics*. He has a wealth of experience in LIFO® training and consulting, creatively designing special programs and exercises for his clients. It has been a joy to collaborate with him.

Al De Leo, a LIFO® licensee, has been a consultant for many years and has worked with international organizations as well as national ones. He has a delightful, charming style that makes it easy to like him and appreciate his ideas. We once began working on a consulting book but abandoned it. However, he then wrote an engaging book on consulting that was published a year ago entitled *The Perils and Joys of Consulting*.

I met **Willie Donald** at an advanced LIFO® training group in London. He evidenced considerable skill and knowledge in using

LIFO® concepts, so I was happy when he volunteered to write an article for this book.

Roger Harris is an American consultant living in Seattle with lots of training experience and major consulting assignments. He attended several LIFO® advanced training conferences, constantly interested in learning as much as possible as he could about the subject. I recently had the pleasure of having a lengthy breakfast with him at the May, 2014, meeting of LIFO® International users and was amazed at the depth of insight he showed about working with highly technical people.

Shirley Murray was working at Toys R Us in Canada when she first joined the LIFO® community. She has been innovative in her use of the methodology and experimented with many uses. Over time, she has become another of the treasured friends that I made while involved in LIFO® training. Her lively and engaging manner invites people to open up and share experiences.

I met **Marijke Theunis** many years ago at a meeting arranged by Jan De Jong, our Dutch agent. An experienced, dedicated, and enthusiastic LIFO® practitioner, she has many years of experience as a coach and consultant. We were pleased that she decided to write an article based on her coaching experiences.

Linda Wiens, has been a friend for many years. I first got to know her and her colleague, Cliff McIntosh, who became the first Canadian LIFO® agents. I spent several summer weeks visiting them at their conference center at Quetico Lake. In a spectacularly scenic locale, we had many sessions that were provocative and powerful learning sessions for me. Indeed, Linda was responsible for stimulating my efforts to create the LIFO® Learning and Teaching style surveys.

Gem Brion Zabala, our intense and highly productive agent in The Philippines, provided me with guided tours of Manila and Corregidor as well as opportunities to meet interested students, trainers, and high-level managers. She has joined our contributors with a delightful article about the Filipino culture and suggestions for how a consultant should expect to adapt techniques peculiar to a culture, different from their own, for effective consultation to take place.

Part One

ABOUT THE LIFO® METHOD

Chapter I

INTRODUCTION

As a consultant, do your clients ever ask you such questions as:

- *Why do you think my executive team can't seem to get along with each other? There's so much discord, yet I've hired the best MBAs you could hope to find?*
- *How can I make sure that our new VP will be compatible with rest of the executive team?*
- *How can I find a new secretary who will work well with me?*
- *How can I stop the conflict between manufacturing and quality control without firing the two managers?*
- *How can I put together a productive team to develop our newest project?*
- *How can our manager of R&D, who is extremely knowledgeable and well organized, learn how to manage his team more effectively?*
- *How can I improve my communications with the VP of Operations, so I can make sure he fully understands me?*
- *What would be the best way to announce new changes to the way we will operate the company in the future?*
- *How can we know whether our ads are reaching the right customers?*

This book will help you to answer such questions and also to implement effective programs for changes that are required to achieve desired changes. It is based on concepts and methods called *The LIFO® Method*. In this book, we will describe the basic components and applications of The LIFO® Method that licensed users and country agents have devised to help you answer these kinds of questions.

VALUE OF LIFO® EXPERIENCES

We began this book wanting to provide a professional treatment of the many subjects and then stopped to take a look at what we had written. It seemed as if we were trying to let our colleagues know the full measure of what we had learned instead of the fun and excitement that people experience when they are in our courses, seminars and workshops. So we decided to shift gears a bit and reveal how people respond to LIFO® seminars and workshops.

"Wow," said one participant, "How did you get all of that information about me from just 72 questions?" Another said, "I found it awe inspiring to realize that some of my faults really reflected strengths that I over-use!" A third, "It was mind-blowing for me to realize that my boss needs to have proposals offered in a highly organized and detailed form when I like to share the spontaneous inspirations I have from new ideas. I realize now that I have to alter things a bit when I am enthused about something new if I want to get his approval and support."

Some other experiences are reported in the following statements: "It seemed so simple for me and a colleague with whom I have had difficulty, to realize that both of us hadn't shown respect to each other, yet wanted it so badly from each other!" And, "I realized that I had been sitting on a very positive characteristic of an ability to see things from many perspectives and I hadn't been sharing that with my teammates!"

On a more personal level, one man said, "I realize now that my caring for my son made me overly critical of any time he failed to progress—and that, in turn, made me do things that blocked him from being able to achieve success."

We also remember some remarks of high-level managers, such as, "It was so easy for me to see how my many interests and requests of staff members made me seem overbearing and unsympathetic to their needs and interests. I simply got excited by many possibilities and didn't realize how overwhelming I seemed to them!"

A CEO of an insurance company remarked, "When I looked at our team scores and saw how concentrated we were in our operational concerns, and how low we were in customer concerns and attentiveness to needs for appreciation and recognition, it was obvious to me how we needed to change!"

Many individuals discovered new things about themselves:

"I was so touched by the LIFO® strength bombardment exercise. I never realized that others saw me as so valuable to the group. I didn't seem to value myself as others did. I left that team session feeling grateful and also proud." And, "Tears came when I realized team members did appreciate how much caring I had shown for them—how much they appreciated my efforts to coach people in some of the refined ways they could interact with others."

In addition to these insights and reactions, you will find in the following chapters that team and organizational performance increased significantly in companies effectively using The LIFO® Method.

THE LIFO® METHOD: A BEST KEPT SECRET

One author was talking with a friend who knew of his consulting work and was asked, "Why don't I hear more, or see so little, about the LIFO® Method? If, as you say, more than 10,000,000 people have participated in LIFO® seminars, there should be more public notice." The author didn't have a good answer. It appears that the LIFO® method is the best kept secret about its value for consulting. This, despite three books and translations of surveys and workbooks into Chinese, French, German, Italian, Japanese, Norwegian, Polish, Portuguese, Rumanian, Russian, Slovakian, Spanish and UK English.

It is true that the LIFO® Method didn't begin in a university and doesn't have a lot of professional articles concerning its effectiveness. Also, many professors were not trained so that they would adopt and sponsor the method, as was the case for Myers-Briggs Type Indicator (MBTI) and the DISC Assessment Method. However, we do have many licensees who are based in learning institutions of considerable fame and are, perhaps, more known in other countries than the United States. Hopefully, they will conduct more research and publish their findings in the future. There are loads of articles, however, on The LIFO® website (www. lifo.co).

We are writing this book to remedy the situation by providing a treatment of basic theory, along with some subtle nuances. The book will also include many practical instances of applications that have been conducted successfully with outstanding results by our licensees and agents worldwide. We, and our professional colleagues who have contributed to this book, hope that we will convince organization consultants and trainers to use The LIFO® Method more frequently in their practices. We believe this book will help them see how they can work on personal, team and organization development issues more effectively. This, in turn should encourage wider use and knowledge of The LIFO® Method.

Very few consultants fit Peter Block's "flawless state." Most consultants are not ideal. Good ones are, in fact, works in progress, starting out with often a single orientation, learning about different theoretical approaches, and expanding their knowledge, understanding and skills with each new consultation. Indeed, we have found it highly enriching to work with consultants who were not grounded in psychology but were students of anthropology, sociology, finance, languages and physics.

Unfortunately, grounding in only one framework may lead to an excessive preoccupation with one perception of events. If so, this needs to be broadened with knowledge of other systems, or it needs to be a framework that allows other orientations and sciences to modify itself. For example, consultants can be so MBTI-oriented that they never consider the issues of congruency in communication, or so focused on a typology of rigid classifications that they neglect such factors as the interaction of role, culture, and situational demands. Unfortunately, training in universities often leads to a biased consideration of the values of alternative theories and approaches because of theories they espouse and advocate.

It is therefore vitally important for the consultant to know his own framework thoroughly and yet to be open to others, to follow experiences rather than be blinded by theories. Each approach, including our own, has, as we will show, its strengths and blind spots.

It certainly helps to have a powerful overall framework that considers the major individual and organizational behavioral characteristics and cultures that prevail. Frameworks help to classify, organize and understand what is happening. In fact, many comprehensive frameworks can be useful. It also helps to have one that cannot only apply to broad-brush areas but to the subtleties of small ones as well. Of course, it is essential that the approach generates predictions that can be verified.

The LIFO® Method provides concepts and tools that provide predictive understanding of individual and group behavior. When introduced, participants develop a language that allows them to deal not only with current problems but to make meaningful plans about future events. What may begin as an operational problem can be translated into many contexts, even affecting such external events such as those involved with marketing and customer services.

Although The LIFO® Method started (for those interested in history—see Appendix B) with a particular structure, it has evolved and changed with the efforts of agents and licensees who have applied the method, reflected about what happened, and then developed new ways of using the old methodology—even causing some revision of theory. In Germany, for example, annual conferences are held to present papers, demonstrate new applications, and extend the range of theoretical thinking. We believe that such openness to new ideas is what should characterize every consultant. It also attests to the vigor of the original method itself, allowing concepts to be modified and changed over time but still retaining basic elements that are valid.

Above all, we wanted this book to be practical, to allow the consultant to view first-hand a variety of successful applications. To this end, we placed an appeal to our world-wide agents and licensees to provide specific examples of how they have used the method(s). We have listed their contributions in the Foreword and will also cite them individually for each specific use, as it is reported in the subsequent chapters.

Chapter 2

WHAT IS THE LIFO® METHOD AND HOW DOES IT WORK?

The LIFO® Method is a set of concepts based on sound behavioral science theory, self-surveys, and seminars designed to help people manage their strengths for more effective interpersonal relationships. It promotes non-judgmental feedback, valuing diversity, and understanding different perspectives. A clear and simple behavioral language allows people to deal with differences in a non-defensive and constructive way.

The term "LIFO" stands for *life orientation*, which refers to a person's basic pattern of viewing, valuing and behaving. The method consists of both a total system for understanding a person's behavior and a set of practical strategies for leveraging skills and strengths to make work and life more productive and satisfying.

The LIFO® Method is based on universal principles that have allowed it to be used with more than 10 million people in 26 different countries and thousands of organizations.

A TOOL FOR MANAGING PERFORMANCE

The LIFO® Method provides leaders, managers, and teams a practical approach to managing individual, interpersonal, and group performance that encompasses the complexities of human behavior within a simple but powerful framework.

Under the pressure to produce, people can resort to quick judgments of others—right or wrong, good or bad, my way vs. your way—without taking into account the complexities of individual and organizational behavior. Acting on these oversimplified judgments often results in costly, unintended consequences. In fact, any behavior can trigger undesirable consequences when used in excessive ways. As you will see in later chapters, strength management begins when you become aware of how you are behaving, realizing the impact your behavior has on others and the situation, and modifying that behavior so it meets the situation in a productive way.

The LIFO® Method is a global tool that provides behavioral insight in the following mission-critical areas:

- Leadership
- Team Building
- Interpersonal Communications
- Productivity
- Selection
- Training

HOW DOES IT WORK?

Based on sound psychological and management theory, The LIFO® Method begins by:

- Inventorying the resources that represent your strengths, focusing on behavior but also examining the relationships between your intentions, behavior, and impacts (the congruency of communications).

- Understanding and appreciating the pattern of your behavior in favorable and unfavorable conditions – recognizing the value of your strengths.
- Recognizing the consequences of over-using strengths and the vulnerabilities created by blind spots in your behavioral pattern, and valuing the strengths of others, especially in areas where you are not particularly strong.

The initial approach is followed by:

- Learning to build productive relationships with others through self-disclosure and sharing of experiences.
- Learning powerful strategies for managing your strengths and those of others.
- Practicing methods to increase the strengths in your blind-spot areas.

COMPARISON TO OTHER METHODS

The LIFO® Method focuses on what people do and how they manage their relationships. It is a highly self-valid and descriptive measure of many aspects of personal, group and organizational behavior. The survey results are readily recognized and provide practical tools for analyzing and problem-solving in business through language that relates to organizational issues.

It does not probe deep personal motivations and self-concepts that are included in The Human Element program and others, such as therapeutically related ones do.

It is non-normative. It describes individual behavior without reference to comparison groups, and treats the individual with understanding and acceptance. People are not treated as normal or abnormal, healthy or unhealthy. It does not use judgmental evaluations.

MAJOR APPLICATIONS

The LIFO® Method can be used effectively in the following areas:

STRATEGIC DECISION-MAKING

- Helps ensure strategies are chosen after sharing various viewpoints and concerns

MARKETING

- Helps to identify marketing targets; aids in developing effective advertising.

COACHING

- Provides a structured framework for behavior change, easy to implement.
- Uses concepts easy to relate to own perceptions and experiences (self validation) that enhance exploration of issues without defensiveness.
- Provides a framework that allows clients to analyze and assess issues on their own, as well as help in follow-up trials.
- Provides coaches valuable information to guard against their own biases.
- Stimulates exploration of underlying factors.
- Provides differentiation between intention, behavior, and impact that allows and encourages coaches to see the complexity of human behavior.
- Allows coaches to check their intentions regarding the coaching process

- As contrasted to the client's style.
- Allows clients to question their own role definitions and what they think the expectations of others are likely to be.
- Enriches the possibilities of behavior choice through use of strength management strategies.
- Encourages asking for feedback from others to gauge how clients' behavior impacts them.
- Helps clients find ways to create the impact that is desired.

LEADERSHIP

- Gives leaders a means of accurately assessing staff and team members that is related to effective interactions.
- Helps leaders to understand different styles of thinking and working of their people.
- Provides hints on how to use strengths of team members from their individual profile information.
- Provides strategies for management of personal leadership behavior and change that is required.
- Provides checks to determine the authenticity of communication (impact of leadership behavior).
- Demonstrates ways of adjusting communications for different people to gain their favorable attention.

TEAM-BUILDING

- Provides identification of team strengths and vulnerabilities.
- Provides description of how teams respond to familiar and stressful situations.
- Helps teams select successful strategies for managing their strengths to improve effectiveness of operations.

- Helps teams assign roles to optimize use of member strengths.
- Helps teams identify strengths needed in new members.
- Helps teams recognize and adapt to changes.

TEACHING AND LEARNING

- Helps teachers understand why some learners show progress and others have difficulties in learning because of their teaching styles.
- Provides strategies to make teaching effective for all learning styles.
- Indicates behavior most likely to help children with learning difficulties.
- Helps learners realize why they find it easy or difficult to learn from different teachers and what they can do themselves to make it easier for them to learn.

SELLING

- Provides self-valid description of selling style successes and failures.
- Gives salesperson a means of understanding customer behavior (buying styles)
- Provides ways to activate different styles when needed to communicate with different customers.
- Provides techniques for dealing with all kinds of customer resistances.
- Provides training in the most effective ways to support customers depending on their needs and styles.
- Provides cues for understanding when customers are responding favorably to sales presentations and when they are not.
- Provides training in ways to close sales, depending upon the buying style of the client, nature of customer concerns and values.

OTHER BUSINESS SITUATIONS

- *Recruitment.* Provides assistance in finding candidates who would be the best fit for teams and situations.
- *Mergers with other companies.* Helps to identify relative strengths of two companies, provide strategies for blending them, make changes smoothly and develop a coherent sense of values and effective teamwork.
- *Improving marketing efforts.* Helps by identifying customer styles and by making advertising communications more customer-style focused and thus more attractive.

THE LIFO® METHOD LICENSEES

There are several thousand professionals who have received advanced training in LIFO® applications, become certified, and used those applications in many different kinds of business situations. Before we go into the specific concepts and applications themselves, we would like to emphasize what may be readily apparent in the list of applications, that there are many different surveys.

In the early use of The LIFO® Life Orientation Survey, we found it helpful to provide guidance on how the various participants should think about their lives. For most business applications, we would stress thinking about behavior in work situations. People sometimes forgot that and pointed out that they do behave differently in various situations, for example, being a boss as contrasted with being a parent or spouse. Subsequently, a decision was made to construct different situational surveys to develop profile patterns most appropriate for that situation and role.

Next.....

In Chapter III, we will discuss some basic concepts of the method. This will be followed by chapters that provide in-depth detail about the LIFO® Life Orientations.

Chapter 3

BASIC LIFO® CONCEPTS

In this chapter, you will be introduced to the basic concepts of The LIFO® Method, including the four life orientations, the strength-weakness paradox, the Golden Rule revised, and the measurement by survey of strengths.

THE FOUR LIFE ORIENTATIONS

The most basic concept in The LIFO® Method is that the behavior of a person is influenced by four distinct "life orientations." A profile can be constructed that shows the relative portions of each life orientation used by a particular person.

The four life orientations are:

1. Supporting-Giving (SG)
2. Controlling-Taking (CT)
3. Conserving-Holding (CH)
4. Adapting-Dealing (AD)

Stuart Atkins was fond of introducing the topic of orientations by reference to an old Italian painting that depicted a square castle perched on top of a mountain. From one side you could look through the windows and see the coast and the ocean; from another, you could see a heavily wooded landscape; from the third, you could see a valley, planted with crops; and from the fourth side, you see some majestic mountains. The total view included all of these, but imagine if you were limited to only one. For you, the world would appear to be only the one you saw.

Life orientations provide a particular view, based on experiences, values and behaviors. When very dominant, they may seem to be too exclusive, like a one-sided view. Fortunately, we are not quite as limited as the one-view scene would suggest. We can walk around the castle of our minds and see different things, even though sometimes it appears as if we don't. So, too, with life orientations. You don't have to be limited to only the dominant one; at times you can afford to take a look at other scenes as well. In LIFO® training, we try to provide such flexibility, appreciating not only the dominant view but also those of others.

Sometimes powerful experiences such as therapy, war, and age open up these other vistas. If we could incorporate all of them into our total outlook at earlier times, we would find our world considerably enhanced with possibilities we hadn't imagined before.

In LIFO® theory, remember there are four orientations: SG, CT, CH and AD. LIFO® theory assumes that each of us has elements of all four orientations in our behavioral profiles. Furthermore, in different situations, the dominance of a particular orientation may change, as well as the other positions. We will use the term *style* for the particular combination that characterizes a person's behavior viewed over many situations. However, it is important to remember that you may exhibit a different style at other times. For example, you may be quite confident and assertive in situations that you have experience with, yet be extremely reserved and obedient in situations where you have to learn new things.

THE STRENGTH-WEAKNESS PARADOX

Eric Fromm, in his book *Man for Himself*, describes a basic principle that is characteristic of human behavior: "A man's weaknesses are seldom more than the excessive uses of his strengths." Stuart Atkins later rephrased this seemingly contradictory concept and re-titled it the *strength-weakness paradox.*

The strength-weakness paradox has several implications for change strategies. For example, a person's effectiveness can be managed to ensure that behavior stays within the boundaries of productiveness and avoids excessiveness. If you can recognize when you are behaving excessively, you can reduce the intensity and return to productivity. Furthermore, by observing another person's excesses, you could even understand what that person's strengths could be.

This concept is often viewed as one of the most outstanding features of the LIFO® Method. As one seminar participant said, "I found it so liberating to understand the relationship between my good qualities and my faults, and realizing I didn't have to change myself but rather manage my good qualities more effectively."

Some excessive behavior is simply the result of overusing behavior that works well for you. If you have been rewarded for being humorous and taking things in a light-hearted way, then you may do it in some situations where it isn't appropriate and then be surprised that people don't appreciate it. Most excessive behavior, however, occurs when people are deeply in conflict with others or under high degrees of stress (intense unfavorable conditions). In that case, the major consulting and coaching strategies would be to:

1. Find out how the person interprets the situation.
2. Identify the excessive behavior and reduce its intensity.
3. Help the person to reinterpret the situation so they can experience it in favorable condition terms.
4. Identify alternative behaviors that could be used.
5. Provide practice and coaching in alternative behaviors.

6. If the issues are interpersonal, facilitating communication of stressful and conflicting experiences, so each person can appreciate and understand the other's position.
7. Reconstruct the situation as one that requires people to understand and resolve their different interpretations, so problem-solving of work issues can occur more readily.

THE GOLDEN RULE REVISED

All of us are aware of the Golden Rule, which is to *Treat others the way you would like to be treated.* This basic view on life is important and has been espoused across most religions. For example, consider the following:

Confucius (551-479 B.C.E.), Chinese philosopher and founder of Confucianism, told this story in the *Analects:* Tse-kung asked, "Is there one word which may serve as the rule of practice for all of one's life?" The Master replied, "Is not *reciprocity* such a word? What you do not want done to yourself, do not do to others."

Muhammad (632-570 B.C.E.), prophet of Islam, said, "No man is a true believer unless he desireth for his brother that which he desires for himself."

Hillel Ha-Babli (c. 50 B.C.E.) wrote in the Talmud: "Whatsoever you would that men should not do to you, do not do that to them. This is the whole law. The rest is only explanation."

In Luke 6:32 from The New Testament (c. 75 B.C.E), it is stated: "As ye would that men should do to you, do ye also to them likewise."

The LIFO® Golden Rule, a phrase that underlies The LIFO® Method, takes a different slant on this. Instead of emphasizing treating others as we ourselves would like to be treated, the LIFO® Golden Rule says, *Treat others the way <u>they</u> would like to be treated!*

To be an effective manager, you must know about others. Indeed, to be an effective person, you must also have this same knowledge. A gift you might like for yourself, for example, may mean nothing to someone who has different interests. A compliment that you deem to be high praise may fall on deaf ears to someone who needs to feel specially recognized for what they value. Criticism that you as a manager feel would be helpful might be experienced as a devastating evaluation for an employee. Knowing what the other person *wants*, *needs* and *values* provides the key to finding effective behavior that will achieve the results you desire. The LIFO® framework can provide such a key.

Reorienting your attitudes through understanding and acceptance requires a willingness to suspend judgment, to forego giving advice, and instead expend efforts toward listening to what others are feeling and thinking. Only then will you discover how they see their world and the events affecting them, and appreciate their strengths. In turn, such knowledge helps you to manage your strengths and learn how to manage the strengths of others. This is not always easy. It takes patience and discipline to fully pay attention to others in the way described above.

A MEASUREMENT OF STRENGTHS: *THE LIFO® LIFE ORIENTATION SURVEY*

The LIFO® Method is a positive look at a person's strengths, striving to make the best use of the strengths the person possesses, to control the excesses, to encourage complementing strengths with others, and to develop new strengths as they are needed. Indeed, our belief is that an organization that provides the maximum opportunities for people to use and develop their strengths in their jobs will gain the most rewards for such an investment.

To help people have a basis for thinking about themselves and their strengths, The LIFO® Life Orientation Survey was created. It would be best described as a tool for understanding your profile of strength usage under two sets of conditions: *favorable* and *unfavorable*. Favorable conditions are those that are familiar to a person and represent the usual range that he or she encounters. Unfavorable conditions are those where the person is in strong conflict with others or feels under pressure and experiences stress. In other words, favorable conditions are those that you know you can handle successfully and unfavorable ones are characterized by conflict and stress, in which the outcomes are less certain.

The Life Orientations Survey consists of 18 general questions with four alternative answers. Nine of the questions relate to favorable conditions and nine to unfavorable ones. You are asked to rank the alternatives in terms of which are most characteristic (4); next most characteristic (3;) next most characteristic (2); to least characteristic (1) of yourself. Each alternative may be assigned only one rank— no ties are allowed. An example is given here:

When given a task to do:

a. I want to know what the task is expected to accomplish, how valuable it is perceived, and I try to give my best to the effort. ( )
b. I quickly get engaged with the task, judge how it should be done and get it finished as quickly as possible. ( )
c. I study what is involved, ask questions to clarify the requirements, lay out a plan, systematically follow them and check their execution against the task criteria for successful completion. ( )
d. I make sure to establish a friendly relationship with the task giver, work cheerfully and may make changes to the task or the path needed for its accomplishment, that I know will please that person, even though that may not be expected of me. ( )

Each of the alternatives represents a different strength orientation: Supporting-Giving (SG), Controlling-Taking (CT), Conserving-Holding (CH) and Adapting-Dealing (AD). A score is derived for each strength orientation under the two conditions, favorable and unfavorable. For the favorable conditions, the maximum score for a particular orientation would be 9 questions multiplied by 4 (most characteristic choice) or 36. The lowest score would be 9 questions multiplied by 1 (least characteristic choice) or 9. Similar sums would be obtained for the 9 unfavorable condition items.

A person's LIFO® score would consist therefore of four numbers, arranged so the top four represent favorable conditions and the bottom scores represent unfavorable ones. You will learn more about the meaning of those numbers in a later chapter.

In the next four chapters, we will be providing examples of profiles in which one strength orientation is dominant. Dominance does not mean that the person may not use other strength orientations but other orientations would appear less frequently, depending upon the role the person is asked to play, as well as the situation that prevails.

Chapter 4

THE SUPPORTING-GIVING ORIENTATION

A CONSULTING SCENARIO

Assume that you have been hired as a consultant to provide coaching for an individual in a corporation who is a brilliant scientist but has been experiencing some difficulties in managing a research group. Your client states that the manager, Bill Stern, has made many contributions to the company's technology but as a manager lacks something to be desired. Morale in his department is low and there have been several requests for transfers to other research organizations within the company. You agree to interview Bill, and discuss the situation with him and his staff before making any suggestions for improvement.

You meet Bill in his office, where you find him sitting behind his desk and apparently busy typing on the computer. He turns to meet you and asks you to sit down. He's dressed more like an academician than the traditional executive and speaks in a quiet and respectful manner. His desk is rather cluttered—apparently he is dealing with a lot of things.

After the introductory process is completed, you ask him to describe what his group does and how he manages his group. He explains that he is in charge of a group of brilliant physicists, chemists and engineers, and generally believes that they are highly competent. Considering their skills and experience, he generally trusts them to be responsible for executing their responsibilities and directing their own activities.

To keep track of what is happening, Bill does ask everyone to submit reports of their progress and keep him informed about any problems or delays that are likely to prevent the timely completion of their work. If someone enters his office to ask questions or requests help, he is happy to provide it. In staff meetings, he requests suggestions and opinions from everyone and tries hard to think about what he has heard before making decisions. For difficult decisions, he is likely to check with his boss before committing to a particular path of progress.

In reviewing work, he is likely to call attention to priorities and standards that need to be met, and asks people to keep in mind the significance of what they are doing for the company and the department. One of his frequent questions is: *What significance does that suggestion have for the work we are doing?*

He admits that he is not the most organized person in the world, although he does keep track of priorities that need to be met by the group. He feels he provides the kind of professional environment for his staff that he prefers, which is the opportunity to do work without someone looking your shoulder and to exercise your own professional judgment as needed.

You ask whether you can interview staff members and request he notify them that you will be contacting them for suggestions on information as to how the department's performance can be improved.

In discussing Bill's behavior with the staff, you listen as they comment on how he has helped people develop their skills and is willing to promote them to higher positions in other departments. They welcome the freedom that he provides for them to function according to their own professional judgment. However, they feel that he expects an awful lot from people, despite the fact that he does not provide clear direction for them. They also complain about his failure to make spontaneous decisions, pointing to his need to check with higher levels of authority before making a decision. They are often surprised, when their work is reviewed, to find him so exacting in his expectations, despite the fact that he never made it clear to them exactly what he did expect. They also feel he is too receptive to demands made by others outside of their department, loading them up with additional work.

One person commented, "He always says that he's receptive to any comments, and when criticized he apologizes and acknowledges guilt. However, he doesn't necessarily change his behavior or the situation."

Nevertheless, the staff feels Bill constantly urges them to improve, to achieve at levels they hadn't realized were possible.

He is modest about himself and willing to give credit to others. But he does get extremely angry when he feels someone hasn't kept him up-to-date. He does not like surprises!

The staff also reported seeing Bill angry when someone falsely accused the department of not fulfilling its responsibilities, especially when this was a criticism after the fact. He does not want to be asked to sacrifice standards for the sake of convenience. In this respect, some people feel he is quite impractical in what he expects and does. He is as hard on himself as others.

With Bill as an example of someone emphasizing the Supporting-Giving orientation as his main preference, let's see what's involved by going deeper into our understanding of this orientation.

UNDERSTANDING THE SUPPORTING-GIVING ORIENTATION STYLE

SG PERSONAL GOAL: To earn the respect of others and live up to my ideals.

SG PHILOSOPHY: If I work hard and collaborate in a principled and ethical way, I will be rewarded. I believe in cooperating with those committed to contributing to significant goals. My motto: *"Anything worth doing is worth doing well."*

To someone who uses this set of behaviors as their dominant one, it is important to be seen as a "good person" doing the "right thing," a worthwhile human being who is doing his or her share. There is a strong desire is to prove one's worth and to be helpful.

The person using this style has a strong belief that ideals and values are important. There is a desire to behave in a way that lives up to their own best intentions and expectations, and a belief that rewards will come when earned. *In excess*, their desire to be responsive to others may result in putting aside their own needs for the "good of the group, individual or situation" and feel resentment if not appreciated.

Those who have a preference for SG believe ideals serve as standards. They may have special standards, which can cause challenges. They can always be comparing self and others to those standards, hopefully meeting them and constantly striving for improvement. This orientation is driven by what they believe *should* be done. There is a strong sense of mission and purpose, and a belief we each have a responsibility to make a contribution to making the world a better place. The SG style is interested in continuous learning and helping others grow and develop.

In excess, there may be a tendency to be idealistic and impractical which can lead to discouragement. This idealism and high standards may be seen by others as self-righteous. In addition, failure to meet their standards and goals often leads to disappointment, disillusionment and even guilt. Others the SG users work with may feel that someone who emphasizes SG behaviors is overly critical, and they can never meet their expectations, particularly when in excess.

As a member of a group, those using an SG style will strive to contribute to enhancing their welfare and reputation. An SG user would expect appropriate guidance and direction from leaders of the group. Leaders and other members would be expected to have personal integrity and have earned their place and respect as a result of their contributions and competence. An SG user believes it is important to "do," not just talk.

In excess, it may be difficult for SGs to say no and disappoint others. This may result in over-extending themselves, leading to further discouragement from not being able to meet their expectations of themselves.

The person who uses SG a lot is modest and does not boast about personal behavior or accomplishments. There is a personal sense of satisfaction derived from being responsive and cooperative that goes beyond any external recognition. Though this style does not request recognition, there will be good feelings when appreciated and acknowledged by others.

In excess, SG-dominant people may overly defer to authority or to those they perceive have more experience. They may delay offering their opinions until they are invited. They may give in when pressed, even if they disagree.

This mode of behavior is accompanied by a basic belief in the value and worth of others. Such a person will make allowances for people and defend their rights. They will trust easily at face value until there is a reason not to trust. *In excess*, they may be seen as gullible, and others may take advantage of them.

Loyalty is very strong for those who favor this orientation: loyalty to the group, the organization, the relationship and of course, ideals and standards. *In excess*, their feelings of loyalty may be so strong they stay in a situation too long, trying harder and harder to make it work.

In conflict situations, there is a desire to deal in a fair and reasonable way with the expectation that their behavior will be reciprocated by opponents. Others will often feel this person is easy to get along with. When they are not easy to get along with, it is because they feel betrayed, or their principles are being violated.

In excess, SGs may be overly accommodating and end up with a situation in which they have lost the argument. They may defer their own needs and yet feel resentment if not recognized or appreciated. In the extreme, they may adopt a martyr or victim posture. It may be difficult for them to ask directly for what they want, expecting that others "should" know.

When there is a crisis, those who prefer the SG style tends to feel overly responsible. *In excess*, they may feel guilty. They may try harder and work to exhaustion, not prioritizing and treating everything as having equal importance, creating time management issues and reducing effectiveness.

Those who prefer the SG orientation are willing to seek and accept advice from others who clearly demonstrate their expertise and mastery. *In excess*, the SG user may overtly defer to authority and those they perceive as having more experience or expertise.

They do not express anger readily or express strong disagreement in conflicts. Indeed, it is often hard for them to say no. *In excess*, they may sacrifice their own interests to avoid serious conflict and stifle anger. However, a sign that something isn't quite right may be referenced in later complaints and resentment for having been unfairly treated. This may result in lack of recognition and loss in credibility for their own expertise, especially from bosses who are confident and assertive.

CHARACTERISTIC STATEMENTS AND QUESTIONS

- What is the ultimate importance, the long-range objective?
- Is this consistent with our standards and values?
- We should be courteous and listen to the views of everyone without interruptions.
- What is your opinion? We need to hear everyone's view.
- We must be fair.
- Something worth doing is worth doing well.
- Are we sure we are doing the best we can – can we exceed expectations?

- What do key individuals say?
- Is this the best decision for everyone?
- What is the long-range impact of this decision/action?
- How can I help?
- We need to work together on this.
- You can count on me.

VALUES

- Living up to the ideals and standards of a group.
- Behaving in as excellent a manner as one can
- Trying to assure the benefit of others through one's actions.
- Being honest and behaving with integrity.
- Being true to one's beliefs
- Respecting traditions and authority
- Being able to make a contribution to one's community, organization, and society. Being able to provide advice, help, and support to those in need.

ASSETS

- Cooperativeness in working with others
- Dedication of effort to achieve goals
- Honesty in revealing errors
- Consistency of behavior with ideals
- Willingness to fully hear ideas of others
- Interest and willingness to provide help when needed or requested
- Concern about benefits for everyone
- Willingness to follow orders and directives
- Adherence to policies

SUMMARY OF PRODUCTIVE AND EXCESSIVE BEHAVIORS: PARADOXES

A summary of productive and excessive behaviors associated with this orientation is listed below. (This does not necessarily mean that someone high in that orientation exhibits all of the behaviors listed.)

FAVORABLE CONDITIONS (FAMILIAR AND COMFORTABLE):

Productive Behaviors	**Excessive Behaviors**
If you use your strength productively, you may be seen as:	*If you use your strengths too much or inappropriately, you may be seen as:*
Accepting directions	Passive
Responsive	Overly committed
Considerate	Self-denying
Idealistic	Impractical
Modest	Self-deprecating
Courteous	Deferential
Trusting	Gullible
Having high standards	Being critical
Loyal	Feeling obligated
Respectful of authority	Being dependent

UNFAVORABLE CONDITIONS (CONFLICT AND STRESS):

Productive Behaviors	**Excessive Behaviors**
Hearing others out	Giving in
Not expressing wishes	Lacking confidence
Influenced by strong suggestions	Gullible
Yielding to authority	Overly concessional
Trying hard under pressure	Overly tired

BACKGROUND CHARACTERISTICS

- You are more likely to be a middle child than the oldest or youngest one.
- You probably had parents with strong beliefs and values and experienced a lot of "shoulds" and "oughts" in your childhood, emphasizing the need to conform to values, be obedient, accept what teachers and others ask you to do.
- There were probably rewards for following parents' and guidance and punishment when you disobeyed them. Punishments may not have been physical but often involved being shamed or judged negatively.
- You are more likely to be somewhat fonder of your mother than your father. In school, you may have experienced strong examples of a teacher's behaviors that you have internalized as ideals.
- Your self-concepts are somewhat modest, and you are likely to be less confident and assertive.
- You respond well to praise and inclusion.

ADDITIONAL CONSIDERATIONS

If you tend to rely on the SG orientation strongly, you are likely to be uncomfortable when there is high tension or emotional behavior (angry situations, especially, are disturbing), or when there is confrontation and you may have to sacrifice your beliefs and values. As a result, you may sometimes give in to the other person, even though what they're asking may not be what you would like to have. You may find it difficult to present your own position strongly and positively-or ask for something directly, hoping the other person will recognize your concerns, and try to meet your needs.

You may feel guilty that conflicts arose and possibly feel anger, although you are reluctant to show it, carrying resentments for a long time. It is easier for you to express anger when you feel the other person has violated your beliefs and values. Other people may feel that you are easy to deal with and overly agreeable.

Important Note About the SG Orientation: Many people lock on to the "excellence" aspect of the SG orientation that is mentioned in some of our earlier writings, but it is not that SGs are driven by excellence, as much as they feel they have to live up to a standard of behavior that is always higher than they can achieve—as if there is no way they can ever meet that standard.

The underlying sense is that of being influenced by what you believe you should be (or by what your parents felt or said you should be) or ought to be; when a person cannot live up to those expectations they feel anxious, guilty or remorseful. Thus it may be harder for you to fully appreciate your own strengths and value yourself positively. (In Chapter XI on LIFO® tools, you will discover an exercise, *Strength Bombardment*, that is especially useful for helping those who find it hard to feel the power and value of their own strengths.)

To understand this and for that matter, all of the life orientations, you need to focus more on the underlying needs and philosophy of the orientation, not only study the behavior itself, but look at what drives it. Sometimes, behavior that looks like it ought to be one orientation might actually be another. For example, helping someone is not always supporting-giving in style. If I *tell* you something will be helpful, that is a CT (controlling-taking) way of helping. This is different than helping you to understand how a particular action might be helpful (SG). The first represents a need for power and control, the second a need to be of help.

BACK TO BILL.....

As you can now see, Bill's behavior certainly is typical of someone whose dominant orientation is Supporting-Giving. You have also seen that some of the behavior falls into the excessive category. In a later chapter, we will present material on strength development and strength management strategies, and discuss what consultants might recommend for each of the cases involved.

Usually, most people show a mixture of the four orientations in their style, although often they are dominated by one that is more preferred than others, as evidenced in Bill's case.

On a Personal Note ...

As you read the cases and descriptions in this and the next three chapters, some may seem as if they are characteristic of your own attitudes, values and behaviors.

As you read the case and descriptions in this chapter, some may seem as if they are characteristic of your own attitudes, values and behaviors. Note them below.

_____

_____

_____

_____

_____

Chapter 5

THE CONTROLLING-
TAKING ORIENTATION

A CONSULTING SCENARIO

You just received a call from the CEO of one of your client companies requesting an appointment as soon as is convenient for you. You
return the call and discover it concerns a newly appointed regional
director of the Northeast area of their electronics business. When
you meet the CEO, he immediately begins to discuss the person,
Amy, whom he describes as a brilliant and innovative individual who
manages to get a great deal accomplished but is somewhat inept in
handling people. There have been numerous complaints, and two
key subordinate managers have threatened to resign unless something can be done about the situation. You then make an appointment to see Amy.

You arrive and notice that she is working on her computer and
her desk has numerous piles of paper. She gets up and greets you,
commenting "It's nice that you got here at this time, since I have
so much to do today!" She wants to know why you have scheduled
this visit and what you need from her. You explain that the CEO
is concerned about the recent requests by two of her managers for

reassignment and suggested that your services could provide assistance in dealing with this issue.

As a beginning, you ask if she would mind briefly describing her responsibilities and how she manages her division. Looking at her watch she says, "Well, it will have to be very brief since I have a staff meeting scheduled in 45 minutes." She states that she is responsible for the overall operation of the area's business. As such, she watches the net performance of the region's business, oversees how each manager handles their area, and reviews regional marketing and business strategies. She is also involved with assessments, disciplinary matters, and rewards for outstanding performance.

She prefers to have managers who are highly capable, can grasp things quickly, need very little review, can function in a highly responsible manner, and can be trusted to get things done according to schedules and promises. She is less inclined to care how things are done as long as they get done. She also expects managers to handle their own personnel smoothly and not create problems. She admits that she tends to provide heavy workloads, assuming capability, and may sometimes not realize when people are overloaded.

In the case of the two people who have threatened to resign, she points out that they seem reluctant to manage, constantly asking questions about how things should be done, requesting written descriptions of assignments and wondering what activities can be minimized if they respond to her immediate requests—in short, behaving like "needy subordinates" rather than as "managers." As further exemplification of her dissatisfaction, she cites their inabilities to meet deadlines and failure to have information when questioned about something in their areas. In contrast, she cites her marketing manager, who seems to take on assignments readily, finds unique ways to handle things, and generally handles matters without requiring direction.

When crises are encountered, she admits that she does become somewhat impatient, and may assume a very personal direction of matters, overriding the manager who seems to be hesitant to do what's needed. She will ask departmental managers who are having problems, experiencing delays, or failing to meet financial goals for information about what is happening. She does grill people until she get the answers she is looking for. Managers who can handle such questioning with answers and can argue their cases cogently are highly valued.

If proved wrong, she can be quick to change her position. She feels the two managers who have requested reassignments are not people she is especially eager to have in their present positions.

When you interview the staff managers, they express their admiration for her energy and drive, although sometimes they feel she is trying to do too many things at once. This sometimes means that priorities get changed, and it is unclear as to exactly what is most important to do first. They like her directness, her willingness to provide freedom to act as they feel necessary to achieve their goals, her support in fighting for the resources needed, and her willingness to defend them from top management criticisms. They have also found her willing to argue with them about issues, to make concessions when they have proved their point, and to provide stimulation for improvement.

They feel she sometimes doesn't pay enough attention to details, minimizes problems they face, and has unusually high expectations for their levels of performance. "She is a tough and demanding boss!" As a result, sometimes directions are not specific enough; she can be overly impulsive about reacting to situations and sometimes results to forceful behaviors when more diplomatic ones would have created cooperation rather than the resistance that was encountered.

You may feel like you'd like to do something to help this person, and in future chapters on applications, we will show you how you can use The LIFO® Method to do that. Meanwhile, let's try to make sense of someone whose main preferred style is Controlling-Taking.

UNDERSTANDING THE CONTROLLING-TAKING ORIENTATION STYLE

PERSONAL GOAL: To demonstrate competence and achieve challenging goals.

PERSONAL PHILOSOPHY: If I demonstrate initiative and act boldly, I will achieve the results I want. I believe in seizing opportunities and taking risks to master challenging situations. My motto is, *Seize the day.*

The CT style is characterized by action and a sense of urgency. The people using this style know what they want and will put their desires into actions quickly, wanting to see and achieve results fast. CT users will seize and take advantage of opportunities or will find opportunities if not readily evident.

In excess, they may be seen as impatient. They may take action too quickly, looking at the "here and now" and short term rather than taking time to look at the long-range impact. Their strengths of taking initiative and responding quickly may result in them acting without thinking of causes or consequences, being enamored by a new idea for the sake of its novelty

The CT users see time as urgent and those who prefer this style move quickly to take charge and direct others to make things happen. They "want what they want when they want it." *In excess,* they may be seen as impulsive and may dominate others. They may sacrifice thought for action in order to see quick results.

Those who heavily use CT behaviors trust their experience and intuitive assessment of a situation. However, if they are in new territory, they will seek out an "expert." *In excess,* CT confidence may be seen as arrogant and domineering. The users of this style may become overly self-reliant and not include others in decisions and plans.

They may cut people off and start "telling" rather than being inclusive.

The CT style users tend to trust themselves and their experience and like to be in charge of what is happening. *In excess,* they may inadvertently suppress contributions of others.

Challenge, variety and change are important for those who prefer acting in the CT mode. They will become bored and disinterested doing the same thing repetitively. They like being involved in many different activities. They show initiative and a tendency to explore. In excess, they may be seen as taking on things for the sake of a challenge. They may seek change for the "sake of change." They may neglect important projects for the sake of the new and different.

Those who prefer the CT style can be competitive in the positive sense. Tell them something cannot be done and they will show you how it can be done! *In excess*, they may take a challenge just to prove it can be done, diverting energy and focus.

It is of paramount importance for one favoring this orientation to feel in charge of what is happening, to be able to direct the course of events, to meet challenges by marshaling resources, focusing energies and overcoming difficulties. There tends to be a focus on being able to get done whatever needs to be done. There is an essential joy in being busy, able to handle and accomplish many things.

It is important for people who use this style to have a free rein and not have anyone looking over their shoulder. *In excess*, they may be seen as overly self-reliant and arrogant.

The CT style can be tough to deal with, when conflicts occur. People who make heavy use of this style enjoy being with other people who favor the use of the CT style and the stimulation of argument and debate. They do not give in readily and will persist and argue for their point of view. In excess, they may be seen as creating a win/lose situation every time there is a disagreement.

There is a willingness to confront differences in a confident and assertive way in order to get one's way and to convince others of the value of the position that has been taken. *In excess*, they may be seen as domineering and overbearing, The CT user learns the value of other viewpoints in this kind of exchange and can make decisions accordingly.

CHARACTERISTIC STATEMENTS AND QUESTIONS

- We are wasting time talking, just do it!
- If we act now, we gain considerable advantage.
- What will it take to make this happen – what are the obstacles?
- This is what we are going to do...
- What's next?
- No problem.... we can handle anything that is thrown to us.
- Who is the expert on this?
- Who is in charge?
- Give me the key points, make it brief, we don't have all day.
- Stop being so cautious...be direct. Call things the way they are.
- What are the opportunities?
- What's the worst that can happen!
- Are you finished yet
- We can't wait for the ideal circumstances to occur, let's take advantage of what we have now and act.
- There's no mountain so tall that it can't be climbed
- Can you deny that what I'm saying is true?
- Don't you believe that this is the only way to go?
- What's the basis for your argument? Prove your case.
- Let's get the show on the road
- Don't promise me anything you can't deliver.
- I'm giving the orders around here.

VALUES

- Competency in subordinates. Trying is not enough – it is doing and accomplishing that matters.
- Urgency. It is not only important to get things done but to get them done quickly.

- Confidence in one's abilities and deeds. Hesitancy and reluctance do not meet the CT user's expectations.
- Taking advantage of opportunities, avoiding loss of benefits both for the person and their organization.
- Willingness to take risks. (This is related to the previous statement in that hesitation to do so causes one to lose advantages.)
- Involvement in a variety of tasks. There is enjoyment in variety, in dealing with changing situations and a sense of boredom in doing the same things repetitively.
- Competition as fun. Nothing can be as stimulating as an opportunity to compete, and even if one doesn't win, feeling that one has given everything they had in the event.

ASSETS

- Expressing desires directly to eliminate confusion
- Indicating specifically what one is looking for
- Making decisions quickly
- Letting others know where they stand with you
- Expressing confidence that other people can achieve what is asked of them (I can do that, I know what can be done)
- Being willing to take risks
- Staying on top of what is happening
- Acting directly to show what is needed
- Confronting differences
- Fighting hard for what you believe in
- "Don't let the bastards grind you down!"
- Taking charge when there is no action
- Acting independently
- Gathering resources and directing them directly against the task

SUMMARY OF PRODUCTIVE AND EXCESSIVE BEHAVIORS: PARADOXES

A summary of productive and excessive behaviors associated with this orientation is listed below.

FAVORABLE CONDITIONS (FAMILIAR AND COMFORTABLE):

Productive Behaviors	**Excessive Behaviors**
If you use your strength effectively, you may be seen as:	*If you use your strength too much or inappropriately, you may be seen as:*
Direct	Domineering
Self-confident	Arrogant
Competitive	Antagonistic
Quick to act	Impulsive
Risk-taking	Gambling
Insistent	Disregarding others

UNFAVORABLE CONDITIONS:

Productive Behaviors	**Excessive Behaviors**
Confronting issues	Putting people on the spot
Expressing views firmly	Disregarding what others have to say
Persisting	Unwilling to concede, even if wrong
Trying to handle everything by self	Failing to delegate—taking over from others
Impatient	Wanting quick resolution
Initiating too many actions	Diffusing and wasting energy
Forcing actions	Failing to recognize difficulties

ADDITIONAL CONSIDERATIONS

If at times you offer ideas and suggestions to someone who favors this orientation, you may be rebuffed or ignored. This may not be a personal rejection but simply reflect the person's involvement with his own ideas. Considering that the focus of someone who mainly relies on this orientation involves concentrating on what they want to achieve—immediately, if possible—this behavior becomes more understandable. Such a person needs to feel your input is related to their interests. Indeed, CTs themselves may view offers and suggestions as criticism, implying they are unable to reach the proper conclusions or solutions on their own. Unless they specifically request suggestions or experience problems beyond their capability or available time, CTs are likely to reject them or express irritation.

It is not that CTs don't value the help but simply that it is not what they are requesting since they believe they can handle most situations by themselves. It doesn't usually occur to them to ask for help. Of course, those offering it, hoping to be perceived as contributing, may feel unappreciated or ignored. Nevertheless the best course for the giver would be to ask if help is needed or wanted—and to accept whatever answer is provided.

Thus, an important key for understanding clients/people who use this orientation is to recognize the sense of pride CTs have in their own capabilities. Often, after you have made a suggestion, you are likely to hear, *I already thought of (or did), that.*

If your help is requested, it is expected almost immediately, especially if you have the expertise that is required to achieve a solution. After all, if you are the expert, you should know. When one of our clients offered alternatives to a CEO who was a heavy user of the CT style, he remarked, "What do you recommend? If I am presented with options, I want the best answer. That's what I'm paying you for!"

In another company, a Vice President of Manufacturing agreed to a test of the effectiveness of more detailed planning before implementing a manufacturing procedure. Two lines were established, both to manufacture the same item. The "Big Plan" group was still planning six months later, but the "Little Plan" group had started manufacturing after three months. Nevertheless by the end of the year both groups were actively producing their materials. However, the number of production defects in the Little Plan group was twice that of the Big Plan group. At the end of two years, the Big Plan group's production rate was almost twice as fast as that of the Little Plan Group. Despite these results, the VP would not agree to a change in the planning process, stating that he couldn't wait for six months before any production occurred.

This need for a fast tempo can often create irritation when others impede it, as if they were blocking the possibility for action. In short, acting itself is prized by CTs even if wrong because the CT user can quickly reverse and try another path. This very speed of ideation can also be a boon for creativity, for being dissatisfied when things are not working properly can encourage innovation. However, thee is also a heavily pragmatic outlook frequently exhibited by those who use a CT style. If something works elsewhere, the CT wants to know about it and see it implemented in his/her own organization. Thus, if involved with strategic planning, heavy CT users view the future in more short-range terms—almost tactical in nature rather than strategic.

In addition, one should appreciate something about the way such a client responds to the environment. Changing conditions and situations are stimulating, and there is a ready flow of reactions and situations that are stimulating, and are likely to be readily expressed. Indeed, in many consulting situations, the CT manager often becomes the co-owner of the consultation itself. (We will discuss this more in Chapter XII on Entry Consulting Issues.)

There is less attention to one's internal world, flowing with the feeling and searching for the profundity of meaning. Thought runs and is apprehended intuitively in relation to the surrounding context. Therefore, those who rely heavily on the CT style often criticize failure in being open and direct. This CT attitude can feel threatening to those who deal with experience in wholly different modes (SG and CH users, especially).

Nevertheless, the person who emphasizes CT behavior can respect a confident refusal to be rushed, providing an explanation is given that makes sense to the CT. For example, in one major retailing corporation, the president ordinarily asks and expects prompt and accurate answers to his questions. At one meeting, he turned to the financial vice-president and asked, "What's the latest situation on inventories versus sales?" The VP, also a heavy CT user, countered, "Do you want an answer you can count on, or just a guess?" The president replied, "One, I can count on!." The VP stated, "I'll have it for you Monday." To which the president added, "Okay – by 11:00 a.m." Both men shared the same orientation but realized that to meet the other's demands, the delay was necessary. Confidence and strength carried the day when both men respected one another but needed to assess the other's convictions and style. A manager with another orientation (SG, for example) might have made the mistake of providing an immediate answer without knowing the accuracy of what he was stating.

BACKGROUND CHARACTERISTICS

- Mothers are preferred more than fathers, although fathers are respected more than mothers.
- You were probably either the eldest child or the only child.
- Parents stressed initiative and responsibility, and provided opportunities for exercising them.
- Achievement is stressed, valued and rewarded.
- Praise is offered for standing up to others; being willing to fight if necessary.

- Boundaries and the basis for rewards and punishments are clear.
- Punishment is swift for violations of those boundaries.
- Often there is a grandparent who has been a very important figure in the family.

On a Personal Note ...
As you read the case and descriptions in this chapter, some may seem as if they are characteristic of your own attitudes, values and behaviors. Note them below.

_____

_____

_____

_____

_____

_____

Chapter 6

THE CONSERVING- HOLDING ORIENTATION

A CONSULTING SCENARIO

The CEO of an aerospace company wants you to help him decide whether or not a particular employee is someone who should be promoted to a newly created position of Manager of Information Systems. He explains that Marlene Daren has been with the company since it was started 10 years ago, has demonstrated loyalty and commitment, and is a highly qualified technical supervisor of a group of programmers. Marlene is 32, a graduate of MIT and has had a lot of experience in designing programs and systems for the company. An appointment for an interview is made after checking with Marlene for a convenient time.

One thing that strikes you when you enter Marlene's office is the neatness of furniture arrangement, the piles of papers on her desk, and her general appearance. She is an attractive person, dressed in a gray suit with white blouse and doesn't wear any jewelry save for a wedding ring. After introductions, she asks you for the specific questions that you want her to answer and how you would like to proceed, and states that she has scheduled an hour and a half for the interview.

You explain that you would first like to know something of her background, her responsibilities, and how she supervises her group. She then asks you, "What specific information re you looking for?" When prodded to begin where she feels appropriate, she provides you with a printed resume that describes her academic background. Work history, accomplishments, and career progress, asking "Are there any questions after reading my resume?"

She doesn't volunteer much beyond what is listed except to describe some of the activities in more detail. Overall, it is a difficult interview. Marlene is responsive, but difficult to engage in any lengthy conversation, rarely volunteering any more than what is asked.

She was recruited by the company's CEO shortly after her graduation from MIT. He described the goals, investment sources and organizational plans, explaining he was interested in her because of her computer and programming sophistication, her excellent academic record, and the recommendations of her professors. She asked many questions and took some time before responding affirmatively. After her interview, she researched the various firms engaged in the business, his background, the investors involved, and the prospects for a new firm entering the marketplace. It took her several weeks to do this.

Her behavior during the acceptance process was typical of her approach to work in the company. She is exceptionally conscientious and thorough in whatever she does. Marlene likes to work systematically and methodically to accomplish her tasks and the assignments she provides for her staff. She keeps meticulous records about everything and reviews that information before attending meetings and having discussions with other corporate personnel. Her staff members have certainly learned her penchant for accuracy and detail by the questioning she does whenever anyone is asked for a report. She wants everyone to follow schedules on time and as specified.

Managers in other departments comment favorably on the quality of Marlene's work, as well as her group's accomplishments.

However, they express wishes that she could be faster in responding to their requests and that, once committed to anything, she is extremely reluctant to make changes. Her exhaustive examination of issues, while appreciated, is nevertheless felt to be somewhat overdone – even boring. They find her non-intrusive, careful to offer remarks only when she feels she has knowledge that is required for a decision. She plans what needs to be done carefully and expects that her staff members will think first before acting.

Her staff feels that sometimes she is overly picky about details, even to the extent of correcting spelling and grammar in what were intended as first drafts. On the other hand, they find her a fountain of knowledge about the technical fields involved and willing to share that with them when appropriate. They also feel that she is extremely slow to make decisions, desiring to "analyze things to death," even when major issues are not involved. Performance reviews are fair and objective, usually backed by a comprehensive review of everything involved. Instructions are usually clear and documented so people know what is expected of them.

When Marlene is under stress she becomes very serious, and her deliberateness and caution become even more evident. She does not get rattled but rather tends to treat issues as problems to be solved if only you do enough thinking before reacting. She will study the situation, establish priorities and organize a systematic attack, weighing pros and cons, before making any decisions. Marlene will also fall back on organizational processes, procedures, and reporting guidelines to support the way forward in a crisis. One can count on her to examine conflicting approaches, question the accuracy of details and information, and question the logic underlying positions. Given her profound respect for knowledge, she can be counted on to check with and value expert experience/information in areas outside of her professional field.

Let's see what is involved in people who rely heavily on this orientation.

UNDERSTANDING THE CONSERVING-HOLDING ORIENTATION STYLE

PERSONAL GOAL: To be careful, to build on current ideas and what already works, minimize waste and make the most of resources. Those favoring this orientation want to be secure and to conserve what they have, minimizing losses and optimizing gains.

PERSONAL PHILOSOPHY: If I analyze the situation carefully and think through the options, I will make steady progress towards sensible goals. I believe in thinking before I act, consolidating what I know, and avoiding mistakes. My motto: *Better to be safe rather than sorry.*

The CH style is characterized by proceeding with care and caution. While those who use the Supporting-Giving (SG) style demonstrate responsiveness and the Controlling-Taking (CT) users are pro-active, the Conserving-Holding user strikes a balance between the two.

A person who emphasizes such an orientation likes working with the tried and true, building on the past and on existing resources. This person uses logic, analysis, practical and realistic considerations of other alternatives. Such users are more concerned with avoiding loss and minimizing risks than making gain. Analysis, planning, systems and routines are used to minimize risk and assure that everything is being handled properly. *In excess*, they may get caught in "analysis paralysis," be seen as slow to make decisions, and appear to be rigid in how they proceed to deal with tasks and problems.

As mentioned earlier, the core of the CH style is also a strategy of caution in most matters; organization and good systematic habits are therefore highly valued. Those heavily invested in using this style do not believe in changing what is working just to find a new or better way of doing something. *In excess*, they may be seen as lacking willingness to explore uncharted areas or to experiment with new ideas and may be sometimes described as "uncreative," especially by CT and AD users. However, many artists have employed a CT approach in their paintings and writings.

In excess, the CH user may be seen as resisting change to new ideas or methods because they may believe it is a waste of resources to change something if there is no real need. However, if something needs to be changed, the CH style can take ideas, try to get the most out of them, and optimize the possibilities in a situation before abandoning it. Once systems, policies and procedures have been established, those preferring this mode will favor following them until someone proves there is a better way – one that makes more sense.

Attention is paid to small details. Consequently there is emphasis on appropriate documentation and information retrieval systems. *In excess*, those who prefer CH behaviors may be seen as stubborn and inflexible, being "nit picking" and overly controlling with details.

The title, Conserving—Holding, tells you something about this style in that the practitioners may be hard to read because they hold on to their opinions until they have thoroughly analyzed the data and weighed the pros and cons. *In excess*, they may be seen as uninvolved or disinterested.

During disagreements, there will be close attention to facts and details. The quality of reasoning is important as well as systematic coverage of all information. Calm and deliberate, the users of this style will not respond favorably to a pure emotional presentation or debate. *In excess*, these style users may be seen as slow to respond. They may take a holding position, disengage from opponents, wait until the opponent "sees the light" and comes to them.

In unfavorable conditions of stress or conflict (or even the threat of stress or conflict), they would proceed cautiously and thoroughly, maintaining a calm attitude, keeping their heads and seeking to limit any possibility of loss. *In excess*, they may not be flexible enough to allow concessions, which would help solve a problem. Their calm detachment may be seen as a desire to avoid involvement with the issue and people who are disagreeing with their approach or plan.

Those who prefer CH style will rarely consider feelings and intuition as data. Facts and figures are data, and these are rigidly separated from and regarded as superior (objective, rational) to any other social or emotional sources of input. *In excess*, they may be seen as uncooperative, stubborn and rigid.

CHARACTERISTIC STATEMENTS AND QUESTIONS

- Why change what already works?
- What are the hard facts to support this?
- How do we know this data is accurate?
- How much time will this take, and what will it cost in person hours and financial resources?
- What is the return on investment?
- Is this practical?
- How can we minimize the risk?
- What are the pros and cons?
- Are we rushing this? We need more time to review.
- How can we build on what exists?
- Do we have a step-by-step plan and a systematic process for follow-up?
- Can we keep emotions out of this? We must stick to the facts and proceed rationally, objectively.
- Haste makes waste.
- Better safe than sorry.
- Let's take things up as listed in our agenda. Starting with the first item.
- Keep calm, stay cool, and you'll be okay.
- Don't just simply tell me what you want. Tell me what you've considered and describe the thinking that guided you toward your decision.
- We can't take on that project until we've completed the ones that are already in the pipeline.
- What data were you using when you advised that course of action?

- We live according to the rules, as specified!
- Systematically review your expenses, but first establish a budgetary plan that will give you a sound basis for deciding whether an expense has been worthwhile or needed.
- You're out of order!
- Let's wait until everyone cools down before saying anything!
- A penny saved is a penny earned!

VALUES

- Being cautious
- Being deliberate
- Thinking before acting
- Systematic habits
- Being risk-conscious. They also value
- Previous and relevant experience
- Acting consistently with routines and procedures
- Research
- Thinking logically
- Following-up, checking to make sure progress is as expected and results consistent with goals.
- Staying focused with one thing fully before moving on to other ones.
- Accuracy, paying attention to facts and details.
- In crises, objectivity and restraint are highly valued, keeping emotions out of the picture as much as possible.

ASSETS

- Establishing a clear work structure
- Planning thoroughly
- Carefully analyzing what is involved before acting

- Establishing schedules
- Double-checking on what has happened
- Documenting what happens
- Calling attention to the need for information before making decisions
- Providing consistent behavior
- Assuring adherence to policies and procedures
- Assuring objective evaluations
- Attention to costs
- Maintaining calmness when crises arise
- Keeping emotions out of conflicts and stress
- Checking facts and logic underlying conflicting opinions
- Examining assumptions and logic when disputes arise

SUMMARY OF PRODUCTIVE AND EXCESSIVE BEHAVIORS: PARADOXES

A summary of productive and excessive behaviors associated with this orientation is listed below.

FAVORABLE CONDITIONS (FAMILIAR AND COMFORTABLE):

Productive Behaviors	**Excessive Behaviors**
If you use your strength effectively you may be seen as:	*If you use your strength too much or inappropriately, you may be seen as:*
Practical	Unimaginative
Firm	Stubborn
Structured	Rigid
Prudent	Overly cautious
Attentive to detail	Fussy
Reserved	Incommunicative
Objective	Unemotional

UNFAVORABLE CONDITIONS (FAMILIAR AND COMFORTABLE):

Productive Behaviors	Excessive Behaviors
Acts rationally	Doesn't attend to emotion
Keeps questioning	Doesn't respond to other person's questions
Acts calm in crises	Is unresponsive and withdrawn
Answers repetitively	Fails to acknowledge opponents' remarks

ADDITIONAL CONSIDERATIONS

Typically, those who emphasize the CH style slow down, take time to consider what is involved, examine the reasoning behind positions, and take care to respond to conflict calmly and objectively. In crises, similar modes prevail. These people do not tend to panic, but rather carefully observe what is happening, consider possible alternatives, and strive to make the best decision possible. They do not care to respond emotionally but rather try to keep emotions under control whenever possible. When confronted by highly emotional behavior, the CH user may retreat into silence, only becoming emotional if there is highly intensive confrontation.

People who favor other styles, especially CT and SG, may feel the tempo and pace emphasized by the CH user is too slow and that decisions tend to be delayed too much. Nevertheless, it pays to keep in mind the unique qualities reflected in this mode of behavior. The users have deep respect for the value of knowledge, for the ability to appraise situations calmly and objectively, to know what information is needed to understand what is happening and to weigh consequences carefully before reacting. While CH excesses may result in what appears to be procrastination and endless fondness for detail, consider what one gains from consistency, and being able to count on predictable and organized behavior. The CH user's quality of thinking and the concern about logical implications are highly useful in planning discussions.

The CH user loves structure and has an immense appreciation for rules, regulations, and procedures. This means that those who prefer CH behavior believe their behavior can be justified by what is known and accepted, and this is reflected by whole-hearted commitment to those frameworks. They may have concerns for deviations that do not make sense or appear to be someone's whims, especially if those deviations violate the rules. While this may seem somewhat antithetical to creativity, they also contribute to new ideas through their interest in considering alternative pathways for determining different ideas that meet the agreed upon criteria for success. Discoveries in scientific research have often been the consequence of such style behavior: the hard work of checking possibilities. It also means that there is a high value on both planning and follow-up to assess the anticipated benefits.

Think of which style user you would like to have at the other end of a rope if you were climbing a mountain. In addition, omissions are less likely to occur, payments will be made on time, budgets met, and both risks and benefits are likely to be considered before making decisions.

On the other hand, one consultant had the exhausting experience of needing the approval of an executive vice president who was responsible for supervising new projects for change. A heavy CH user, the VP insisted on no less than 17 revisions of the original proposal before he would consider submitting it to the executive board. Detailed reports were demanded of every phase of the activity. As a result, the project took 18 months longer to complete than took place in a more CT styled company. On the plus side, the detailed proposal was highly instrumental in getting another company to accept a similar organizational change project.

BACKGROUND CHARACTERISTICS

- Children preferred the parent who was the non-disciplining one, more often the mother than the father.
- Children were expected to follow the rules as given.
- Neatness and order were emphasized: "A cluttered room is symbolic of a cluttered mind"
- Children were praised for thinking clearly and asked to give explanations for their behavior.
- Faulty thinking was criticized
- Family activity was scheduled and predictable: similar times for meals. going to bed, waking up, etc.
- Punishment was used more often than rewards and praise.
- Expectations were made clear and punishments for violations
- May have a female parent who punished by outbursts of anger that are sudden
- Low frequency of expressed affection, such as hugging and kissing, sharing of feelings

On a Personal Note ...

As you read the case and descriptions in this chapter, some may seem as if they are characteristic of your own attitudes, values and behaviors. Note them below.

_____

_____

_____

_____

_____

_____

Chapter 7

THE ADAPTING-DEALING ORIENTATION

A CONSULTING SCENARIO

Imagine you've received a call from a potential client who would like to interview you about your services. When you arrive at the company building and announce your name, the receptionist asks you to take a seat, makes a phone call, and in a few minutes a secretary comes for you and takes you to the client's office.

Immediately, the client leaves his seat and comes to meet you, offering his hand and introducing himself. He invites you to take a comfortable seat and wants to know how you found the trip, since he knew you came from the other side of town. He asks whether you would like some coffee or tea, and while he calls his secretary, you take a brief moment to look around the office. It is nicely decorated with a wall covered with pictures, one you notice showing him with a U.S. Senator.

The client is well dressed, wearing a tie to match his suit color and a white shirt. He wears a golden college ring and an expensive watch. He asks several questions about you, your consulting experience and family. He explains that the company has moved from a startup to one of the largest technological companies in its field, and that the rapid growth has caused some growing pains. As you describe your background, he acknowledges what he has heard, compliments you on your experience and suggestions, and generally creates a comfortable atmosphere for discussion. When you mention some feelings about the situation he describes, he explores them with you, acknowledges your concerns, and tries to address them in a positive way. As you describe the methodology that you will use, he picks up on your plan to do personnel assessments and suggests several approaches that could be taken to make people comfortable about the idea.

When he describes key players in the company, he tries to present them in a positive way, even though he feels in some circumstances they are responsible for some of the problems the company faces.

Finally, when discussing fees, he confesses that he hadn't quite expected that the consultation would be so costly and attempts to negotiate the fee downward. When he sees that you are somewhat firm about that, you describe some extra benefits he might derive from the consultation. When still faced with disagreement, he smiles and agrees. He goes on to tell you more about himself, and is interested in you and your personal life. He describes his own department and their efforts in a highly favorable way, expressing considerable enthusiasm for what they have accomplished

When you leave, he assures you that there will be a lot of new and interesting people that you will be meeting and hopes that everything can be done in a friendly and considerate way. In addition, he reminds you that the prestige of an effective consultation with his firm will only enhance your reputation.

You had a basically positive impression of the executive you just met. However, as part of the consultation, you interviewed every member of that executive's team and discovered another side of his behavioral repertoire. One member commented, "Mr. X is full of himself, believes he is responsible for much of the group's success and is not above adding his name to authorship of some major reports about the group's successes." Another said, "Mr. X is often very sensitive to any hint of personal criticism so that those group members reporting to him are reluctant to offer suggestions for change or to report any outside criticisms from other departments." Several also stated, "We seem to chase a lot of ideas, to the point of losing focus on some of our major responsibilities." Several added, "It's difficult to know when you are being criticized, since he often couches his remarks in a very positive style!"

On the positive side, group members also stated, "Mr. X is very sensitive to morale, has parties to celebrate events, remembers personal things about each group member and is careful not to hurt anyone with his remarks. He also provides a lot of enthusiasm for what we are doing and keeps himself open to new ideas, willing to explore interesting possibilities and concerned that people are able to handle relations smoothly."

A senior executive related a bothersome experience with Mr. X reporting, "He often tends to relate jokes and humorous comments when we are discussing serious issues, apparently trying to relieve tension, with the result of distracting us from focusing intently on what we are reviewing." Three of department heads commented, "It's difficult to know where we stand with him, since he can tell us one thing one time and another later. He seems to change his opinions with the wind." A related comment was: "He tells one of us one thing and tells another the exact opposite!"

Let's look at the orientation that the behavior described in the case illustrates:

UNDERSTANDING THE ADAPTING-DEALING ORIENTATION STYLE

PERSONAL GOAL: To be seen as flexible, adaptable and creating harmonious relationships - to get acknowledgment and acceptance from others.

PERSONAL PHILOSOPHY: If I adapt to new situations, experiment with new ideas and gain acceptance, I can help bring about exciting results. I believe in being sensitive to the needs of others and creating win-win solutions. My motto is, *When in Rome, do as the Romans do.*

The AD user relates to the world through the ability to understand and work with other people. They gain the acceptance of others through their empathy with others' feelings and thoughts, and knowledge of what others require. They express appreciation and respond readily to them. *In excess*, they may be seen as overly social and manipulative.

It is important for those who use the AD style to be able to be able to transact easily with all kinds of people. They use a light touch and personal charm to win people's regard. They use humor to keep tension low and smooth over disagreements. Through such means, they may diffuse tension and then try to influence others to their way of thinking.

Tact, empathy, humor and social skill are easily recognizable behaviors of this style. The users place heavy emphasis on harmonizing, compromising, and pulling people together. Their humor may indeed diffuse tension. Their ease of use of empathy enables them to see all sides of an argument. They make attempts to mediate and negotiate differences and enjoy gaining agreement and consensus. They exhibit a willingness to give and take. They can deal with those who are considered "difficult."

In excess, they may be seen as appeasing, avoiding confrontation, lacking conviction. Their tact and empathy may create mistrust with others as to their true thoughts and feelings.

The AD style is open to new ideas and new experiences. They are enthusiastic and willing to experiment with new ideas and alternative approaches. This orientation user will look for options and will want to keep options open. They will be flexible when relating to people and also when considering alternatives. *In excess*, they may be seen as aimless, always trying the "next new idea." They may be so willing to experiment that they always have the latest "new draft" but not a final decision. They may have too many options, confusing others and slowing down decision-making.

In a conflict situation, the strengths of this style are expressed in trying keep a balanced, innovative approach to problem solving, and an avoidance of conflict and disharmony. *In excess*, there may be a reluctance to engage in healthy conflict. Others may feel their concerns are not recognized or "covered over," resulting in a failure to really resolve problems.

Their optimism can be inspiring. *In excess*, it could be misleading and deluding. Nevertheless, their use of humor may often be helpful in maintaining good relationships despite differences.

The AD style user demonstrates flexibility and facility in adjusting to the requirements of most situations. These orientation users are quick to adapt to the requirements of most situations, changing positions and feelings as necessary. *In excess*, they may be seen as inconsistent, unprincipled or not standing for anything.

Those using the AD style want to impact others as likeable people and to receive friendly acknowledgment For them, a positive value is to be on the winning side, and to be adaptable to the environment for success. *In excess*, they may be seen as too adaptable, raising questions as to where they really stand. This can impact on their credibility and trustworthiness.

CHARACTERISTIC STATEMENTS AND QUESTIONS

- Can we experiment to find an alternative? It might even be better than we thought.
- We can always change it.
- What do others think about this?
- Whom do we need to influence – get consensus from?

- If we do this, do you think there will be lots of unhappy people?
- Can you see the humor in this!
- What do you want? We can work this out together.
- Let's try to be more easy-going and less serious and intense.
- What does the customer think?
- That is an interesting point. That's really helpful! That's a great idea!
- What I understand you are saying is….
- We can make this interesting and fun…you'll see!
- We can feel our way through it, play it by ear.

VALUES

- Being empathic and expressing empathy to other's statements.
- Making as many friends as possible
- Being Flexible
- Adapting readily to new situations and changes in old on
- Willingness to explore new paths
- Encouraging creativity
- Expressing positive regard for people, ideas, and accomplishments
- Enjoying humor
- Liking to have fun with others

ASSETS

- Expressing appreciation for efforts
- Sensing feelings and acknowledging them
- Initiating social contacts
- Making people feel welcome

- Listening to new ideas in a positive way
- Encouraging flexibility and experimentation
- Building harmony and friendly relationships
- Providing information on how people are likely to feel if treated in a particular way
- Awareness of customer needs and attitudes
- Willingness to see the other side of the issue
- Negotiating in a positive and win-win manner
- Expressing remarks that make people feel good about themselves
- Providing a sense of fun in what is being done
- Expressing and encouraging enthusiasm and optimism
- Willing to approach changes in a positive way
- Dealing positively with the public and other groups
- Tactful and diplomatic in dealing with delicate situations

SUMMARY OF PRODUCTIVE AND EXCESSIVE BEHAVIORS: PARADOXES

A summary of productive and excessive behaviors associated with this orientation is listed below.

FAVORABLE CONDITIONS (FAMILIAR AND COMFORTABLE)

Productive Behaviors	**Excessive Behaviors**
If you use your strength productively, you may be seen as:	*If you use your strengths too much or inappropriately, you may be seen as:*
Flexible	Inconsistent
Adaptable	Compliant
Humorous	Frivolous
Empathetic	Insincere

UNFAVORABLE CONDITIONS (CONFLICT AND STRESS)

Productive Behaviors	Excessive Behaviors
Sensitive	Defensive
Resourceful	Tricky
Negotiating	Giving more than is needed
Striving for win-win	Failing to resolve key differences

Driving this style is a strong need to be admired and liked. People who emphasize this orientation in their behavior have learned to sense feelings, perceptions, values and thinking of others and guide their own behavior accordingly to achieve the satisfaction of this need.

Life is viewed as a matter of give and take. AD users enjoy negotiating and dealing with people. Generally they believe that it pays to go through life making as many friends as possible and keeping one's options open.

AD users value a friendly and optimistic attitude. They believe it is a basic requirement for success, giving acknowledgement and appreciation for efforts that others have made.

As illustrated earlier in the consulting scenario, they value humor, the ability to see the light side of things. They also value optimism and a willingness to try new things. A related guiding principle is to avoid making enemies and creating unwanted criticism and loss of status.

ADDITIONAL CONSIDERATIONS

Some people do not appreciate those who use an AD approach (especially if they favor other ones). The term "wheeler-dealer" sometimes seems to stick in people's minds for this style. Indeed, it can be argued that a better title would have been more appropriate (Flexible-Sensitive, for one). Regardless, the following material may help to change your mind about the value of this orientation.

As a means of broadening your view of the AD style, imagine what life would be like without the ameliorative and sensitive remarks that characterize the behaviors of this orientation. In such a world, phone calls would all too often be like those that one author received when his teenage son's friend would call on the telephone. The caller usually stated, "Larry?" When the author asked, "Who's this?" the answer followed: "I'd like to talk with Larry!" There was no "Hello," no identification, no "Thanks." Typically, when his son's friends entered the house, they entered and left rooms without any acknowledgment of who was there—no greetings, no goodbyes. In a sense, other people didn't seem to exist, save for the immediacy of the teenager's needs or tasks. We have sometimes encountered managers who behaved in similar ways!

Think of the reactions to your own work or contributions. Without the AD behavior, there would be little or no complimentary words, appreciation, recognition or spontaneous remarks that would show you that your good points and contributions had been noticed. People would say whatever they wanted to without regard for your attitudes, feelings, and sensitivities. After all, from other points of view, "What difference does it make?"

If you didn't understand what others were saying, they would simply repeat what they said, rather than inquiring about what you did understand or not, and trying a different approach.

When new ideas are proposed, those who fail to use the AD style would criticize them immediately. They would look for finding whatever flaws exist rather than playing with the possibilities and imagining what would happen if the ideas could be realized—in short, forget about the fun and excitement of creative thinking. People would concentrate only on their own ideas (something that occurs in many staff meetings).

If disagreements occurred, people wouldn't bother to listen to you, try to find out what you're concerned about and the reasons supporting your position, or try to acknowledge what you have been saying. They would simply look for the first opportunity to drive their point home and force you to concede.

People who don't invest much in this orientation would seldom bother to demonstrate any interest in what is happening to you, failing to recall anything about your personal life, family, or experiences. They wouldn't share much in the experiences you're having together, enjoy humor, laugh at jokes, or examine other views that might lend perspective to what is being experienced. When visiting other countries, they would behave exactly as they behaved at home, not interested in learning the language, appreciating local customs, taking account of special sensitivities or telling people what they enjoyed about them and their countries.

It sounds kind of stark, doesn't it? Not just for personal life but also in business worlds as well. As you can see from the foregoing examples, it is the AD behavior and attitudes that give a totally different character to relationships. They provide a tone to experience that makes it possible to enjoy relationships and reduce tension and antagonisms. In fact, many of the different training experiences that are offered emphasize the necessity to acquire AD skills, even though they are not known by the AD name. Sensitivity training, listening practice, feedback training, improving communication and feedback skills, managing interpersonal relationships, Synectics, negotiation skills, managing conflict, selling and presentation skills are only some of the many programs that are used to compensate for peoples' failure to employ these skills in their personal and business lives. (You will learn later about LIFO® developmental strategies for similar training.)

Perhaps some of the negative attitude concerning AD behavior comes from the judgment that it represents a rather shallow approach. We suspect this comes from observing an excessively defensive bit of behavior when the style is used to avoid conflict and reduce tension. The depth of this orientation however, shouldn't be ignored. It is reflected in such attitudes as, *Being different is okay!*, and *One ought to see what is of value in what other folks are saying before disagreeing with them!* as well as the desire to find ways to integrate differences rather than proving to others that you are right. Clearly, these kinds of attitudes are extremely valuable for teamwork and collaboration. In many Western cultures, we may tend to over-value orientations that are more power-focused, reflecting a CT approach to the world.

We feel that in world politics today as well as in companies, new approaches (more AD centered) are required that rely not only on what is right and wrong as what is valuable about differing ideas— one that views things in terms of complexities rather than in either/ or terms.

BACKGROUND CHARACTERISTICS

- Generally from single-parent households
- Larger family sizes
- Emphasis on behaving so people will like and/or admire you
- Punishment using shame or withdrawal of love

A NOTE ON THE DIFFERENCES BETWEEN SG AND AD ORIENTATIONS

In earlier writings and lectures, we tended to make an artificial distinction in the orientation that characterized SG and AD users as "people-centered" and CT and CH users as "task-centered." We now feel that such a distinction was overly simple and indeed inaccurate. All of the orientations are concerned with life issues. What they reflect are differences in values and strategies for dealing with them. For example, an SG user may offer advice as something that might be of interest, a CT user as something that should be done, a CH user as something that the analysis of data proves is useful, and an AD user as something that would have additional benefit in your particular condition. To judge any of these behaviors as being people-oriented or task-oriented isn't really helpful to an understanding of The LIFO® Method.

EFFECTIVE ORGANIZATIONS NEED ALL FOUR ORIENTATIONS

Effective organizations require a mixture of individuals who exhibit a variety of styles that, when combined, add value and move the business forward successfully. The following chart summarizes the assets that each style offers. It also indicates liabilities associated with excessive uses.

STYLE	ASSET	LIABILITY
SG		
	Helpfulness	Gives too much
	Idealistic Goals	Impractical
	Trusting	Gullible
	High Standards	Overly critical
	Developmentally-	May sacrifice action for training oriented
	Accepts direction	Passive
	Highly responsive	Over commits, can't say no
CT		
	High initiating	Starts too many projects
	Acts quickly	Impulsive
	Takes risks	Gambles with high stakes
	Confident	Arrogant
	Provides direction	Overly controlling
	Accomplishment-	May lose sight of values focused
	Assertive	Dominates

CH

Thorough	Too involved with details
Systematic	Too bound to procedures
Analytic	Analysis paralysis
Composed	Unfeeling
Tenacious	Can't let go
Highly organized	Compulsive
Cost sensitive	Penurious

AD

Flexible	Aimless
Open to ideas	Indiscriminate
Enthusiastic	Overly pushes for ideas
Sensitive to feelings	Overlysolicitous
Empathetic	Loses distinction of self
Negotiates	May give away too much
Sense of humor	May not be serious enough

You may note how the strengths of some can counteract the excesses of others. This will be an important feature to think about when we discuss teamwork.

STRENGTH APPRECIATION

As consultants, we believe we need to provide appreciation for all of the strengths available in an organization, recognizing when the concentration may be so overwhelming in one area that it creates a major deficit. For example, one company selected all of its managers on the basis of their CT and CH strengths, yet suffered from excessive competitiveness between managers, organization, impulsive actions and lack of attention to their customer's needs. Therefore, the proper balance of strengths is essential for organizational effectiveness. More about the dangers of selecting similar styled users in later chapters. In essence, you can have too much of a good thing in your team!

EFFECTIVE LIFO® CONSULTANTS DO NOT THINK IN TYPOLOGICAL TERMS!

While trained consultants use shorthand symbols for description, they do not think that it is an absolute indicator of behavior. To properly classify behavior requires knowledge of the underlying orientation, the particular behavior chosen, the person's role, and the perception of the situation.

While an interest in *helping* others is often associated with the SG style, someone emphasizing the CT style, for example, may provide help by steering another person along a particular direction. A CH user may offer a recommendation based on proven research. An AD user may provide an example of an un-thought of possibility because he feels friendly to you.

Similarly, you can *control* through questions raised for consideration (SG), direct commands (CT), by choosing the result of a thorough analysis of alternatives (CH), and an AD might do it enthusiastically based on his knowledge of your interests.

You can *conserve* because you are concerned about the economic status of poor people (SG), because it can get others to grant approval for a desired action (CT), or because you know such a concern will be appreciated by a customer whom you want to keep as a repeat client (AD).

You can *adapt* because you see the benefits of the change for the organization (SG), because it will enable the person to gain more rapid achievement of their goals (CT), or because it will result in a reduction of expenses (CH).

Analysis might be done by an SG user by reference to experts, by a CT by considering what the pay-offs of an action are likely to be, by a CH through an exhausting examination of relevant data, and by an AD by exploring possibilities.

Adapting may be done by an SG user through guidance by an influential leader, by a CT user because the behavior chosen did not solve the problem, by a CH user because the rules were changed for guiding behavior, and by an AD user because it provides so much fun and pleasure. In another book, *Learning Dynamics*, Katcher and Czichos even describe different kinds of humor that could be exhibited by each of the styles.

It is behavior that is emphasized in current descriptive categories, not traits. To properly understand what orientation is involved, you need to ask *how* the behavior is being demonstrated. In short, The LIFO® approach assumes everyone can use all of these stylistic approaches, although many prefer only certain ones. Indeed, this fact enables us to train people to increase the frequency of least preferred behavior to increase personal effectiveness. You may remember that this is also reflected in the LIFO® Life Orientation survey results—there are no zeros to indicate a complete lack in any of the orientations.

To use the LIFO® Method fully and accurately, the professional LIFO® consultant therefore needs to take a dynamic and holistic approach to understanding behavior.

On a Personal Note ...

As you read the cases and descriptions in this chapter, some may seem as if they are characteristic of your own attitudes, values, and behaviors. Which characteristics are those that you possess? Write about which characteristics of the AD orientation you find in yourself.

_____

_____

_____

_____

_____

Now, Construct Your Own Personal Profile:_

Reviewing all of the four LIFO® Orientations, how would you construct your own personal style profile, assuming a range of 9-36 for each orientation?

Dealing With Favorable Conditions:

SG:

CT:

CH:

AD:

Dealing With Unfavorable Conditions:

SG:

CT:

CH:

AD:

Chapter 8

LIFO® THEORY: CONGRUENCY

In this chapter, we examine LIFO® congruency theory in the first half; and in the second half, an article by René Bergermaier, *Congruence and "Intention, Behavior, Impact" of The LIFO® Method: The Competitive Advantage,* examines the research on congruent communication.

LIFO® CONGRUENCY THEORY

As a consultant, you probably meet people who on the surface seem well intentioned, warm and open, yet aren't trusted by others for what appears underneath their words. For example, one of the authors had a boss who would habitually say, "Don't you think this is the only way to go?" obviously intending a direction, not a request for an opinion. Another example would be a manager who wanted to be supportive of his subordinates but was nevertheless viewed as a terribly critical person who reviewed reports submitted with a string of fault finding remarks and never a word of acknowledgment or praise.

How we think we are being perceived isn't necessarily the way we are perceived. Information about why this is so can sometimes be provided by an analysis of the answers to questions on The LIFO® Life Orientation Survey. Such an analysis can determine *congruency* or *incongruency* of a person's communications, and therefore his or her effectiveness.

There are three sets of results available from The LIFO® Life Orientation Survey that give additional depth to the meaning of the total results. Analysis of these three sets of results focuses on *intention, behavior* and *impact* to determine congruency or incongruency. *Intention* refers to statements that reflect a desire to accomplish something (what you want to do). *Behavior* refers to statements that reflect what you do to have the effect(s) you want. *Impact* statements reflect how your behavior affected the person who was targeted by the behavior.

When these three results are similarly weighted, it would appear that a person is *congruent*, meaning that their intentions are reflected accurately in their behavior and the result is exactly what they intended. A person who is congruent is generally easier to understand and more probably seen as authentic. Someone whose behavior and impacts are different than what was intended may be perceived as difficult to understand, possibly insincere, and may find it hard to be accepted as credible. Such a person's communications would be, in LIFO® terms, *incongruent.*

As an example, consider the following situation that occurred in a leadership-training course for Air Force officers who commanded crews that operated radar sites. During an exercise in which officers debriefed their crews' behavior, the officers had to demonstrate that they were interested in the comments and suggestions of their crews for improving operations. A number of simulated programs were conducted that reproduced situations similar to those they might actually encounter, and the crews were using radar information that would be the basis for their regular operations. Some commanders couldn't seem to stimulate discussions that were productive, even though they were trying to solicit information from their crews.

Videotapes of the discussions reflected some incongruencies between the commanders' behaviors and their intentions. Behavior alone wasn't sufficient; it had to match the intention and reflect what the commander wanted to do to get the effect he desired. If the crew sensed that their commander really wanted to tell them what he thought happened and the improvements that needed to be made, that sense would undercut the statement that the commander used: *I am interested in your perceptions about what happened during the exercise.* The discussions would then result in frequent silences and ultimately lead to an unproductive debriefing.

For example, a commander might say to his crew, "I want to make sure we're able to improve the way we handle information. I want to have everyone participate in this discussion." However, this statement (*behavior*)—because of the underling *intention* of the commander wanting to tell people what he thought and wanted—had the *impact* of being perceived as an order, and resistance was evidenced by the crew's silence. After reviewing this behavior on videotape with the training consultants, the crew commander made this statement to his crew: "I really don't know what happened in the exercise but sure would like to see if we could handle things better. I need your inputs and suggestions to make things improve since you are the ones who have the key to what happens." This statement resulted in a lot of discussion about what had taken place, seeming to match the officer's intention of wanting to get the crew to offer solutions to problems. The commander, in turn, seemed more sincere (*impact*) to the crews in the requests being made for participation. Alternatives for different behaviors can improve congruency. In addition, practice is needed to bring about desired results.

Western Air Lines once decided to improve their customer service and requested all flight attendants to smile when speaking to customers. They even advertised that any passenger who didn't receive a smile when being addressed by attendants could receive $1 by mailing a letter to the company and providing the name of the attendant. Many attendants who, in performing their duties, were hassled by passengers refusing to comply with rules were highly annoyed by this official request and complained bitterly. The company, after realizing that a false (incongruent) smile didn't really communicate sincerity, dropped the campaign.

FURTHER ANALYSIS

Results in the three dimensions of behavior, intention, and impact can be compared to each other to yield important and helpful information about a person's congruency or incongruency.

Intention as it relates to behavior: When behavior scores are significantly *less* than intention scores, it may mean that you lack experience in that area or you haven't practiced enough. There are many instances, such as the Western Air Lines example and from listening training, that demonstrate if you want to improve relationships, simply smiling or listening doesn't provide the results that are sought—unless attendants/trainees really feel that they want to provide help and are committed to practicing the appropriate behavior. In many instances, consultants can help coach people on how to smile and identify the situations where such behavior is appropriate. In listening training such efforts would also teach clients not only to pay attention to words but also to feelings—to the music, not simply the notes.

When behavior scores are significantly *more* than intention ones, it may mean that you excessively rely on certain behaviors despite situational differences, meaning your habits get in the way. It may also mean that you are not aware of your true intentions (see the previous example of the Air Force crews). Sometimes a person's remarks are seen as angry, even though there is no threat in the behavioral statement, because the person addressed may feel personally insecure.

Behavior as it relates to impact: When impact scores are significantly *less* than behavior, you may be using the wrong behaviors. If you are using the correct behaviors, you may not using them effectively or, as in the above example with the airline, appropriately. In some instances, you may have an idea of appropriate behavior that differs from those conventionally held by others. This can be particularly true in cross-cultural circumstances. For example, in the film *The Inglorious Bastards*, a faux-pas is committed by an American spy when he orders drinks for three by using the index finger and the neighboring two fingers, instead of the thumb and the two adjoining fingers, as would be the German symbolic indicator for three. Those from European and other continents can provide many other examples.

Incongruency can occur because of familial cultural experiences. For example, one manager lowers his voice and speaks slower when angry because that is how his English mother and father communicated when they became angry. However, his American staff and colleagues had difficulty recognizing that behavior as indicative of anger. This may have been true for his early family experiences with parents, but it isn't true for many others.

It is interesting to note that sometimes our reputation for a strong orientation in one area may also cause our behavior to be misinterpreted. One woman manager has very high CT scores. In the SG area, her *behavioral* scores are much higher than her *impact* scores. It seems that people interpreted her helping behavior as "controlling," a carry-over from her strong CT style. Such a difference suggests for consultants that this may be an area worth additional training.

When impact scores are significantly *higher* than behavioral scores, the behavior is likely to be very intense, or the "reputation" of the other score areas, as in the above example, is causing the behavior to be misunderstood. For example, one manager had very high CH impact scores. His AD intention numbers were high, his AD behavioral results were medium, and his AD impact results were low. His ordinarily serious and rational manner made it hard to recognize when he was flexible and humorous. For him, it may take an even greater increase in AD behavior to achieve the desired effect. Alternatively, he may need to add some preamble statements to his colleagues and staff to assure better understanding, for example, *This is a joke*, or *Despite the approach I feel we ought to take, I am willing to consider other alternatives*.

Intention as it relates to impact: When the impact scores are significantly *greater* than the intention scores, either you are using more intense behavior than you realize, or you are relying on incorrect behavior to get things done. Things may be different than you realize, or you might be underestimating your own intentions. When the results are reversed, it would be an indication that you are not exhibiting enough intensity or too much intensity in your behavior.

Remember the example of the Air Force crew commanders! In a similar instance, a CEO of an industrial company never did change his behavior, despite considerable training. Characteristically, he tended to communicate in a directive tone. When interviewed, it was evident his real intention was to dominate and control his group, not to solicit suggestions and comments (his stated LIFO® intention). His intention score was over-estimated by him. He never did succeed in developing better relationships with his staff. However, using a strategy we will discuss later (*augmentation*) he allowed a vice president, whose behavioral results matched his intentions, to lead meetings that resulted in improved discussions.

Sometimes our expectations influence our behavior. We feel we should use more of a specific behavior because of what people expect or because it seems appropriate to the role. Placed in a new position, one manager was having serious problems with his professional staff. His CT intention results were lower than his CT behavioral ones. The impact results matched the behavioral ones but not those of his intention. Such behavior, verified by his staff, was deeply resented. When he saw the survey results, he was very troubled. Discussions revealed he felt that as a manager he thought he was supposed to be in charge all the time and to let others know it, which is why he was using his CT behavior excessively.

From a LIFO® point of view, if you are getting impacts that appear surprising, ask yourself (or review with your colleagues or consultant coach) the following questions:

1. Are there areas in which I need to control or modify my behavior in order to achieve the results I want?
2. Are there areas in which I need to develop skill in using particular behaviors?
3. Are there areas in which I need to be more aware of my impact—to check with others how they experience my behavior?

LOOKING DEEPER

Consultants are sometimes made wary by clients, who indicate that they do not want them to use psychological approaches. However, when discussing LIFO® Life Orientation Survey results with clients, we find that they often try to explain their behavior by reference to previous training and life experiences.

The feeling of being understood and not judged, emphasized by The LIFO® Method, seems to encourage personal exploration of such issues. This often begins a journey to understanding the complexities of dynamic forces underlying behavior. As the client searches for reasons, they often learn much more about the real forces underlying their behavior.

There is, however, a more obvious use that has practical utility for modifying behavior and feelings. After all, it is behavior that creates impact—this is tangible. For situations dealing with bosses, colleagues, customers and clients, it is behavior that makes the difference, especially when behavior is congruent with desires (intentions) to establish good relationships. "I couldn't care less about what you think as long as you treat me decently," said one patient in a dental office. However, as we have indicated, some dentists may require considerable training and self-understanding to make that happen.

UNDERSTANDING CONTEXTS

Consider the statement: *I felt I didn't mean much to you when you didn't respond to my comment.* When questioned this way, another person replies, "I'm sorry you felt that way, but I was still reacting to the terrible news I received today. I lost my brother in a car accident." The questioner hurries to say, "I'm sorry—I didn't realize anything like that had happened." They might also add, "I wish you had told me that before we started our meeting!" Clearly, our reactions change when we understand what is going on with the other person.

The LIFO® Method is influenced by the concepts of Carl Rogers, and so it encourages such dialogues about context and situational understanding between individuals and group members. The theory is that when we understand the context that governs a person's thinking and accept it, we can encourage more productive behavior and relationships. This is not always easy. Even an experienced psychotherapist as Rogers states that he sometimes finds it difficult to allow himself to suspend judgment and evaluation to fully hear what the other person is saying and feeling. It requires a special attentiveness based on concern that what the other person is experiencing is of primary importance.

We hear statements about people being well intentioned but inept about what they say and do (differences between *intention* and *behavior*). If we have accurate knowledge about a person's intentions, and understand and accept them for what they are, then a lot of behavior can have a different impact. Furthermore, consultants and coaches know that providing feedback about impact (describing what is happening) often enables those with good intentions to modify behavior. They often say, *I had no idea that you might see it that way.*

The more people can mutually share both their desires and knowledge about impacts, the more they are likely to see their relationships improve.

We also have to recognize that behavioral impact may be due not just to the originator, but also due to one's own self. For example, a person with a poor self-image might interpret any remark about their behavior as a personal rejection rather than a difference in point of view or information. Our reality is, after all, only a subjective one, save for agreement about common perceptions. In fact, extremely intense reactions may be due to the symbolic triggering of our unconscious memories.

We should also mention the importance of congruence. When a boss clearly states he wants to be on top of things and make the major decisions, a group is more likely to accept him than if he pretends to be "democratic" but rejects all signs of initiative. People respect the integrity of congruency.

Relationships of trust and long acquaintance provide other contexts that mitigate some of the negative impacts of behavior. They may either allow us to diminish the impact by knowing how the other person tends to react or feel, as well as realize that a temporary incidence of behavior does not indicate a permanent change in the relationship. Examples of statements that indicate this: *She always gets angry when she is asked to change her behavior.* Or *Although that sounded terrible, I can't imagine that she meant to hurt me.*

A useful ground rule might be extended from the implications of the above paragraphs, namely that one should first grant the other person the best of intentions. Providing feedback about the impact of their behavior and checking the stated intention can then determine if any more appropriate reaction was needed. A hostile intention may well merit a fight, although it might be meaningful to explore further the reasons for the hostility. A sharing of feelings about the issue and the differing perceptions involved might allow for some problem solving that is mutually acceptable (more AD behavior).

When members of a team share their LIFO® profile information, it fosters more teamwork and collaboration.

To help in behaving this way, consider the table below of general intentions associated with the four LIFO® orientations.

Intentions of the Four Styles

Supporting Giving

Favorable Conditions	Unfavorable Conditions
Helping others achieve their goals	Producing positive outcomes by working hard and adhering to ethical principles
Achieving excellence through dedicated, collaborative effort consistent with organizational values	Reducing conflict through sincere efforts to build mutual understanding
Creating a trusting, cooperative team spirit in which everyone helps one another achieve shared goals	Addressing legitimate complaints and resolving problems in ways that are fair to everyone
Making sure people realize the importance and significance of what they are being asked to do	Obtaining help from staff and guidance from experts when problems arise
Making people aware of the standards that should be achieved	Deferring to higher authorities to make sure that the organization's goals are achieved
Encouraging people to get involved in offering suggestions and ideas	Making sure everyone appreciates the seriousness of the situation
Being modest in how you talk about yourself, your team, and your achievements	Making sure you do not have to sacrifice your principles or values to give others what they want
Encouraging others to live up to high ideals	Avoiding exacerbating conflict and reduce it as soon as possible

Controlling Taking

Favorable Conditions	Unfavorable Conditions
Getting results through decisive, vigorous action	Responding quickly and expending intense personal effort to overcome difficulties
Seizing opportunities before they pass you by	Clearing the air by confronting disagreements
Persuading others to follow your lead and help you achieve your goals	Overcoming others' objections so progress can be made
getting people to follow your direction	Protecting yourself and your organization from being exploited by others
Getting people to take risks to gain benefits	Making sure that goals are achieved even if you have to take over others' responsibilities to do so
Discussing issues in a straightforward manner without wasting time in excessive conversation	Demanding that others prove their point in order to win your support
Encouraging independent action but letting others know you want to be informed when critical issues or problems arise	Advocating your own views vigorously until you win the argument

Obtaining immediate and competent response to your directions	Fighting hard for what you believe

Conserving Holding

Favorable Conditions	Unfavorable Conditions
Creating and maintaining order through well-organized systems and procedures	Solving problems through careful analysis and methodical reasoning
Building up resources to ensure a secure future for yourself and your organization	Maintaining a calm, reasonable atmosphere in which differences can be discussed objectively
Making well-reasoned decisions based on thorough research and accurate facts	Staying on course by relying on what has been proven to work in the past
Staying on course by relying on what has proved to work in the past	Making sure everyone stays calm until all the facts are known
Getting people to follow organizational policies	Developing a plan for meeting the challenge and following the plan, paying strict attention to schedules and costs
Making sure that plans are thought through before action is taken	Refusing to continue a discussion unless others adopt a calmer, more rational approach
Justifying what you do with sound logic and facts	Persisting in debate until your opponent presents a better argument, additional facts, or more accurate information
Documenting your plans, activities, and communications with others	Abstaining from making comments unless mutual respect and common sense prevail

Adapting Dealing

Favorable Conditions	Unfavorable Conditions
Making sure others are pleased with the situation and satisfied with the outcomes	Experimenting with many approaches until a solution is found that everyone can accept
Creating a harmonious and sociable environment in which everyone gets along	Keeping tension low by using a light touch to smooth over disagreements
Adjusting to new ideas and changing circumstances so friction is kept to a minimum	Maintaining enthusiasm and optimism about the outcome of conflict
Welcoming change, experimenting with new ideas, and trying different approaches	Keeping your options open and trying anything that will reduce the stress
Communicating an upbeat view of events and an optimistic attitude towards the future	Keeping morale up by encouraging people and appreciating their efforts
Understanding the organizational politics	Assuring others that things will work out all

and behaving accordingly	right and coming up with a solution that will meet their needs
Maintaining and enhancing your reputation and the standing of your team or organization	Keeping arguments friendly, using humor and alternative perspectives to keep tension low
Making sure that everyone has fun and enjoys working with one another	Finding solutions that will satisfy everyone and enable people to save face

You can see that if we start by assuming one of these productive intentions is involved, it becomes easier for the other person to explain what they want when questioned. Further, there is less likelihood that a disagreement will escalate into major conflict. To demonstrate how a congruency analysis is made, we offer the following case:

INTENTION-BEHAVIOR-IMPACT CASE ANALYSIS

Favorable Conditions:				**Unfavorable Conditions:**			
SG	CT	CH	AD	SG	CT	CH	AD
Intention							
8	11	5	11	7	9	6	8
Behavior							
8	10	6	10	6	10	8	6
Impact							
7	6	7	11	7	11	9	3
TOTAL							
23	27	18	32	20	30	23	17

Favorable Conditions:
Major Discrepancy: C/T

Unfavorable Conditions:
Major Discrepancy: AD
Minor Discrepancy: CH

One possibility for the major discrepancy of the CT behavior under favorable conditions is the intensity of the AD itself. So much energy may be expended to gain approval and acceptance that it generates a "masking" effect on other behaviors. The CT behavior is likely to be a persuasive manner that seems so full of good will that it may not be received as directive. The dilemma for this person is that he may not experience compliance with his requests, since there are times he may not be taken as seriously as he intends. It is as if he fears that if he were to take too strong a stand, he might create enemies. Trust may sometimes be affected by his AD excesses—people may feel that "too much selling" is occurring.

Almost the reverse pattern occurs under unfavorable conditions. Despite desire to be well viewed, the intensity of the CT behavior may prevent others from recognizing the desire to compromise or preserve amicable relations. When conflict occurs, the basic uneasiness about creating unpleasantness results in more caution (note the higher CH preference). Certainly, if the opponent is critical and unfriendly, defensive stubbornness may be intense (*There's nothing to lose!*).

In the profile, the issues of power and harmony seem to be central. It is interesting and valuable to explore these dimensions with the survey participant, to see how they play a role in the person's life and serve his or her needs. In addition, one could help the person examine alternatives that would provide more of the impacts desired. It would also be useful for the person to check such an interpretation with colleagues and staff members.

꧁꧂

Congruence and "Intention, Behavior, Impact" of The LIFO® Method: The Competitive Advantage
by René Bergermaier

All LIFO® surveys are built on an *intention-behavior-impact* (IBI) structure. This structure is followed under favorable conditions (when things go well) and under unfavorable conditions (under stress/conflict). This structural and conceptual element of The LIFO® Method is one, if not the key differentiator of The LIFO® Method from competitive instruments in this field.

Some might ask what the scientific basis is for the *intention-behavior-impact* of The LIFO® Method. In the following article, the experience of LPC (LIFO® agency for German-speaking countries), as well as the theoretical basis of The LIFO® Method, is described in order to help the LIFO® Analysts (certified licensees of The LIFO® Method) understand and explain the concept to their clients and participants. This also will help to fully utilize the possibilities within The LIFO® Method without stretching them beyond its intent.

LPC LIFO® PRODUCTS & CONSULTING EXPERIENCE

During 20 years in the market, LPC has never experienced any difficulties or negative attitudes regarding the explanation of IBI. Indeed, our experience demonstrates that clients react to the explanations of The LIFO® Method as being highly enlightening. We stress that it is better to have congruency (without forcing it on people) between intention, behavior, and impact (almost self explanatory). The measurement of the questions *what I intend*, *how I behave*, and *how others see me* is simple and readily understood. With the impact questions, you have to explore later with the clients how much feedback they receive from others, and the reasons offered for the kind of feedback they receive. However, incongruence will often lead, one way or another, to uneasy feelings by the respondents, regardless if their perception of their impact is perfectly correct or slightly distorted.

I have indicated below some of the important scientific and research findings that are relevant to the congruence concept and intention, behavior and impact (IBI) of The LIFO® Method.[1]

HEIDER

Congruence and incongruence, balance and imbalance, refers in the literature to individuals, groups, or social systems. In Heider's (1946) case, he refers to individuals and how they get into *balance* or *imbalance*. Heider's theory is one of the Cognitive Consistency Theories which dominated social psychology in the 1960s. He has given a nicely phrased description of balance by saying, *My friend's friend is my friend; my friend's enemy is my enemy; my enemy's friend is my enemy, my enemy's enemy is my friend.* Heider shows the balance on the relationship between three things: the perceiver, another person, and an object (where the third can also be a person). By knowing the pattern of all dyadic relations, it can be determined whether the formed triads are balanced or not. Now this becomes tricky, as The LIFO® Method favors the advantage of heterogeneity in groups, as the use of different styles in the group will be advantageous for the outcome. However, an appreciation of the different styles leads to liking and balance in the group.

OSGOOD AND TANNENBAUM

Osgood & Tannenbaum (1955) extended the ideas of balance in a way that enabled more precise predictions. However, this is purely with respect to attitudes. Their Congruity Theory is explicitly oriented to communication and persuasion. Their theory holds that incongruity (like imbalance) is unpleasant and motivates people to

---

1   For this write-up on this subject, the content is based mainly on Wikipedia (http://en.wikipedia.org/wiki/Carl_Rogers), Communication Institute for Online Scholarship as part of the (http://www.cios.org/encyclopedia/persuasion/index.htm), and Rapp (2008); see also for an overview Fishbein & Ajzen (1975)

change their attitudes. They used measures with regard to the intensity of an attitude. Using numbers to measure attitudes permits a more precise analysis of balance.

Their Congruity Theory also has some unexpected advantages. It predicts that incongruity can change the attitude toward the concept (or object at hand) as well as the attitude toward the source (of the message/information), which was demonstrated by research. Second, Congruity Theory predicts that more polarized (extreme) attitudes will change less than moderate attitudes. This prediction was also confirmed by their research.

Limitations of the Congruity Theory are that it ignores the content of the message. It says that the source makes an assertion, which is a message, but the theory tells nothing about the nature of that message. There is ample evidence that message factors, such as strong arguments or evidence, influence persuasion. Congruity Theory only classifies messages as either associative or dissociative, with no consideration of the relative strength of messages. It would be easy to propose that messages with strong arguments would produce more or less incongruity and therefore more attitude change than messages with weaker ones. However, Congruity Theory only covers whether the source is favorable or unfavorable toward the attitude object.

FESTINGER

Another theory in this direction is the Cognitive Dissonance Theory, developed by Festinger (1957). Festinger argues that there are three possible relationships among cognitions (thoughts, ideas): consonance, dissonance, and irrelevance. Dissonance Theory is similar to Balance Theory. It is somewhat like the assumptions of Congruity Theory, except that Dissonance is not limited to situations in which a source makes an assertion about an attitude object.

Dissonance theory has been refined in later work (Aronson, 1969; Brehm & Cohen, 1962; Festinger, 1964; Wicklund & Brehm, 1976).

One of the advantages of Dissonance Theory is that it can consider more than two cognitions at a time. Another advantage is that it acknowledges that some cognitions are more important than others, and that the importance of cognitions influences the amount of dissonance. Dissonance is influenced by two factors: 1) the proportion of dissonant and consonant cognitions; and 2) the importance of the cognitions.

For example, if you know four bad things and six good things about a person/topic, you should experience more dissonance than if you know one bad thing and six good things. Also, the importance of these good and bad things makes a difference. Thus, dissonance theory considers all of the relevant thoughts at once, considering both the proportion of consistent (consonant) and inconsistent (dissonant) thoughts and the importance of those thoughts. Balance Theory and Congruity Theory can consider only one idea, and neither theory accounts for the importance of ideas.

Dissonance theory suggests that there are three ways to restore consonance. First, one may change cognition to reduce dissonance. Second, a person who experiences dissonance can add a new cognition. The third way to reduce dissonance is to change the importance of cognitions. One important limitation of Dissonance Theory (unlike Congruity Theory, for example) is that Cognitive Dissonance does not predict how dissonance will be reduced in any situation.

An obvious implication of Cognitive Dissonance Theory is that if someone wants to change another person's attitude, that someone should try to create dissonance concerning the person's attitude and hope that the desired attitude change would result. However, there are other implications of Cognitive Dissonance as well.

Festinger states in his theory that dissonance is unpleasant, and that it will encourage us to change our cognitions in order to reduce it. Another implication is that people may attempt to avoid situations that are likely to create dissonance. Thus, Dissonance Theory predicts that people will try to avoid exposure to information that they suspect may arouse dissonance—and they may seek out information that is consonant, or consistent, with their attitudes. In addition, research has revealed that people seem to avoid potentially dissonant information (Cotton & Hieser, 1980; Olson & Zanna, 1979). That is, we are selective about the information to which we expose ourselves. We tend to seek out consonant information and avoid dissonant information.

However, dissonance is only one factor among many that influences our exposure to information. For example, curiosity may lead some people to seek out information that disagrees with their current beliefs and attitudes. Second, if we believe that certain information is likely to be useful to us, we may decide to acquire it rather than avoid it (Freedman, 1965). Third, there may be a fairness norm that operates in some situations (like trials), encouraging us to seek out relevant information regardless of whether it is consistent with our current beliefs. Thus, a desire to avoid dissonance may sometimes encourage us to be selective about the information we seek, but other factors may also mean that in other situations we may not try to avoid dissonant information.

Another area of dissonance concerns what happens when we engage in behavior that is inconsistent with our attitudes or beliefs. A classic study was conducted by Festinger & Carlsmith (1959). They asked a subject to perform a very boring and repetitive task, pretending that the researchers were studying that task. Actually, they wanted to know whether attitudes would change when subjects experienced dissonance. After performing the boring task, subjects were asked to help the experimenter to convince another subject to participate in the study they just completed (some were given $1 to convince the next subject, and others were given $20). The subjects who were paid $20 could easily rationalize their action. Therefore, the key principle of induced compliance is that the less justification provided for performing the counter-attitudinal behavior, the more attitude change.

One important limitation is that Dissonance Theory makes no predictions about how dissonance will be reduced (e.g. through additional consonant cognitions, changing dissonant cognitions, altering the importance of cognitions), but surely persuaders want dissonance to be resolved in a way that furthers their goals. It seems likely that some people can tolerate dissonance more than others. Some individuals may be more mentally "tidy"(e.g. Conserving/Holding, in LIFO® terms), while others may be willing to put up with some inconsistency in their thoughts (e.g. Adapting/Dealing, in LIFO® terms). Dissonance theory does not take into account such possible individual differences (actually, this limitation applies to all consistency theories). In this respect, The LIFO® Method and the differences of style profiles overcome, to some extent, this limitation.

All Consistency Theories are about the relationship of the thoughts or ideas ("cognitions") in a person's mind. The basic idea is that people prefer harmony, or consistency, in their thoughts. Furthermore, consistency theories hold that when we have inconsistent thoughts, this inconsistency (also called *imbalance* or *incongruity*) motivates us to change our thoughts to restore consistency. Inconsistent cognitions often, but not always, lead to attitude change.

Persuasive messages, in general, try to persuade us to change our minds or our attitudes (at times they also may try to strengthen or reinforce our existing attitudes). When a message disagrees with us (tries to persuade us to change our minds), there is discrepancy, or a difference, or an inconsistency, between the message's position and our attitudes. If there is a reason to like or agree with the message (liking for the source of a message, for instance), this can translate into pressure or motivation to change our attitude, to bring it in line with the message. Consistency theories are designed to understand how and when inconsistencies are in our thoughts.

CARL ROGERS

Carl Rogers was among the founders of humanistic psychology. When reading Rogers' works one should take into account that his major work focused on psychotherapy. (Initially he called his approach *non-directive therapy* but later replaced the term "non-directive" with the term "client-centered" and then used the term "person-centered.") His work also included topics and areas like theory of personality, interpersonal relations, education, nursing, cross-cultural relations and "helping" professions and situations, as described in Wikipedia[2].

In Rogers' personality theory, he was looking at the compliance between ideal self and actual self. Rogers emphasized the need for unconditional positive regard (defined as accepting a person "without negative judgment of ... [a person's] basic worth"). Furthermore, he looked into congruency and incongruence from an individual viewpoint, and described congruence as "accurate matching of experience and awareness" (Rogers, 1961, p.339). The experience of emotions Rogers explained as follows: "The emotion and the cognitive content of the meaning of this emotion is grasped within their field of experience. This term thus refers to the unity of cognition and emotion, as this is indivisible experience at a given moment." (Rogers, 1991, p.23). The experience includes the experience of emotions beyond anything that is potentially amenable of becoming aware, and shall include perceptions, memories, and events of which the person is not immediately aware. Rogers developed a theory of personality development that included the constructs of congruence and incongruence and their importance for the development.[3]

Rogers argues that when people have a positive regard for themselves and are fully congruent, they are able to lead lives that are authentic and genuine. Incongruent individuals, in their pursuit of

---

2 http://en.wikipedia.org/ wiki/Carl_Rogers; taken at September 12, 2012

3 The LIFO® Method places also emphasis on the importance of positive regard (e.g. the positive descriptions of strengths, the use of strength appreciation in individual and group development, etc.)

positive regard, lead lives that include falseness and do not realize their potential. Conditions put on them by those around them (e.g. through their upbringing) make it necessary for them to forego their genuine, authentic lives to meet with the approval of others. (Elias Porter, who collaborated at the beginning with Stuart Atkins and Allan Katcher on the development of The LIFO® Method, provided, in his doctoral dissertation (1941) the evidence of the effectiveness of the client-centered approach of Carl Rogers by using the recordings of therapeutic sessions between Carl Rogers and his clients).

Incongruent individuals cannot be open to all experiences, and they are not functioning ideally. They work hard at maintaining/protecting their self-concepts, but since their lives are not authentic, this is a difficult task. They deploy defense mechanisms to achieve this through two mechanisms: distortion and denial. Distortion occurs when the individual perceives a threat to his or her self-concept[4]; then the individual distorts the perception until it fits the self-concept. "They live lives that are not true to themselves, to whom they are on the inside." From the point of view of The LIFO® Method, incongruence in the LIFO® scores does not mean to suggest a therapeutic intervention but to be used as a signal for additional exploration of the meaning of one's behavior.

Rogers postulated that people tend to strive for self-actualization, which is fairly well achieved in the healthy development of a person. Rogers formulated a theory of a fully functioning person, stating that the fully functioning person has a tendency towards constant self-actualization and was described by the following behaviors:

- Being open to all of one's experiences
- Accurately symbolizing personal experiences
- Constantly changing with changes in experience

---

4 ttp://en.wikipedia.org/wiki/Carl_ Rogers; taken from Wikipedia, September 12, 2012

- Rating experiences unaffected by others, and highly flexible in this assessment
- Not judging oneself nor others
- Being highly adaptable
- Changing constantly one's own assessment process to form a trustworthy basis for one's self
- Lives in positive relationships with others

The construct of the incongruence describes a limited correspondence between the self and the experience, and means an inner psychological gap. Mismatches are not necessarily pathological. The experience of mental suffering is always associated with mismatches. Mental suffering arises when mismatches are seen as threatening to the self. The suffering itself corresponds to the extent of this self-threat.

Rogers describes situations where a person is in a state of incongruence between self and experience, and considers this from an external point of view. We see the person as vulnerable (if the person is not aware of this discrepancy), or we see them as threatened (if the person is aware of the discrepancy). Considering the person from a social standpoint, it means this incongruence is a psychological maladjustment. The individual considers himself or herself, however, as adjusted (if they are not aware of the discrepancy), or as threatened (if the discrepancy has forced the awareness).

The development of incongruence between self and experience is described by Rogers (1959) as follows:

- Because of the need for self-respect the individual sees his/her experiences selectively, according to the judgment conditions that have arisen in him/her
- Experiences that are in line with the judgment conditions are perceived and correctly symbolized in his/her awareness

- Experiences that contradict the conditions of assessment are perceived selectively or distorted, just as if they were meeting the assessment conditions or they are partially or completely denied to awareness
- Consequently, some experiences arise in the organism which are not recognized as self-experiences that are not incorporated correctly and not symbolized in the self-structure correctly
- From the time of the first selective perception with regard to the conditions of assessment exist to some extent conditions of incongruence between self and experience, of psychological maladjustment and vulnerability.

SPEIERER

One additional concept is described below in order to cover a pathological model, as well and to provide the full spectrum on congruency and incongruence. However, The LIFO® Method was not intended to be applied and used in this direction. Speierer (1994) extended incongruence with the concept of a Differential Incongruence Model (DIM), and he describes it as follows.

In the center of the DIM is the concept of Rogers (1959) of incongruity, i.e. between the experience and the self-concept. Speierer expands the existing concept of the self, the experience, and incongruity by differentiating the terms regarding their causative sources and their origin, their development, their forms, and their interactions (Speierer, 1994, p.22). Incongruence in psychotherapy as described by Rogers is understood by Speierer in contrast to the theories of the psychology of motivation in his Differential Incongruence Model. Incongruence is seen always as a mismatch between the experience and the self. Furthermore, in DIM, equating the experienced incongruence with the perceived importance of self-threat, seems essential.

Speierer, coming from the field of psychopathology, writes that symptoms occur, "... when the compensatory suppression of the incongruence perception is not succeeding due to perceived threatening experiences" (Speierer, 1994, p 87). He names as a result of it the following symptoms of incongruity:

- Feelings of psychophysical tension
- Vulnerability or hurt
- Feelings of worthlessness, hopelessness, and despondency as in relation to depressive disorders
- Anxiety, resulting from experience limitations and phobic disorders and obsessive-compulsive disorders
- Abrupt realization of personality as strange behavior of incongruence
- Disintegration of own personality, which is associated with anxiety, tension and confusion
- To feel like not being "the master in one's own house"

After the psychotherapeutic perturbation theory, seven areas of mental functional limitations are differentiated (following Speierer, 1994, pp. 35):

1. Feelings
2. Direct experience
3. Experiencing incongruence
4. Self-concept
5. Experience constructs
6. Relations towards problems
7. Relationships with people

These seven functional areas are also in the process Rogers has developed (1961) for the assessment of a successful therapy process.

Originally, socially-communicative sources of incongruence were seen by Rogers as the sole condition of formation of mental disorders. Since biological and socially justified life-related sources of incongruence were not named, the client-centered psychotherapeutic treatment theory first assumed that all mental disorders are based on social communications and could therefore be treated only by becoming socially communicative. This uniformity assumption no longer holds for the DIM.

Spierer differs with respect to the development of psychological disorders on three sources of incongruence that may interact in a specific way:

1. Dispositional source of incongruence
2. Social communicative source of incongruence
3. Life event-based source of incongruence

Spierer describes the dispositional sources of incongruence as the "organismic psycho-physical inventory of a person" (Spierer, 1994, p 54). He sees the dispositional incongruence as essential for organic disorders, mental retardation or other disabilities, psychophysical suffering states, and eventually in a subset of schizophrenia, some types of delusional disorders and some types of depression. For dispositional incongruity he also counts perception of incongruence that arises independently of socially communicative conditions by disturbances of information processing, the body perception, and of thought, feeling and action. The fourth kind of dispositional incongruity he names a permanent irrelevance between experience and self-concept, which he postulated as some dissocial personality disorder.

The social communicative sources of incongruence remain as essential sources of incongruence; they can interact significantly with the other two sources of incongruence. The influence of social-communicative sources of incongruence is assumed to be effective over the entire life span of a human being. Disorders appear on the basis of consciously experiencing incongruence from the three sources of incongruence that add up and can interact. They will be in a painful awareness when experiencing incongruence in very high psychological distress.

The live event-driven mismatch is caused by the occurrence of critical events in life that cannot be set directly in relation to social communicative sources of incongruence, such as accidents, illness, or any other change in a situation that can be experienced as threatening.

The experience of incongruence can be compensated by certain mechanisms. Spierer describes these mechanisms as incongruence tolerance and incongruence coping strategies. Spierer's model extends the previous approach, which had been limited to social communicative sources of incongruence in the form of insufficient relationship conditions and assessment conditions, respectively, as well as those for implementing incongruence fostering values and norms.

THE LIFO® METHOD

The LIFO® Method has been developed during the humanistic psychology period and can be considered as a product of this period. In addition to Fromm and Drucker's concepts on strengths (developmental and managerial), the concept of congruity (Rogers) has been adopted. Different from Rogers, The LIFO® Method never assumed any therapeutic goals.

The main goals of The LIFO® Method are to create: awareness of the styles the respondents are using in different situations and roles, as well as the styles others are using; an appreciation and liking of the different styles; strategies to develop and extend particular styles; possibility of reducing the excess use of styles; possibilities and pitfalls of different styles; and having trustworthy communications and collaborations with others. Last, but not least, The LIFO® Method wants the respondents to have more choices available to them than without The LIFO® Method. As illustrated in the first section of this article, recommendations are made for participants to check the consistency of their behavior with the perceived impact on targeted people. When impacts are not as intended, then the respondent is asked to explore other possible behaviors that can achieve what is desired.

Generally speaking, more knowledge about one's own styles and those used by others tends to lead to greater acceptance and approval.

The LIFO® Method makes no demands on the individual to change. It does, however, help by offering suggestions and encouraging explorations of alternative behaviors to increase a person's effectiveness. In addition, certified LIFO® analysts are asked to refrain from "playing" therapy unless they have a fully professional background for such practice.

The LIFO® Method offers in its model the description of favorable and unfavorable conditions, as well as that of congruent behaving (intention, behavior, impact).

The LIFO® Method should be considered for individuals, groups, and organizations.

For Individuals. With its distinction of favorable and unfavorable conditions, The LIFO® Method offers an assessment of behavior in different circumstances.

Similar to Osgood & Tannenbaum (1955), The LIFO® Method is also oriented to communication and persuasion. The intensity of using particular style behaviors can be seen by the LIFO® scores distribution (profile). The elements (concept, source) of Osgood & Tannenbaum can be seen as being covered by The LIFO® Method. The assumption of Osgood & Tannenbaum that the more polarized (extreme) the assessment the more difficult a change is also holds for The LIFO® Method; the change of behavior is one goal but not the prime one of The LIFO® Method, it is awareness and appreciation of own styles and the ones of others.

Different from Osgood & Tannenbaum, The LIFO® Method covers with its different questionnaires and dimensions (e.g. Leadership, Learning, Service Orientation) the content of the message. Often training efforts are directed towards increasing the congruency of the person's communications. At times, one can try to make clear to the client why the particular intentions occurred—that is, to understand the frame of mind of the communicator and thereby, subsequently help the recipients of the communications.

Similar to Festinger's Cognitive Dissonance Theory, The LIFO® Method can consider more than two cognitions. The strategies Festinger is suggesting to restore consonance (e.g., add consonant cognitions, change dissonant cognitions, etc.) can also be applied when working with The LIFO® Method. In addition, The LIFO® Method has the advantage of offering change approaches based on the behavioral styles as well as taking into account the different style resistances. Furthermore, The LIFO® Method offers specific change possibilities to get into congruence (e.g., just imagine Supporting/Giving vs. Controlling/Taking styles). According to Festinger's theory, people try to avoid being exposed to information that may evoke dissonance but attend to information that is consistent with their attitudes (with The LIFO® Method, their behavioral styles).

Having said all this however, The LIFO® Method does not suggest focusing on things to avoid dissonance and aiming for congruence but to make communication more understandable to the respondents. In addition, it aims to provide them with more choices (as illustrated in the first part of this chapter). Coaching can build on these perceptions to assist in changing behaviors for more effective communications.

Congruency can be seen as the desired state. While Rogers views congruence for leading lives that are authentic and genuine, The LIFO® Method assumes that those people are more likely to be seen by peers as authentic and genuine when their communications are congruent. According to Rogers, incongruent individuals live lives that are not authentic; they use distortions and/or denials more frequently than congruent people. The LIFO® Method provides the individual with knowledge about which aspects of incongruence he or she has to work on to assure better understanding.

Another form of balance is found in the literature around the concept of Work-Life Balance. A new survey is the LIFO® Work-Life Balance Survey which focuses on six dimensions: health; financial Security; communication and Interaction; self and values; business-related activities; and private activities. It could be that IBI scores of a particular person show imbalance. The LIFO® Method suggests that the person would find it useful to think about the possible reason for imbalance.

To give an example out of the LIFO® Work-Life Balance Survey and its underlying process model: A very sports-minded male has a sporting accident that makes it impossible for him to engage further in this sport. He also can't work for more than six months, which substantially harms his financial security. This further influences negatively his private activities including his marriage as a consequence. This imbalance example of Work-Life Balance shows clearly the multi-causal relationship for imbalance and that the process for balance and imbalance often must be considered.

For Groups. In the following, a definition (i.e. characteristics) of a group is spelled out. A group consists of two or more people who are interacting and are not simply at the same place; they have most different roles and functions; norms which are described by expected behavior; a mutual task, borders towards the outside so group members know who belongs to the group and who doesn't; in addition, they have some stability over time.

In this respect, the LIFO® analyst and the client are also a group. Respecting or liking one another is a prerequisite for successfully working together. Some years ago, Rogers (1957) attempted an organized theoretical statement in which it was hypothesized that three characteristics, when adequately communicated together, constitute the necessary and sufficient conditions for change and effects. These three conditions were that the therapist[5]:

- be a genuine or self-congruent person within the therapeutic hour.
- experience an unconditional positive regard for their client.
- experience and communicate a sensitively empathic understanding of the client's phenomenological world.

Accurate empathic understanding means that the therapist is completely at home in the universe of the patient. Milton Erickson has phrased it similarly by stating that a therapist has to understand the model of the client; when having achieved this, the therapist is part of the client's model and so can generate change, providing the client with more choices than the client currently has. The communication is not only by the use of words that the client might well have used, but also by the sensitive play of voice qualities which reflect the seriousness, the intentness, and the depth of feeling. An accurate empathic grasp of the patient's conflicts and problems is perhaps most sharply contrasted with the more usual diagnostic formulation of the client's experiences.

If these three conditions (defined above) exist, then a process of therapy will occur in which the client deeply explores himself and comes to know and experience the full range of their being[6]. This should be kept in mind, even not getting deeper into this subject here.

---

5 Remark: Keep in mind that Rogers worked as a therapist
6 see www.centerfortheperson.org/pdf/ 1967__Therapeutic_Conditions_Antecedent_to_Change.pdf

After understanding and accepting one's own behavior, congruency or not, one has to understand and accept the behavior of the other person and/or the members of the group. Otherwise incongruence toward the other may come into place. The goals to be achieved, the roles, the functions, the mutual tasks, and the interaction necessity are also affected by the congruency of communications. This first has to be considered by a group of two persons and is much more complex for a group of more people. The tasks and the goals will get more dominant; however, the effectiveness of the group will depend more on the understanding and respecting of the behavioral styles of group members, the differences of the individual group members' (including IBI, role specific behaviors under favorable and unfavorable conditions), and the strengths they bring into the play to achieve the tasks and the goals.

Unless there are similar, non-complex tasks that are driven by systems and equipment/assembly lines, heterogeneous groups are better, that is, more effective than homogeneous "Behavioral Style" groups. One further step is the interface to people outside of the group including clients (for example, service requesters). Here the style differences of the clients become relevant plus the impressions and "readings" the clients have of the group when doing their work and delivering the service.

Some of the balance and congruence models will not work as effectively as The LIFO® Method which not only shows a good understanding and appreciation of one's own behavior but also those of the other group members, their styles, and the best usage of the styles for the objectives and tasks at hand.

Rogers' person-centered approach could be used for groups as well. As a matter of fact, it became the basis for intensive group experience known as the encounter group. However, it is questionable if this can be used nowadays in a business environment where members discuss their feelings about one another and through the group process, grow as individuals.

For Organizations. In organizations, it is critical to understand the workflow and the interfaces: why things are followed or not followed in the way they are supposed to be followed. Again, it helps if one's behavioral styles are understood (including Favorable and Unfavorable Conditions, IBI, etc.) and also the advantages offered by the different styles of other group or interface members. However, this is not enough (considering for example corporate approaches for service excellence, where differences in the group can help, but each of the employees must have an understanding and appreciation of the different service requesters). This can be achieved following The LIFO® Method.

For organizational applications, some more variables have to be considered which go beyond individual and group considerations (see above). First of all there is a communicated strategy for the organization or a positioning of the company (for example, service excellence), or an organizational culture, etc. These organization-wide valid topics must be fully understood by each and every employee within one company/organization (what it means for his or her work). In addition, it must be understood by every client the company/organization has and by the people who are in contact with clients and/or employees of the company/organization. Clients judge the experience they make with the company and with the representatives of the company/organization.

In addition, the social media offer an easy accessible platform for everyone to compare the experienced behavior or result with the communicated promise, strategy, goals, outcome, etc. Both can have a substantial impact to the company/organization inside-world as well as to the company/organization outside-world.

All these issues have to be considered for the good of the company/organization; starting with understanding one's own behavior under Favorable and under Unfavorable Conditions, one's own intention, behavior, impact as well as the ones of colleagues and clients.

Chapter 9

STRENGTH MANAGEMENT STRATEGIES

In the past few chapters, we have provided information that is primarily diagnostic and/or related to developing a useful tool for communication, both for understanding oneself and understanding others. For the consultant, that is only one part of the demand for services that exist. All too often, the consultant is asked to help particular individuals change or get teams to change behaviors and relationships. The LIFO® consultant has several strategies he can employ. Individuals can also use them for their own self-development.

CONFIRMING AND CAPITALIZING ON STRENGTHS

The most powerful and easiest strategy to us depends on confirming and capitalizing on our strengths. In effect we are trying to capitalize on our best resources. We can make things happen more readily if we can rely on our best powers, bring them to bear when called for, and seek opportunities to use them. Indeed, there is research that strongly stresses the value of doing just that as contrasted to working on one's weakest strength. Clifton and Paulsen cite a study of specialized reading training for two groups: one with well developed reading skills and another with poor reading skills. Training exaggerated the differences: the good became superb and the poor became average!

Thus, the first step begins with *strength confirmation*. Indeed, the primary goal for use of the LIFO® Life Orientation Survey was to help people identify their strengths. The further goal of development was to ensure a feeling of positivity about those talents and skills. Evidence exists that the more confident a person is about a characteristic, the more likely that person is to use it and develop additional skills.

In our LIFO® seminars, we ask people to write positive descriptions of their behaviors, attitudes and achievements, and then speak about them to the rest of the group. As might be expected, many people feel hesitant to do so, but as they continue to talk, they start feeling more confident, especially when they realize others see those strengths as well, or questions are raised when the person behaving responds differently than they expected.

As will be mentioned later in Chapter XI on LIFO® tools, we often use an exercise called *strength bombardment*. In the exercise, we ask a working team to take turns expressing appreciation of each individual's positive traits—of contributions made, pleasant impressions, helpfulness, etc. Admiration and praise flow. The effect of this experience is powerful; people feel terribly touched to receive such wonderful treatment and appreciation. The experience is intended to leave everyone with a reservoir of confidence and assurance about their strengths (believing in self) and encouragement to use them whenever there is an opportunity to do so. In addition, some people learn that other people see particular behaviors that they exhibit as additional strengths. This often surprises the recipients of such praise since they didn't value them as part of their major skill repertoire. They might have had that skill but lacked confidence about its value.

In a sense, confirming involves knowing that you have strengths that have a value and feeling confident about their use. When we have an internal image of success or confidence, it enables us to use a strength with vigor whenever it is needed. Bass & Associates found that confidence was a major factor in the expression of leadership behavior. Crowell, Katcher & Miyamoto found that self-confidence was a major factor in the expression of leadership behavior. They also found that those who regarded their communicative skills highly were more active and successful communicators. However, simply knowing you have strengths isn't enough. People have to find opportunities to use that strength, as doing so helps it be noticed by others, thus making it more available for use.

A second step is *capitalizing on strength usage*. We tell our clients to use their strongest skills whenever they can: If you're intuitive, trust your judgment and act on it. If you have fine reasoning skills, examine possibilities and provide your recommendations. If highly social, help others understand what is happening, volunteer to write letters and work on public relations. If there is a chance you could help out – do so – volunteer yourself. In short, we emphasize the value of capitalizing on your strengths.

In one company, the death of a personnel manager created a huge void. Yet one engineer who had a fine reputation as a supervisor for dealing with her people volunteered to take over while the company found a new person for the job. In a few weeks, it was evident that she was handling things as well, if not better, than the former personnel manager. The company awarded her the position permanently.

In an imaging processing company, the personnel manager was excellent in studying trends, writing reports, and establishing policies and procedures. However, he was somewhat insensitive and inept in dealing with people's feelings and concerns. Fortunately a position opened up in one of the research departments that required the administrative skills he possessed, and the company took the opportunity to transfer him. He was much more satisfied with his position, and the company felt that he made more of a contribution there than he did as the head of the personnel group.

In a small microchip company, a new chip was being developed that required an innovative design which would have implications for a whole new range of products. At the outset, one of the engineers volunteered to take charge of the new project. Although the company was considering someone else, the assertiveness of the request intrigued the president who decided to appoint him as the project manager; he never regretted it. The product became the leading moneymaker for the company and the project was completed on schedule and within budget.

To capitalize means people shouldn't be afraid to let others know about their skills without being arrogant. It may bring a person to the mind of higher management when a new situation develops. Being too passive and assuming others will recognize your worth (an SG excess) often doesn't pay off.

In a way, these confirming and capitalizing strategies are the easiest strategies to employ. They require little change, merely the greater use of strengths already developed. The consultant can help to identify and inventory strengths. He can also assist in examining the fit of individual strengths to those required by the various jobs.

MODERATING

It is important for the individual to gain a sense of what is the appropriate use of strengths in a given situation, and learn to alter and adjust the intensity as is appropriate. Moderating is the strategy for accomplishing such an objective. It does mean that you have to learn to gauge the impact of what you're doing on the people to whom you have addressed the use of the strength. For some, really hollering means you get heard, while for others a mere mention of what is desired will suffice.

One of the authors had a habit of expressing dislikes in a slow, quiet voice. This was often misinterpreted by people who felt that if he were really bothered by something, he would raise his voice. He had to learn to do that when he was irritated or bothered by something, to be fully understood. While increasing strength may be one aspect of moderating, decreasing strength would be the other. People who express everything in enthusiastic terms may have to temper their feelings to allow statements to be fully understood.

SUPPLEMENTING (AUGMENTING)

There are times when the strengths available do not cover the situation and there is clear need for contributions from others who can bring to bear the "uncovered" skills and easily handle whatever is involved. This doesn't require any change in behavior, only an appreciation of those skills and a willingness to employ them. This is precisely the case where "two heads are better than one." It does require an attitude of valuing all kinds of strengths and recognizing that no one person can handle everything, and a willingness to use the help others can provide.

For example, a non-systematic, often casual manner combined with impulsiveness often leads one of the authors to undesired consequences. However, in serious business situations he employs (supplements) attorneys and accountants to do the analytical and planning that provides the necessary attention to take care of matters properly.

In each of the consulting cases described in the styles' chapters, the prevalence of such a dominant use of a style would argue for having some other people who represent strengths in other areas to allow for wider inclusion of different views, methods and ways of communicating. Thus, for the individual who was least vested in Conserving-Holding, having someone on the team who was heavily vested in other styles would help complement the team's style. For the overly AD case, more CT and CH styles would help considerably, etc.

Supplementing requires, therefore, that people are willing to accept their own skills, recognize their own weaknesses, and appreciate the skills of others. They need to feel okay about not being able to be successful in everything, as long as there are others who can help.

The worst mistake managers can make is to select everyone in their own image. It makes it more comfortable to deal with such people but leaves a terrible vulnerability in the group, especially in those strength areas that are used least. A confident investment group, emboldened by several aggressive decisions, was dominated by principals with high CT orientations. However, they failed to stay close to changing market conditions, didn't analyze market trends, and suffered some severe losses. They later hired managers who could track events in detail, slowing decisions but optimizing results.

Belbin has experimental verification of the superiority of team decision-making by groups with varied orientations, contrasted with ones who contained those of only one or few orientations.

EXTENDING STRENGTHS

The consultant can find occasions when people may not have help but can be trained to learn more about their least used skills and practice them more frequently. Impulsive people can learn to use checklists, schedule events, review expenses, and make contacts. Hesitant people can be trained to make more rapid decisions. People focusing only on their own views can be trained to hear other's views and feelings, to seek compromises rather than win-lose outcomes. Indeed, the presence of thousands of management courses attests to the need and value of extending our styles, assuring that we don't experience surprises, failures, and loss unnecessarily. It is a strategy, however, that requires effort and discipline!

BRIDGING (BLENDING STRENGTHS)

When working with one or more people whose style is different from yours, it often becomes necessary to modify and/or extend your style, to enable your statements to be understood easily by the other person. Likewise they will need to modify theirs as well.

Essentially this *bridging* of styles enables each person to meet each other in a way that is acceptable and productive to both. When working together it will be necessary to make sure that ideas and proposals meet the value conditions of both sets of styles.

Experience has demonstrated time and time again that working in teams comprised of different styles produces a productive synergy. This reflects what we call a *blending of styles between individuals* (as distinct from a blending of styles in your own LIFO® style). In a productive team we see a willingness to merge orientations into a *new collective style* that takes advantage of all of the strengths present. Thus a mixture of CT and AD in one person and that of CH and SG in another may mean that no decision will be made before solid planning has taken place, is practical and within budget and likely to receive approval and acceptance by those likely to be affected by it.

CONTROLLING EXCESS USES OF STRENGTH

This is the hardest strategy to follow since we often overdo things when driven by habit or unconscious factors, especially when threats are perceived in situations. Certainly, if people have had a great deal of success using a particular approach, they are naturally likely to use it as many times as possible. They may not recognize, however, when it is inappropriate. In this instance, there is "too much of a good thing."

Defenses can also trigger intense responses that may be inappropriate. Encountering resistance from a potential customer, a salesman pressed so hard that he drove the customer away. A modest request may cause some administrators to respond immediately because they are afraid that failure to respond may lead to unfavorable comments about their performance. An accounts manager insists on assiduously following procedures, despite the fact she is under severe pressure to come up with an immediate progress report.

Asked a question by a critic and fearful of appearing uninformed, a manager provides so lengthy and detailed an answer that he bores his colleagues.

Consultants can help clients to control such excesses by using the following strategies:

Helping them to recognize the impact of excessive behavior. If you offered help to someone, but they reacted as if you had criticized them, you'd wonder why, providing you noticed their reaction. Consultants advise: Pay attention to your audience. If they are not responding as you hoped, if they respond negatively, the chances are you're behaving excessively! When that happens, it is necessary to stop the behavior as soon as possible and respond to the person's concern in a different manner.

Making sure they ask for feedback. This is another way of gaining such information. Sanction others to let people know when behavior is being used too frequently or is too intense. A consultant can set up exercises that demonstrate this and allow for practice, or instructions can be provided for individuals to practice on their own.

LIFO® consultants often use team-building programs to stress the importance of allowing others to help when a person's excesses are not appropriate. Exercises can help clients gauge reactions and warn of excesses. A team of two sales people were observed dealing with a customer: If one of the pair was too abstract in his presentation, the other would pat his head; if the other was too detailed, his partner would look at his watch. These were feedback signals designed to alert the person speaking that he might not be getting the effect he wanted or over-using some behavior—a signal to shift into another mode. In one instance where the other person wasn't getting the signal, the partner broke into the conversation to make a smooth transition. A communication team *par excellence!*

Helping them to understand their own reactions and be alert to signals. If a client is feeling tense, under severe strain and working awfully hard to make a point (like pushing a huge boulder up a hill), they may put too much into replying and acting, and be affecting others negatively. In such situations, a consultant can help the client practice being their own observer(s) for such signals, thus controlling or modifying their behavior accordingly. Practice exercises in recognizing signals of distress are contained in the LIFO® Workbook that is used in introductory courses.

Make sure to stop the ongoing behavior. The most common thing to do when frustrated is to persist. When feeling attacked, one tries to defend intensely. A person may find it useful to listen to feelings, stop the behavior, and see if there isn't something else that could be done. Stopping might involve a request for a temporary break, cutting the behavior off, or even acknowledging feelings that something doesn't seem to be going as expected and exploring the rationale for the other person's behavior. When we visited a manager who had attended a recent seminar, we saw a plaque on his desk. Written in bold letters was the statement: *YOU DON'T HAVE TO RESPOND NOW!* He found that an effective reminder to control his impulsivity.

Helping them explore alternative interpretations. The consultant can help a client learn to assess his reactions by raising such questions as: *Did you want the other person to feel you were criticizing him? By offering so much explanation, were you really telling your staff member that he was stupid? Or were you trying to help because so much rode on this situation? How clear did you make that to that person? When a person barged into your office and asked you to do something for them, were they rude or just over-concerned about something at the moment?* The consultant, presumably, wants the client to learn how their interpretation of the situation influences the response that occurred, especially if the situation seemed threatening.

Additional questions that might be posed are: *What was the perceived threat? How did you feel when it happened? Why did you feel threatened?* During such a questioning period, the consultant is expected to listen intently without judgment, trying to sense the attitudes and feelings that arise and letting the client explore possibilities for alternative behavior.

Kenneth Finn has developed a therapeutic model called *Recharacterization Therapy* that consists of having people try to reframe their views of what is happening. By changing one's interpretation, putting a more positive cast on it, perhaps a longer range view, things can seem quite different. The different perspective may enable a person to bring a more productive response to bear on the situation.

For example, invited to take a scenic tour of Chicago in a small private plane, one of the authors was panicked by every bit of turbulence that was encountered and pleaded with the pilot to return to the airport. He calmed down when the pilot said, "Allan, these are only bumps in the air road. Think of the bumps you run into when driving in a car!" This was enough to change the whole experience, not only for that short flight but for other longer flights when a plane is rocked by rough air.

Using humor can help, too, pointing to what is funny about what is happening; for example, saying, *If we deliberately tried to mislead each other, the two of us wouldn't be as successful as we are now!* Again, a consultant might ask the client questions, such as: *Since we often tend to think of things from our point of view, how might it seem to the other person? What would happen if we would extend the benefit of the doubt to the other person—if we thought they were trying to help us instead of making us appear foolish?*

Consultants can also help people handle fears and stress by having them consider avoiding stressful situations by delegating to others or refraining from an encounter. One manager has a friend with a sailboat who generously invited him for a day's excursion. The friend became anxious whenever the boat heeled and felt a little seasick.

He forced himself to go several times more (he didn't want to seem unappreciative) but never felt comfortable. Finally he decided not to accept any more invitations: "I really don't see the sense of making myself anxious and calling it pleasure!"

A distinguished and highly experienced marketing manager could never make a decent presentation to the board of directors. He would hem and haw, fumble over words, talk low, and generally make a mess of it. Finally, using a supplementing strategy, he designated one of his assistants who was an extremely gifted speaker to be the department's presenter. The marketing manager would assist by answering questions or providing additional information (activities which he could always handle) but never again made a speech.

These interventions are extremely valuable to help clients manage their excesses. This is regarded even more highly when people find themselves creating undesirable impacts, unable to cope with situations, and behaving out of control.

Chapter 10

STYLE COMBINATIONS

The following article was written originally by **Betty Forbis** as a chapter in the handbook she used in her LIFO® training activities.

❈

We Are One Thing and Another
by Betty Forbis

It is tempting to think of everyone as using only one or two of the four life orientation styles—only the ones that we see, hear, and feel most often, the ones with the highest impact. However, each of us has access to all four styles. The lowest result in the LIFO® Orientation Survey categories possible is 9.

There is no zero!

Our full LIFO® profile identifies our preferences in a hierarchy, showing a *priority* of values on which we base our behavioral preferences. The priority differs for each person or profile. For example, the priorities of a CT user with an AD backup style will look, sound, and feel very different than a CT user with a CH backup style. Often, one or two style preferences appear to be a higher priority, meaning we hear it, see it, and feel it more than the others. However, it's important to remember that we are not one style *or* another—we are one style *and* another!

In the following examples of well known individuals, we have identified them by not only their "highest priority" LIFO® style preference, but also attempted to give examples of how other LIFO® styles are included as part of their profile.

PEOPLE WHO APPEAR TO REPRESENT EACH LIFO® STYLE

In the examples below, you may recognize one style as the most visible; however, as you look and listen, you will hear the impact of the overall profile.

SUPPORTING-GIVING (SG) EXAMPLES

Nelson Mandela – A strong anti-apartheid activist. Convicted of sabotage, he was sentenced to life imprisonment and served 27 years in prison. Following his release, he led his party to negotiations to establish democracy in 1994. He served as President of South Africa from 1944-1999, the first president to be elected in a fully represented democratic election.

Nelson Mandela Quotes:

- *A good head and a good heart are always a formidable combination.* (CH and SG)
- *For to be free is not merely to cast off one's chains, but to live in a way that respects and enhances the freedom of others.* (CH)
- *Money won't create success—the freedom to make it will.* (CT)

Steve Jobs – Entrepreneur, inventor, technology visionary. He and Steve Wozniak co-founded Apple Computers, pioneering a series of revolutionary technologies.

Steve Jobs Quotes:

- *Be a yardstick of quality. Some people aren't used to an environment where excellence is expected.* (SG)
- *I want to put a ding in the universe.* (CT and SG; making it happen, thinking big, making a difference)
- *Our goal is to make the best devices in the world, not to be the biggest.* (SG)

Martin Luther King, Jr – American clergyman, activist and leader in the African-American civil rights movement, using the non-violent teachings of Mohandas Gandhi.

Martin Luther King, Jr. Quotes:

- *...And when this happens, when we allow freedom to ring, when we let it ring from every village and every hamlet, from every state and every city, we will be able to speed up that day when all of God's children, black men and white men, Jews and Gentiles, Protestants and Catholics, will be able to join hands and sing in the words of the old Negro spiritual: Free at last! Free at last!* (SG)
- *Our lives begin to end the day we become silent about things that matter.* (CT; speak out, risk)

CONTROLLING-TAKING (CT) EXAMPLES

Margaret Thatcher, Baroness Thatcher - The longest-serving (1979–1990) Prime Minister of the United Kingdom of the 20th century, and the only woman ever to have held the post. A Soviet journalist nicknamed her the "Iron Lady," which became associated with her uncompromising politics and leadership style. As Prime Minister, she implemented Conservative policies that have come to be known as *Thatcherism*.

Margaret Thatcher Quotes:

- *I love argument, I love debate. I don't expect anyone just to sit there and agree with me, that's not their job.* (CT; put it on the table and deal with it)
- *I'm extraordinarily patient, provided I get my own way in the end.* (SG and CH; patience. CT; getting own way. Patience as a means to an end.)
- You might wonder if this speaks to AD tact and diplomacy when she said, *You don't tell deliberate lies, but sometimes you have to be evasive.*

Sir Richard Branson, Inspirational entrepreneur, Virgin Records, Virgin Atlantic Airways, Virgin America Airways, Virgin Galactic, and over 400 other Virgin-branded enterprises. He has been successful in business since age 16.

Richard Branson Quotes:

- *My biggest motivation? Just to keep challenging myself. I see life almost like one long university education that I never had – every day I'm learning something new.* (CT; challenging and SG; believing in the importance of learning and developing)
- *Business opportunities are like buses; there's always another one coming.* (CT; opportunities, as in if there's not one there, go find one.)
- *You don't learn to walk by following rules. You learn by doing and by falling over.* (CT; jump in, be willing to risk)
- *A business has to be involving, it has to be fun, and it has to exercise your creative instincts.* (AD fun with CT being involved).
- *I am prepared to try anything once.* (CT and AD)

Donald Trump – is an American businessman, investor, television personality and author. He is the chairman and president of The Trump Organization and the founder of Trump Entertainment Resorts. Trump's extravagant lifestyle, outspoken manner, and role on the NBC reality show *The Apprentice* have made him a well-known celebrity.

Donald Trump Quotes:

- *As long as you're going to be thinking anyway, think big.* (CT)
- *In the end, you're measured not by how much you undertake but by what you finally accomplish.* (CT)
- *I try to learn from the past, but I plan for the future by focusing exclusively on the present. That's where the fun is.* (CH; build on what exists. SG; future long range planning, an example of a CT way of having fun)

CONSERVING-HOLDING (CH) EXAMPLES

Thomas Edison is a good example of CH creativity. CH demonstrates creativity when there is a need – when something is not working the way it was intended to work.

For example, there was a light bulb already invented, but it was not efficient or reliable. Methodically and systematically, Edison went through hundreds of models until he found success.

Thomas Edison Quotes:

- *Discontent is the first necessity of progress.* (CT)
- *I have not failed, I have found 10,000 reasons why it won't work.* (CH; systematic testing of options)
- He also said, *Hell, there are not rules here, we are trying to accomplish something.* (CT)
- *Many of life's failures are people who did not realize how close they were to success when they gave up.* (SG; to try harder)

President Theodore Roosevelt was the 26th president of the United States and the youngest. Known for his exuberant personality and wide range of interests and achievements, he was also only one of three sitting Presidents to win the Nobel Prize.

President Theodore Roosevelt's Quotes:

- *Do what you can, where you are, with what you have.* (CH; practical, CT; seems to say, "Don't just be but do something!")

- *Keep your eyes on the stars and your feet on the ground.* (SG and CH)
- *The most important single ingredient in the formula of success is knowing how to get along with people.* (AD)
- *In any moment of decision, the best thing you can do is the right thing, the next best thing is the wrong thing, and the worst thing you can do is nothing.* (SG ideals, and CT concerns.)

> **Stephen William Hawking**, CH, CBE, FRS, FRSA is a British theoretical physicist and author. His key scientific works to date have been a collaboration with Roger Penrose on theorems of gravitational force. Hawking has a motor neurone disease related to amyotrophic lateral sclerosis (ALS). He is almost completely paralyzed and communicates through a speech generating device. He continues to use his remarkable mind, humor and persistence in exploration of science and space.

Stephen Hawking Quotes:

- *The whole history of science has been the gradual realization that events do not happen in an arbitrary manner, but that they reflect a certain underlying order, which may or may not be divinely inspired.* (CH; systems, order)
- *One cannot really argue with a mathematical theorem.* (CH; fact based, objective*)*
- *There ought to be something very special about the boundary conditions of the universe and what can be more special than that there is no boundary?* (CT; no limits. AD; talking, experimenting, exploring new ideas)
- *Mankind's greatest achievements have come about by talking,* (SG; collaborating) *and its greatest failures by not.*
- *Life would be tragic if it weren't funny.* (AD; humor)

ADAPTING-DEALING (AD) EXAMPLE

Robin Williams –Think of the varied roles to which he has so flexibly adapted ...*Good Morning, Vietnam; Good Will Hunting, Patch Adams, Dead Poet's Society, Birdcage, Fisher King*, to name only a few. Flexible, adaptable, playful, optimistic, experimental, empathy, and humor as his hallmark

Robin Williams' Quotes:

- *Comedy is acting out optimism.* (AD)
- <u>*You're only given a little spark of madness. You mustn't lose it.*</u> **(AD)**
- *No matter what people tell you, words and ideas can change the world.* (SG, CT)

President Bill Clinton – Probably a combination of SG, CT and AD. His AD "connects" with people; strong eye contact, tunes in to the person, tactful, diplomatic, goes for win/win. His SG is devoted to raising the standards of quality of life in the world. He has done more good in the world since he left office. He uses his network of relationships (AD) to "make things happen" (CT).

President Bill Clinton Quotes:

- *We cannot build our own future without helping others to build theirs.* (SG; helping, cooperating, responsive to needs of others)
- *If you live long enough, you'll make mistakes. But if you learn from them, you'll be a better person. It's how you handle adversity, not how it affects you. The main thing is never quit, never quit, never*

quit. (CT; never give up. SG; try harder. CH; persistence. AD; try another way)

- *I may not have been the greatest president, but I've had the most fun these eight years.* (AD)

> **Dr. Seuss** – writer, poet and cartoonist, most widely known for his children's books also loved by adults. You will recognize The Cat in the Hat, Green Eggs and Ham, Oh, the Places You'll Go!

What do you think Dr. Seuss' LIFO® profile is? If we look at some of his quotations, we can see that they represent all four of the styles:

- *Step with care and great tact, and remember…life's a great balancing act!* (CH)
- *You have brains in your head, you have feet in your shoes. You can steer yourself any direction you choose.* (CT)
- *Today is your day, your mountain is waiting, so…get on your way!* (SG, CT)
- *From here to here, and here to there…funny things are everywhere.* (AD)

LIFO® STYLES REPRESENTED BY POPULAR SONGS

The following popular songs can be seen to represent the four different styles:

SG - SUPPORTING-GIVING:

- "Imagine" – John Lennon
- "Impossible Dream" – Man of La Mancha
- "I Have a Dream" – Abba
- "Change the World" – Eric Clapton

- "Superman" – Five for Fighting
- "Do You Hear the People Sing?" – Les Misérables

CT - CONTROLLING-TAKING:

- "We are the Champions" – Queen
- "My Way" – Frank Sinatra
- "We Will Rock You" – Queen
- "I Want it All and I Want it Now" - Queen
- "A Hard Day's Night" - Beatles
- "Master of the House" - Les Misérables

CH - CONSERVING-HOLDING:

- "The Element Song" – Tom Lehrer
- "50 Ways to Leave your Lover" – Simon & Garfunkel
- "The Twelve Days of Christmas"
- "100 Bottles of Beer on the Wall" (if you sing the entire song!)
- "We Didn't Start the Fire" – Billy Joel
- "Three to Get Ready and Four to Go" – Dave Brubeck

AD - ADAPTING-DEALING:

- "Always Look On the Bright Side of Life" – Company from Spamalot
- "Don't Worry Be Happy" – Bobby McFerrin
- "Dancing in the Street" – Mamas and the Papas
- "A Little Help from My Friends" – Beatles
- "We Can Work it Out" – Beatles
- "We're Going to be Friends" – Jack Johnson

Chapter 11

LIFO® TOOLS AND EXERCISES

The most memorable experiences with The LIFO® Method come from experiences with LIFO® tools and exercises. These include surveys, the reports of profiles, explanations of interpretations, and explorations of relationships. In addition, there is the use of LIFO® Strength Feedback charts to illustrate individual and group characteristic behaviors; workbooks to gain additional knowledge practice uses of LIFO® concepts and understanding the various LIFO® strategies for personal development and change; and a Slide-A-Style device that allows you to identify the style from the behavior as well as identify behaviors from the style selected.

THE LIFO® LIFE ORIENTATION SURVEY

The basic survey is called The LIFO® Life Orientation Survey. It is available both in paper form and on the Internet. From the summary results, interpretations of your style of behavior can be made either individually, by written report, or via a computer report.

A cautionary note: The LIFO® Life Orientation Survey provides data that allows us to pose sets of provocative questions for use in coaching and training our clients. Since the statements in the survey are ones the client indicates are characteristic of him or her, they need to be verified when checking with the client, and with those acquaintances and colleagues that know the client. In and of themselves, they do not necessarily reveal anything inherent in the client; the results are always subject to verification by the client.

Survey construction. There are a total of 72 items that are ranked according to their accuracy for representing your style. These are organized into 18 categorical statements: 9 for identifying behavior under favorable conditions and 9 for unfavorable ones.

Typical directions are: *You will be given a descriptive statement followed by four possible endings. You are to indicate the order in which you feel each ending applies to you. In the blank spaces to the left of each ending. Fill in the blanks with the numbers, 4, 3, 2 and 1, according to which ending is most like you (4) to the one that is least like you (1), the others being ranked as 2 or 3. There can be no ties.*

For example:
Most of the time, I am:

1. respectful and helpful
2. confident and full of ideas
3. practical and careful
4. lively and popular

As mentioned earlier, the survey provides information about the extent to which you use each of the four LIFO® orientations. Actually, each statement reflects one of these, with the first representing the Supporting-Giving (SG) Orientation, the second the Controlling-Taking (CT) Orientation, the third the Conserving-Holding (CH) Orientation and the fourth the Adapting-Dealing (AD) Orientation. Sums are calculated so that a 4 is assigned to the most characteristic statement, a 3 to the next highest one, a 2 to the next, and a 1 to the least characteristic choice. The highest result for the nine items in each orientation category would be 36 and the lowest 9.

LIFO® population study results. People whose results fall in the top and bottom profiles show consistent results when retesting. There is more change for those whose results are in the middle ranges. Almost no one who has a very low result ever moves from the lowest rating to the top. A similar case exists for changes from the top to the lowest. Over 90 percent of people tested felt their profiles truly represented them.

In our trainings, we sometimes ask people to pair off and discuss ways in which they handle life and work problems, and relate that discussion to their LIFO® profiles. Another way is to use a Colleague Dialogue Survey, based on incomplete sentences that allow the individual to complete them according to the way he or she normally handles the issue everyday. The surveys are completed privately and then discussed. As a result, pairs readily see the validity of the profiles or inquire further when there appears to be no correspondence. Often the explanation lies in the interpretation of the specific item involved in the survey.

The following shows the LIFO® test results:

9% use primarily a single dominant orientation.

18% use primarily one main (highest result) orientation and another high orientation.

54% use primarily two dominant orientations.

14% use equally often three different orientations.

5% are equally balanced in use of four orientations.

In about half of the population, the *unfavorable condition* profiles differ significantly from those revealed under *favorable* conditions.

Taking the survey — some changes. Initially, the LIFO® Life Orientation Survey was the only survey available. We found it most meaningful to instruct people taking the survey to think of behavior that was most generally characteristic of their behavior. When working with business groups, however, we suggest that participants think of the behavior they characteristically exhibit in the work situation. We made that change because we discovered that different instruction sets yielded somewhat different results.

Other LIFO® Surveys. A later development was the construction of surveys designed for different situations: coaching, consulting, customer preference, leadership, learning, marriage, parenting, reactions to change, selling and teaching. Each survey is constructed identical to the LIFO® Orientation Survey, save for changes in the content appropriate to the role. Instructions are also the same, save for the role reference.

In the special situation type surveys, the instruction requires participants to think of that particular situation and the most generally characteristic behavior that the person exhibited in that role. We recommend that consultants examine all of the surveys, considering the roles and situations they face, rather than relying only on the LIFO® Life Orientation survey.

VERIFICATION EXERCISE-DIALOGUE WITH COLLEAGUES

Members of a group are paired, preferably with someone that they know. Everyone is asked to complete a 40-item incomplete sentence survey with such sentences as:

- When I feel my boss has confidence in me, I _____
- When I experience difficulty in my work, I _____
- I enjoy work most when _____
- When I find people disagreeing with me, I _____
- When I join a group, I expect the leader to_____
- When I'm experiencing time pressure, I _____

The pairs are instructed to exchange papers and take turns reading each answer. Finally, they are asked to relate the findings to their LIFO® profiles.

WORKBOOKS

Workbooks can help people understand how to interpret their own survey results and have discussions with others to develop further understanding, especially if in natural work groups. This can also help them confirm the interpretation or modify it, so it can represent them more accurately. In addition to the basic workbook, special workbooks are available for other applied surveys, for example leadership styles, selling styles, etc.

COMPUTERIZED REPORTS

Based on many professionally written reports, a computer version of the survey results provides a written document that can be used as a personal reminder or as a basis for discussion with others. The report is based on the LIFO Life Orientation Survey Results (a sample report can be viewed at the LIFO® website, www.lifo.co).

We recommend to our clients that they use it as a starting point for discussions, subject to modification if any statements do not accurately or thoroughly represent the person's style of behavior.

SLIDE-A-STYLE DEVICE

The Slide-A-Style device is constructed to resemble a slide rule. There are two such "slide-rules" that provide information, listed below. By moving the slide rule so the indicator identifies a particular style, you can get insights about a) communications or b) strategies for compatibility:

Regarding *communications*, information is provided about:

1. What a person using this particular style wants to know.
2. What approach makes them "tune in."

3. What approach makes them "tune out."
4. How to communicate with an employee of this style.
5. How to communicate with a boss of this style.

Regarding *compatibility strategies* information is provided about identifying benefits, challenges, and solutions of style combinations:

1. Between your most preferred style and the most preferred style of another person.
2. Between your two most preferred styles.

Many people keep these devices for years as a vivid reminder of their LIFO® experiences and useful tools when encountering new people that seem difficult to understand.

TINKER TOY EXERCISE

A box of Tinker Toys (or any other child's construction tools) is emptied onto the table and pieces randomly distributed to each of the people involved in the exercise. The group is asked to construct a model of what they feel would represent the best leadership imaginable. They are given one hour to complete the task. If possible, their behavior is videotaped.

At the end of the exercise, the group is asked to indicate the degree of satisfaction they felt about their model and describe the group process that led to the final construction. They are also asked to discuss why they assigned such ratings.

As a final step, the scores of each member of the group are arrayed in column form such as in the example below, and the group is then asked how the behavior that occurred is related to the LIFO® data.

SAMPLE TABULATION OF GROUP RESULTS

	Favorable Scores:				Unfavorable Scores:			
	SG	CT	CH	AD	SG	CT	CH	AD
1.	26	30	14	20	28	27	15	20
2.	30	20	20	20	20	30	25	15
3.	22	28	12	28	20	30	14	26

For example, which people seemed to disagree most? The answer would be: those who had high CT scores under unfavorable conditions. Of the three listed above, all could be cited, with #3 being more willing to compromise after a disagreement. How about participation? Probably everyone contributed, if scores were similar to the three cited. Additional questions related to group performance could also be raised, and the group scores could provide a basis for understanding how the group manages tasks and decisions.

SUBMITTING ADVERTISEMENTS

If a program lasts more than one day, participants are asked to find examples of each style in advertisements that appear in the newspaper or magazines. When they return, each member is asked to place his advertisements in the appropriate style category written on a board. The group examines the accuracy of the placement, different ways styles can be expressed, and the probable likelihood of gaining a favorable response from the targeted audience. They are also asked to think of how the advertisement could have a better probability of receiving a favorable response from the targeted audience.

THE HUMAN GRAPH: *WHO ARE WE?* EXERCISE

Four categories of LIFO® Survey result possibilities are placed on a blackboard or Easel Papers with a fair distance provided between the categories, for example, 9-17, 18-26, 27-31, 32-36. Members are asked to stand underneath the category that represents them (based on their LIFO® survey results), for each of the following times (separately): 1 for their main style, 2 for their backup, and 3 for their least preferred styles. When there are ties, they are asked to make a choice.

They do this both for their behavior under favorable conditions and also for their behavior under unfavorable conditions. As the array is demonstrated, the group is asked to comment on what has been illustrated, its validity in terms of perceptions, and the respective differences between people.

INDIVIDUAL HAND-WRITTEN REPORTS

These are similar to the computerized ones, except that the consultant can add examples from the specific work or life conditions of the client, and enhance the impact and utility of the report. In coaching, reviews of such circumstances are made more meaningful because the client can realize the specific impact of his or her behavior. Especially when reviewing situations with two or more people who know what happened, new possibilities for productive resolution of differences can occur because people are more aware of why and how things happened. They also have learned to understand and accept each other more.

STRENGTH FEEDBACK CHARTS

The Stress Feedback Chart represents all four of the LIFO® orientations, along with descriptions of some productive characteristics and also some excessive ones. An example of such a chart is provided below:

LIF◐ Strength Feedback

Supporting Giving	Adapting Dealing
Considerate	Flexible
Idealistic	Tactful
Modest	Sociable
Trusting	Empathetic
Cooperative	Enthusiastic
Helpful	Adaptable
Receptive	Inspiring
Responsive	Experimental
Seek excellence	Negotiating
Loyal	Animated

SG AD
CH CT

Tenacious	Directing
Practical	Quick to act
Economical	Confident
Reserved	Seek change
Factual	Persuasive
Steadfast	Forceful
Thorough	Competitive
Methodical	Risk-taking
Detail-oriented	Persistent
Analytical	Urgent

Conserving Holding   **Controlling Taking**

CONDITIONS	SG	CT	CH	AD
NAME [_____]				
Favorable	☐	☐	☐	☐
Unfavorable	☐	☐	☐	☐

In the exercise, a separate chart for each participant is posted on a blackboard. Most consultants then ask each person to go up to the chart with their name and indicate with a red crayon their own rating of the behavior on a scale from 1 to 10, where 10 is most and 1 is least. Then every other member of the group goes to all the other charts and indicates their ratings of the particular member's behavior.

Each participant then stands by their chart and describes what they have learned, asks questions for elaboration of ratings or qualifications, and then summarizes the major findings of their own chart.

In another use of the chart, members can mark characteristics on every chart for behavior they would like to see more of (using a blue crayon) and behavior they would like to see less of. In a work group situation, this often promotes a general discussion of specific instances that have been experienced.

In team-work programs, such charts are used as described above.

STRENGTH BOMBARDMENT EXERCISE

Members of a team group are gathered together in a circle with their hands on each other's shoulders. Each member offers him or herself to the group for comments. The instructions for providing such comments are as follows: "Look directly at the person and think of those things you admire, have impressed you, or have made a positive impact on you or others. Try to state those impressions in as positive a way as possible. You are not to make judgments but rather to be specific in your mention of events or consequences."

After everyone has received such treatment, the behavior and feelings are discussed. This provides a very positive influence on group morale and on personal feelings of acceptance and acknowledgment.

(This will be discussed more in Chapter XV on teamwork applications.)

LEADERSHIP STYLE STRENGTH FEEDBACK CHARTS

These are similar to the other charts, except that they display leadership behavior under each of the four orientation labels. They are designed to accompany experiences with the LIFO® leadership style surveys.

Part Two:

APPLICATIONS OF THE LIFO® METHOD

Chapter 12

ENTRY CONSULTING ISSUES

In Part Two, we will describe some of the major applications that have been used and are available for The LIFO® Method licensees. In this chapter, we begin with the methods use for enhancing initial contacts with clients.

INTRODUCTION

When meeting new clients, consultants vary from being wary, confident, unsure and sometimes committed to a particular methodology that they believe will be of value to their clients. In our practice, we have found The LIFO® Method a valuable tool for enhancing the initial contacts with clients, quickly demonstrating the client's capabilities and vulnerabilities. It also provides a firm basis for continuing the consulting relationship.

Clients frequently have concerns about the consultant regarding credentials, experiences working with similar clients, and manner of working with people. Questions may arise such as: *Will the consultant expose certain people, make things difficult, or upset established practices and procedures? Will he or she really help us solve our problems?* and *Can we afford what is recommended?*

We are presuming that the consultant will want to establish a continuing relationship with the client and hopes to do that by getting the client to understand what is happening, how the executive team processes information and makes decisions, and how committed the consultant is to working on existing problems. The client probably hopes that this can be done with a minimum of personality upsets and within a reasonable time.

Consultants have many ways to be introduced, but let us assume that this is the first meeting. With a LIFO® approach predominating, the consultant would try to gain acceptance for an initial study period. During that period, the consultant would ask to have each executive (or team member) take a LIFO® Life Orientations Survey and be interviewed about their perceptions of the key issues faced by the group.

VALUE OF THE LIFO® METHOD IN ENHANCING INITIAL CONTACTS

The following describes the many values provided by The LIFO® Method in new situations:

Non-evaluative way of describing behavior. In many cases—for example, in a family-owned firm or one in which a key person has built the business—such a process as we describe would be done with that individual, privately. In an executive group, individual reports would be prepared for each participant. These provide descriptions of behavior patterns characteristic of each member under favorable and unfavorable conditions in non-judgmental terms, along with some recommendations for ways in which the person could manage their behavioral pattern for increased effectiveness, both for himself and in relation to others. A group profile would be constructed, providing information about the key strengths the group has for dealing with problems, possibilities for over-relying on some ways and ignoring others, and vulnerabilities caused by the particular combination of individuals that comprise the group.

Checking for confirmation and agreement. The material provided would be subject to review by individuals and the group. If there is any disagreement with the statements, attempts would be made to understand the nature of the disagreement, and when justified, amendments made. During the process, some of the information revealed by the group would be related to the material provided by The LIFO® Method.

Feeling of being understood and accepted. Often, after listening to the information provided by the LIFO® Survey and Report, group members will proceed to cite instances that corroborate, disconfirm, or elaborate further about what has been revealed. They are often motivated to talk at length about issues that concern them and the executive group.

Reinforcing consultant credibility. Since the method provides concrete and objective material that helps explain the client's perceptions of issues, the credibility of the consultant is reinforced beyond his or her credentials and references.

Gaining insightful information on how to communicate with client or client group. There is often a predominant style evident in the group profile. This happens because key executives have the tendency to hire staff members who resemble them, who share their values and concerns, and who can understand them readily. This leads to a concentration of strengths in a particular area; for example, in one major bank, confident behavior, quick decision-making, and willingness to assume risks as contrasted to a computer company where thoughtful deliberation, detailed planning, and sharing of information is prized. For the first company, the consultant would realize that he'd need to communicate in a similar manner to be readily accepted and understood by the individual or group. For the latter group, evidence of sound planning, a slower and more careful communication pace would be more successful.

Sometimes, where there is a major split within the group, the use of two differently styled consultants might be advised. Flexibility and familiarity with different styles would be extremely valuable for the consultant(s). By having more balance in strengths (including AD), it might be easier to shift as required by different member's styles. This will be especially helpful in dealing with two dramatically different individuals. Having a consultant to work with the person whose style mirrors his own can enable rapport to be quickly established and gain agreement and acceptance.

However, the most convincing factors are the LIFO® surveys and interpretations themselves. The experienced LIFO® consultant recognizes that the method provides a lot of valid understanding of how one behaves.

For example, the president of one international company asked, "We have just gone through an experience with the Management Grid—why do we need The LIFO® Method?" The consultant replied, "I'm sure you must've had a meaningful experience with the Grid, but I don't know of any better way of comparing the two systems than to ask you or someone on your staff to complete a survey and send it to me. I will provide you (or him or her) with a personal report that can demonstrate the value of The LIFO® Method." The client replied, "I'll take it myself!" (The consultant thought to himself, *We're going to have a new client!*)

When the CEO received the computerized report (which was influenced by things that had been observed during a company meeting), he called his executive vice-president and told him, "I just received this report. What do you think about it?" They then spent over two hours discussing the impressions and reviewing some incidents.

A similar experience occurred when he shared the report with his wife. What impressed him was that the report made clear the nature of the problems experienced by both him and others, as well as pointed the way to possible solutions. He was impressed that the feedback was helpful, that it acknowledged his strengths and offered helpful suggestions for managing them effectively. The president then requested that all executive staff members complete the surveys, including the heads of all international divisions, and promised that there would be a discussion based on the results at the next international meeting.

At the international meetings, spouses were often left on their own to do sightseeing and visit stores to purchase local goods and souvenirs. However, they had expressed some interest in having learning experiences as well. Therefore, it was decided to ask them to also complete surveys, and a separate discussion was held for them. At the end of the afternoon when the discussions were scheduled, the levels of noise and involvement were highly evident of the value, as husbands and wives discussed their profiles with each other. Subsequently, consultation was requested by other international executives for similar workshops with their staffs.

MARKETING THE LIFO® METHOD

The term LIFO® is abstract and forces the consultant to get into a description of the concept when there are other and better ways to impact a client. The best advice is to not be hasty in prescribing LIFO® programs, unless you have identified the critical issues that are involved, and have created the opportunity to obtain survey results and had reports available for the executive group.

Clients are concerned about benefits, specifically what the methodology and training can do for them. This requires some knowledge of client concerns, problems, and behavioral approaches. We generally try to discover these by meeting with a client before we make any presentations and become familiar with their business situation, observe the working environment, and, if possible, sit in on a business meeting,

Clients also want to understand how The LIFO® Method will provide the benefits. Therefore, you have to demonstrate a concrete tie between what you are advocating and how it can help to understand a situation or predict certain outcomes. We have found that if we can do that, the Method sells itself.

A further clincher is the use of the orientation names to identify certain practices and uses. The language is extremely user-friendly, and participants will readily employ the names themselves. Demonstrations of how excesses lead to undesirable results and the importance of strength management strategies are easy to point out after observing meetings or when training is introduced. Getting people to think, *How can we best use our strengths to be productive?* becomes a powerful tool for thinking effectively.

EXTENDING THE BENEFITS

Satisfied clients often ask for help in selecting or promoting candidates, coaching for executives, or help in communicating more effectively. By far the largest use has been in team-building. The experienced LIFO® licensee and consultant recognizes that The LIFO® Method provides a set of valuable tools that can be used in solving personal, group and organizational issues.

When we don't have the luxury of the above, we try to arrange a demonstration. This can be as simple as asking them to answer a few general questions about how they behave at work, to asking a group to tackle a small exercise program, for example, the Tinker Toy exercise. During the analysis, it is easy to demonstrate the different approaches, problems solved and created by the individual styles, and implications for their direct work experience.

It needs to be emphasized that the successful salesperson in this instance needs to understand favorable and unfavorable styles, their excesses and deficiencies, and to be spontaneously able to comment on them accurately. Before you reach that high level of experience, you can use questions to build awareness and demonstrate from the answers what different approaches exist, and use answers to indicate how they are effective or not.

We are concerned that the client(s) recognize the significance from their own experience. Usually the survey, an interpretation, and a sharing with some significant other are the clinchers.

NEW BUSINESS OPPORTUNITIES-REFERRALS

In many instances, requests come from previous client experiences, both where such clients have moved to new companies and because of some acquaintances. It certainly doesn't hurt to be able to cite several Fortune 500 companies that are active users or a particular company that is well known to the potential client.

In some instances, where there has been an especially favorable experience, we ask the client whether they would know of anyone else who could stand to benefit from such an encounter. We have found clients willing to make referrals, even though in our initial consulting, we were reluctant to ask.

DEALING WITH CLIENT QUESTIONS

Some sophisticated clients want answers to questions such as reliability, validity, etc. While we can and do answer those questions, we try to spend more of our time answering the underlying issue concerning the validity and meaningfulness of the surveys, and the subsequent experiences.

TARGET

Our preference is to influence the key person or persons involved in directing the organization. In most cases, we did not find the human resources director or training director the most useful contact, except where they designated some line organization as a possible first venture. Sometimes a positive consequence for a poorly performing team can lend instant credibility.

If you are dealing with trainers and training directors, remember that you have to demonstrate how the program can be of benefit to them, that is what their people will gain from the training, how trainers can be readily trained to conduct the programs, how the programs can fit into their budgets, how easily people can use the concepts, and how managers and employees will value their experiences.

SOME ADDITIONAL MARKETING AREAS

- *Companies in the communications business*—making sure they are attracting the right customers and practicing behaviors that will be appropriate in style.
- *Customer service training.* We're now designing programs for brokers and clients with respect to attracting and retaining clients, for resolving issues, and increasing the scope and kinds of investments.
- *Sales divisions.* There are LIFO® sales programs that can make a difference, particularly in demonstrating how resistances of various styles can be overcome.
- *Management training programs*—developing awareness of how behavior influences planning, decisions, actions and motivation; and providing a basis for improving training, counseling, and team behavior that can be demonstrated in changed behavior.
- *Coaching and counseling.* This is a rapidly expanding area, and LIFO® concepts are exceptionally helpful here.
- *Improving school and industrial training*—use of concepts from Learning Dynamics
- *Patient care*—using LIFO® concepts to increase empathy and understanding of caretakers' prescriptions and advice, and to enhance practice-management.

- *Teamwork.* The LIFO® tools and programs are especially useful for helping teams diagnose interpersonal problems, use resources more effectively, and enhance communication and cooperation between members. In fact, in more than 50 instances team-building experiences led to increased business. The LIFO® reports also provide valuable information and tend to be recommended for others outside the experience.

KEEP ASKING OTHERS AND SHARE SELLING EXPERIENCES

This article reflects our experience. Undoubtedly, those with other styles may have found other approaches equally or more effective. Learning to market and sell LIFO® programs is a study in and of itself, so talk to as many people as you can about how they were able to be successful. And remember, it's not simply about copying but more about adapting ways that are compatible with your style. It would make sense to compile a manual of successful selling experiences of others for additional guidance.

Chapter 13

ADVERTISING APPLICATIONS

In our LIFO® seminars, we emphasize the importance of understanding people's styles and communicating to them in the "style" language that is most likely to attract their attention and interest. Thus, if I were presenting a proposal to a boss who had a heavy CH preference, I would be received best if I organized my presentation, made major points clear, offered rationales for what I wanted to do, and provided data and experiences or research that justified my position. However, if my boss heavily emphasized a CT orientation in his behavior, I would try to be brief, headline the major points, and confidently state the proposed action steps, waiting for his approval. If SG, I would stress ideals, long term goals, or request needs for help. A witty and friendly approach, suggesting new possibilities would be most likely to be of interest to someone espousing AD behaviors.

What is true generally for business and personal communications is equally appropriate for advertising. Many ads you see can be classified as to the language used and illustrations chosen that fall readily into the LIFO® orientations. For example, advertisements for refreshments emphasize having fun, people enjoying themselves or relaxing (AD). Advertisements for cereal are pitched more to parents who buy them (SG) and characteristically emphasize the "good-ness and taste" that is offered by the product (frequently, in these days, emphasizing low calories, low fat content and vitamins – "to make you healthier"). Some automobile manufacturer's emphasize the power, speed, and control of their machines (CT), while some advertisements, like for banks, stress safety, consistent returns, and error-free performance (CH).

On the other hand, if one wanted to appeal to managers and high level executives who emphasized the CT orientation, stress-ing the quick start for the day, the surge of energy that one feels, the ease with which it can be served would be key factors influ-encing their choice. A CH oriented cereal would stress the re-search that had been done, the diet conditions that should prevail, presented in a neat and clearly legible manner. An AD one would emphasize the fun, the prominent people, usually sports and film idols, who eat the cereal and how you could increase your chances of acceptance by the particular crowd of people by eating that particular cereal.

As we pointed out in the previous paragraph, automobile ad-vertising often emphasizes the speed and handling of cars (CT). However, advertising also appeals to other orientations (different segments) stressing the structural integrity and family safety (SG), the research that has occurred to develop the product (CH), and the elegance that attracts attention and admiration (AD). Note too that some companies use a mix of advertising styles for the same product, thereby increasing the potential number of buyers.

On a trip to China, Allan was addressing a group of marketing people, talking about the value of LIFO® concepts for achieving ad-vertising goals. Having noticed that most ads viewed while entering Shanghai dealt with the technical aspects of items and the nature of the product preparation, he decided to illustrate the excessive use of this style by asking the group to design an ad for his Nikon camera, which he held up for the audience to view. The ads they produced generally emphasized the sturdiness of the camera, its reputation, the quality of its lenses, the durability of its shutter mechanism, etc.

When he asked the audience why none of them seemed to directly address the person who would use the camera (AD), there was an instant of awed expressions as the group realized the bias of their approach. One could have mentioned that it would be easier to have quality photos of one's family (SG), that it would enable the photographer to quickly select items from a well-structured menu (CT), or that others would regard the photographer as an accomplished photographer (AD).

In fact, in our seminars we often ask participants to bring in examples of advertising they find in newspapers and magazines, post them on the wall under the various orientations, and then ask them to indicate why they classified them in the particular category they chose (to check on their understanding of style behavior). Another advertising learning task is to write ads to different kinds of people.

Seminar experiences like these inspired one participant, a vice president of marketing for a Puerto Rico branch of Citibank, to put this knowledge to practical use. At the time, the bank was in competition with many banks for new depositors. A sample of depositors in the Puerto Rican Citibank was given the LIFO® Life Orientation Survey and then studied. The vast majority of those who deposited money were CH oriented. This was further tested by showing ads that emphasized different orientations. The CH oriented people clearly chose the CH ads over the others. Consequently, the bank decided to stress heavily the years they had been in business, the steady payments, the absolute safety of leaving money in the bank, etc. (all CH qualities). Despite the fact that some competitor banks were offering higher rates, Citibank outperformed other banks and also saw a surge in deposits as compared to previous years. The ad that was used read, *Citibank, through its guaranteed savings program, enables you to have the money you need for Christmas presents, for your retirement, for emergencies, or other needs that may arise in your life.*

When viewing advertisements, there are some other important things to remember. In the Citibank case, the buyer's style was clearly identified and the product suited to the buyer's needs. The time period was not turbulent. For example, in the midst of economic crises, perhaps deposits might be more influenced by another type of advertising (SG offering special loans to depositors). Advertising applications of The LIFO® Method require LIFO® measurements of the current buying target population as well as the characteristics of the product offered.

Sometimes, a product that could be useful to many possible purchasers may not sell because the advertising message doesn't appeal to the desired buyer's style. Sometimes the mistake is made by using only one style, instead of trying different ads with different styles (could possibly increase the product's appeal). In fact, skilled salespeople take the opportunity to talk with customers and get to know something about their needs, values and general buying habits, before making a sales presentation. In essence, the LIFO® surveys provide a similar tool for understanding target populations. The sales advertisement might be quite different for an auto mechanic, racecar driver, aspiring manager, or someone with a large family. Yet, there are some products or services that might be attractive to all kinds of orientations.

This is as yet a wide-open area for LIFO® consultants, and we feel knowledge of our concepts and methods can be extremely helpful. We now have special surveys for sales personnel and for customers, that provide even more detailed information which can be used for advertising and other marketing purposes.

Chapter 14

USES IN SELECTION

In this chapter, you will read two articles describing the application of The LIFO® Method in the selection process: ***Recruiting a New Manager*** **by Gerrit Knodt, PhD,** and ***Hiring, Powered by The LIFO® Method*, by Shirley Murray.**

INTRODUCTION

The LIFO® Method provides a framework for evaluating compatibility of an individual with members of the candidate's potential work group and organizational constellation. It does not test the technical skills required by a job but rather predicts behaviors used by the person in satisfying their needs.

It can also be used to help a manager focus their thinking about the requirements for a successful candidate. This would be even more useful if a previously successful person had also taken a LIFO® survey; better still, if there were a pool of successful people who had LIFO® profiles and reports related to their job performance.

The LIFO® Method provides a description that is used to conduct discussions with a candidate concerning his characteristic patterns of behavior. It is non-normative. It will not identify an "ideal fit." Instead, it encourages and facilitates discovery of creative approaches toward_ensuring that a person's responsibilities allow full use of their capabilities, singularly and in concert with others. It is an effective teambuilding tool, not a test.

The LIFO® Method will also help orient both the selected person and the team to which they will belong to think about the best ways to use the strengths that the candidate possesses. It can also be used to help in dealing with that person when exhibiting stressful behavior. It is at its best when both parties understand the LIFO® framework and the methods for encouraging interpersonal effort toward common goals. Therefore, this methodology provides insight into the degree and frequency with which individuals use the behaviors that ensure desired results. No individual profile will be ideal. The method provides insight into tendencies that are only relevant when viewed in the context of other people's tendencies.

The LIFO® Method is a valuable tool for interviewing candidates. Since it usually provides a description that is reasonably valid, it encourages the candidate to talk more fully about him or herself, and the conditions that make for successes and failures. Such an interview would begin by providing a report (as shown in the example provided later in this chapter by Gerrit Knodt) of the survey's results and an interpretation. (For a sample of the computerized reports that are available, see www.lifo.co/resources.) The next phase would be to ascertain the candidate's agreements with the statements. The candidate would then be encouraged to correct statements that seem inaccurate, provide examples of job situations where various behaviors occurred, and think about how they might react to situations that would not be ideal. In particular, insight could be gained into how the candidate viewed their strengths and weaknesses.

This comprehensive report would be related to comparable information about the potential boss and/or those people the candidate will manage. These discussions tend to be unusually candid and revealing with minimal deception. In part, this is due to the effort to provide descriptions that are positive and the accepting attitude that the interviewer demonstrates to the candidate. Since the report is usually viewed by the candidate as a pretty valid description of his/her behavior, this also contributes to a very open discussion. In addition, a discussion of the candidate's congruence (see Chapter VIII) in communication and possible ways that it could be improved further enhances personal self-disclosure.

Unlike many testing situations and regardless of the outcome of the selection process, the candidate will obtain something of value from the selection method experience. The interview discussion that occurs and the additional data provided presents information that can help the candidate's further growth and personal development. One candidate who was not hired wrote a letter that stated: *I must commend the company for providing the interviewing experience that I had about the meaning of The LIFO® survey and the review of my behavior. It certainly left me with a very positive feeling about the company, even though I was not able to be successful in obtaining the position I wanted.*

Some companies include as part of their selection process an interview between the candidate and the group to which the candidate is being considered for membership. A common understanding of the LIFO® concepts provides a more meaningful basis for discussion of how they might work together.

The following article by LIFO® licensee Gerrit Knodt illustrates the use of the LIFO® Method for the selection process, particularly when teamwork and team building are of paramount concern.

Recruiting a New Manager
by Gerrit Knodt, PhD

In my more than 30 years of working in the areas of recruitment and teambuilding, I have found the application of The LIFO® Method most effective in getting the necessary insights into an individual's behaviors (not technical competencies). Such procedures have to do with behavioral "fit," and this fit is a major prerequisite for harmonious team membership and productivity.

Consider the case of Harold Right, a candidate for manager of a technical group responsible for new product innovations. The company wanted a person of high reputation who could command the respect of the group, communicate readily and diplomatically with other department heads and outside agencies, and be able to develop a highly productive team.

This case will be described in some detail, including a LIFO® Executive Report on the prospective manager's behavior under favorable and unfavorable conditions. While the search does not find an "ideal" candidate, it illustrates how The LIFO® Method would be used, especially when a desirable but not "best-fit" candidate is found. In the latter case, the Method provides a way of helping that kind of candidate to prepare for the team experience, as well as informing the team how they can help the candidate to function at their highest level of productivity.

The company, through research, had identified Harold Right as a technological leader, the inventor of some new methodologies, and the author of very prestigious articles in his field. He was employed by a competitive company but became intrigued by the hiring company because the position offered higher pay and would allow him, for the first time in his career, the opportunity to manage a group.

Harold was informed that as part of the selection process, he would be asked to take the LIFO® Life Orientation Survey, and that all members of the group he would be managing had already taken the same survey. He was also advised that this was not a test, but it would provide information both for him and others about his behavior in a variety of situations. He was told that he would then be given an opportunity to discuss the interpretation with a trained professional to assure understanding and accuracy.

When Harold arrived for the LIFO® session, he appeared friendly and expressed interest in what was going to happen. He wore a tan sport coat and dark brown trousers, white shirt and an appropriate tie. He was courteous and responded eagerly to the material that was discussed.

Below are the LIFO® Life Orientation Survey results of Mr. Right.

LIFO® EXECUTIVE REPORT OF HAROLD RIGHT

LIFE ORIENTATIONS:

Supporting-Giving	Controlling-Taking	Conserving-Holding	Adapting-Dealing

FAVORABLE CONDITIONS:

Supporting-Giving	Controlling-Taking	Conserving-Holding	Adapting-Dealing
28*	21	17	24

UNFAVORABLE CONDITIONS

Supporting-Giving	Controlling-Taking	Conserving-Holding	Adapting-Dealing
24	25	21	20

*numbers can range from a low of 9 to a high of 36

FAVORABLE CONDITIONS (WHEN THINGS ARE GOING RIGHT):
Dominant Style: Supporting-Giving (high)

Back-Up Style: Adapting-Dealing
Least Preferred: Conserving-Holding (low)

UNFAVORABLE CONDITIONS:
Dominant Style: Blend of Controlling-Taking and Supporting-Giving
Backup Styles: Conserving-Holding and Adapting-Dealing

INFORMATION ABOUT CONGRUENCY OF COMMUNICATIONS:
FAVORABLE CONDITIONS:

	SG	**CT	CH	*AD
Intention	8	10	5	6
Behavior	10	5	6	9
Impact	10	6	5	9

**Incongruent
*Mildly incongruent
Dominant Style: Supporting-Giving
Backup Style: Adapting-Dealing

UNFAVORABLE CONDITIONS (WHEN THINGS ARE NOT GOING RIGHT)

	**SG	*CT	CH	**AD
Intention	5	7	8	10
Behavior	11	8	6	5
Impact	8	10	7	5

Very high incongruencies appear in the Supporting-Giving and Adapting-Dealing Areas, some incongruency in the Controlling-Taking Area.

LIFO® PROFILE SUMMARY

Favorable Conditions. It is important for Mr. Right to be respected by those who belong to the group he feels most identified with, to be responsive to others, and to pursue high ideals for performance. In addition, he has some desire to be influential and popular, to be exploring new possibilities.

Unfavorable Conditions. Under these conditions, he is strongly desirous of asserting his own position, defending views strongly unless proven wrong factually or logically, and concerned about not wanting to offend others in conflicted or stressful situations

BEHAVIOR UNDER FAVORABLE CONDITIONS

Productive Style. Mr. Right's managerial style would provide evidence of concern for people, a collaborative work-orientation, and strong desires for significant achievements. Highly intuitive, he readily senses issues of concern and importance. There is interest in being responsive to requests, showing respect for high scientific standards and soliciting input from others.

Overall, there would be a strong sense of teamwork and concern for achievement of organizational goals. He likes to feel needed and that projects on which he works on are significant ones.

Projects that are not of immediate relevance are not as likely to receive his full attention and commitment. Once committed to goals, however, he tries to gain commitment of others to those goals.

As a manager, he would have implicitly high expectations for the products of his work group. Participation would be encouraged, and he would expect a high level of involvement from all group members. He welcomes new ideas.

In group activity, there would be both an active involvement on Mr. Right's part and a firm commitment to delegation of responsibility and authority. Staff member training and development would be encouraged.

In addition, he shows sensitivity to others' concerns and areas of interest. His communications are likely to be flexible according to his audience. He is aware of events in the social substructures of his group and is likely to take a personal interest in his staff members as well as a professional one. He is open to new ideas and willing to explore alternative solutions.

When in meetings or with colleagues, Mr. Right is likely to be seen as a friendly and active participant, and a facilitator of idea exchanges. He encourages member involvement and tries to ensure that all viewpoints are expressed.

When involved in change efforts, he would desire to be an active participant from the initial phases onward. Enthusiasm and enjoyment of the new and different, as well as a ready acceptance of the challenges posed, would gain his active commitment. Participation in the formulation phases would ensure his commitment. Though he would enjoy the opportunity to contribute to a worthwhile task, there may be some reluctance to become involved at the detail level. Preference would be given to outlining the broad guidelines for plans, checking their acceptance, and involvement in the implementation phases. However, the involvement in the specifics of planning would not be his forte.

Least Preferred Style. Bureaucratic and administrative matters may not receive the attention to detail they require. At times, details might slip through cracks because of the way he organizes things.

Facts and substantiating information of his plans and suggestions may not receive close attention. Overall, systematic and methodical functioning is not characteristic of the managerial style he might exhibit if he were in that role. Expectations may not be stated explicitly, thereby causing occasional misunderstandings or disappointment with results.

Some Possible excesses of the productive style. Mr. Right can become overly critical of himself and others when results do not meet expectations. Idealistic concerns may gain his involvement without sufficient attention to practicalities and benefits.

Mr. Right may encounter time management problems due to his ready involvement with many varied projects and a willingness to lend assistance whenever asked, even if insufficient time is available.

Occasionally there may be a tendency to "manage-by-crisis" due to his high level of responsiveness to situations as they develop.

BEHAVIOR UNDER UNFAVORABLE CONDITIONS

Fight style. Although an infrequent initiator of confrontation with others, he will, in such circumstances, state his views with confidence and be willing to argue with conviction. This will be especially true if he feels core values are being attacked or betrayed. He will initially listen to opponent's views and, if values are shared, may be willing to concede.

However, conflict is a serious matter for him, and he will wish to resolve matters as rapidly as possible. Because of this, he will try to state his views in a direct and serious manner, exploring the other person's views and beliefs, seeking clarification and striving to jointly problem-solve differences.

His opponents will be given a fair and thorough hearing, and he will expect similar courtesy in return. If he finds that there has been a misunderstanding and the other person is very upset, he is likely to back down. However, he can respond heatedly if attacked on personal grounds or on matters of principle. He will persist in the situation, following through until a clear resolution is reached. Though possibly ardent in his defense, he would not be likely to allow matters to reach the point where he risks alienating the other person or endangering relationships. When appropriate, concessions and compromises would be explored

In excess, he might be perceived as defensive and emotional, particularly if, as mentioned previously, feeling threatened or confronted in a highly aggressive manner. On matters of principle, he is likely to be unyielding. There may be a tendency to be highly critical in heated exchanges, possibly causing conflict to escalate. However, he would not be comfortable if this happened.

Stress Style. When encountering stressful situations, Mr. Right takes a highly responsive and visible stance. He will endeavor to use all available resources, including full use of his subordinates' talents and expertise. Indeed, he would exercise more control than would be typical of his behavior under favorable conditions. His level of personal involvement in direction of staff and co-workers will be high. Staff members will be expected to dedicate a high level of energy into problem-solving and overcoming difficulties through joint efforts.

Though there will be heavy emphasis on resolving immediate problems, he will also be concerned with finding lasting resolutions that meet organizational needs and goals. He is persistent in dealing with such situations, dedicating a great deal of personal effort and time to matters at hand until the situation is relieved and back in balance.

In excess, there may be a touch of management by crisis if he acts without prioritizing his objectives and reacts to each problem as it arises. He risks diffusing efforts by trying a number of possible approaches rather than evaluating his alternatives and acting upon the most promising one.

IMPROVING COMMUNICATIVE EFFECTIVENESS WITH MR. RIGHT

Mr. Right will be receptive to communications that are direct and open. However, he may enjoy a moderate amount of social interchange before getting into business matters. He would particularly appreciate expressions of personal interest and care. When discussing business matters, he would expect a serious overall tone, but would enjoy creative expressions of ideas and occasional light touches to break the monotony. Receptivity to long expositions of data and information would be low. Preference would be given to bottom-line impacts and expected results.

Under unfavorable conditions, it will be helpful to avoid bringing up additional problems until the ones he is currently dealing with are resolved. Avoidance of overloading him with input and clearly establishing priorities for suggestions would be beneficial.

In regards to improving his own communicative effectiveness, it will be important for Mr. Right to logically sequence his ideas when explaining them to others, especially in dealing with new issues or when dealing with unfamiliar ones. Occasionally he may tend to skip from one idea to the next without filling in the gaps to bridge the thought pattern.

Developing a more systematic framework for presentations could prove useful in gaining acceptance of his ideas. Particularly when dealing with others of a more analytical and data-based orientation, supplying supporting documentation for his statements would strongly aid his case.

People may not always realize what he wants, even though they may sense an underlying interest. This appears evident in the fact that his intentions for exerting control are much higher than the behavior he shows and the impact he has on others. This is an area worth exploring; in particular, how he presents his command of what he wants.

In addition, he may seem more flexible than he really is. Making sure to clarify his position might also be of assistance to others in knowing what he really wants.

Under unfavorable conditions, it will also be important for him to state his needs more clearly and also state his requirements explicitly for different situations. He may be somewhat incongruent in this area, apparently showing more concessional behavior than he really believes he should.

Setting and communicating his priorities and letting others know what criteria will be used to evaluate performance will be helpful to staff and co-workers.

When in a leadership role, he may need to explore the use of more direct means of control and follow-up. Particularly in the areas of administrative and bureaucratic functioning, some backup by staff or systems could be necessary.

He may need to consciously work on being more assertive so that his ideas will be heard and valued. Overall, there is a strong team-oriented style that could serve both his organization and those with whom he works in good stead.

OTHER RECOMMENDATIONS

Particularly when in conflict with more assertive individuals, Mr. Right could take a bolder and more confident approach to sell his position or recommendations.

Crises could be handled more readily by establishing clear priorities and assessing alternatives before taking action.

Part of the alternative assessment and information gathering process will require greater receptivity to new and innovative approaches, and reserving judgment until ideas have a chance to be explored and ferment. Increasing attentiveness to data and available information would also prove beneficial.

INTERVIEW DISCUSSION WITH THE CANDIDATE

Harold was given this written report and provided time to review it. Major points were then reviewed by him, and an in-depth discussion was held concerning his reactions and opinions.

Harold tended to agree with the LIFO® interpretation, although he wasn't sure about what his behavior would be as a manager since he had not functioned in that role and had rather served independently as a principal research scientist.

He agreed that bureaucratic and administrative concerns were not a high priority, and were usually handled by others. He felt that if he were manager of the group in this company, he would need an administrative aide and/or be able to use a manager who was more strongly invested in such preoccupations to assist him.

Subsequently, when he and the group shared profile information, he expressed such a need, and it was agreed that members of the ream would be willing to assist in this regard.

CONDITIONS:	FAVORABLE: SG CT CH AD	UNFAVORABLE: SG CT CH AD
Team Member 1	15 25 25 25	21 26 22 21
Team Member 2	19 23 26 22	20 21 26 23
Team Member 3	19 31 23 17	20 25 24 21
Team Member 4	18 22 28 22	19 25 29 17
Team Member 5	20 24 27 19	17 31 21 21
Team Member 6	19 30 21 20	15 29 25 21
Team Member 7	19 20 27 24	25 17 19 29

Note that the highest scores in the profile are in CT and CH under favorable conditions. The lowest scores are in the SG area. This means that they like to function independently, doing what attracts their interest and what they feel needs to be done. There is also a fairly strong desire for functioning in a well-structured situation, where policies, procedures and strategies are planned in detail, and executed according to plans. They feel most comfortable when provided with responsibility, given a fair amount of autonomy to do the work and have opportunities to review progress in detail.

When disagreement occurs, it is a hard group to influence unless one is confident and has both facts and reasoning to back up one's statements and opinions. There is little willingness to make concessions but a bit of concern about criticism and disapproval that could influence them.

FIT OR NO-FIT

In examining the profiles of Mr. Right and his prospective group, there would appear to be some conflicts that are likely to occur, especially involving teamwork, and willingness to listen and function more intuitively to facilitate innovation.

In a sense, Mr. Right foes not fit with the prevailing style of the group, since he relies less on Controlling-Taking and Conserving-Holding behavior in productive situations. This might have proven highly unsatisfactory, except for the facts that he complements the group with a strong sense of concern for meeting high standards, providing empathy for thoughts and feelings, encouraging experimentation, and using a lighter touch in serious moments.

In turn, the group provides strengths that make up for his tendencies to use more assertive and organized approaches. They may reinforce his high CT intentions and thereby encourage more decisive actions.

While their styles might not be comfortable, in a team sense he and the group cover all of the four major areas. This became apparent during the team meeting where the group and Mr. Right exchanged profile information (each of the group members had taken a LIFO® survey some time previously). Since the company's management had already decided to hire Mr. Right, it became necessary to engage a consultant to help build an appropriate sense of teamwork within the group, both by helping members to share information in terms that would be understood by each other and the new manager. It became clear that the manager would have to do more personal checking, ask questions for opinions and ideas, and arrange for problem-solving discussions that would encourage creativity, minimize defensiveness, and use the individual strengths of the group.

The outcomes of the discussions confirmed the value of the decision to hire Mr. Right as the new manager, a decision which was highly regarded by those who witnessed the team's progress and achievement.

⌗

In the next article, you will see a more traditional type of application but nevertheless highly qualified by the extra steps taken by the consultant in the use of The LIFO® Method for selection.

Hiring, Powered by The LIFO® Method
by Shirley Murray

BACKGROUND

Owned by the major Canadian breweries as a distributor for their products, The Beer Store (TBS) is a retail company that has been in operation since 1927. It has approximately 440 stores, a head office, and 16 distribution centers in Ontario. Stores vary in staff size from 32 employees in large, high-volume locations in major centers to as few as 5 employees in more rural locations.

There are just fewer than 7,000 staff at all levels of the organization. In the stores and distribution centers, about 80% of the workers are hourly and are represented by Local 12R24 of the United Food and Commercial after they are hired.

THE ISSUE

While TBS has been a good employer for 85 years, having had thousands of employees with rewarding careers, they were looking to implement a consistent and structured procedure for hiring Customer Service Representatives (CSRs). Store Managers were looking for a tool that would allow them to always hire the best possible candidates—employees that would provide the highest levels of customer service and engagement with beer consumers. The hiring tool they desired would streamline the hiring process, removing redundant time-consuming procedures and ensuring that only outstanding customer representatives would make it through to the final interviews. As consultants who worked with TBS on other projects and were familiar with the organization, we were asked to help them develop a tool to improve their hiring.

PROJECT OBJECTIVES

The main objective to be addressed was to improve customer service and productivity by hiring CSRs who were a "better fit" for the job and the organization. This was seen to ultimately translate into higher sales and greater profits.

Secondary objectives were to:

1. Develop and implement a standardized hiring procedure which would provide consistency for managers in selecting staff.
2. Provide training for Store Managers in how to hire and what to look for in selecting people who would be good organizational "fits."
3. Minimize the amount of work the Store Managers needed to do in hiring while still allowing them to make their own hiring decision based on relevant criteria.
4. Minimize turnover which would also reduce costs.

THE PROJECT

To meet the objectives, it was first necessary to understand the desired behavioral traits of what the company defined as "good CSRs." We were asked to develop a new tool to "test for fit" when hiring.

Since 2002, much of the management of TBS had gone through training in The LIFO® Method as part of their Leadership Program, so they were familiar with the LIFO® concepts and how they could be used effectively in understanding behaviors. Rather than develop a totally new tool, it was decided to determine if the LIFO® Survey could be used to develop the "best fit" profile.

If the LIFO® survey could be used as a successful predictor of "fit," it would also be used for hiring in order to understand the behaviors of the candidates in relation to the ideal profile. Recognizing that people adapt their behaviors, the ideal profile would not be used to exclude candidates. Rather, it would provide a framework for interviewing candidates to determine whether they appeared to have enough of the appropriate strengths to function successfully in the CSR role.

THE PROCESS

A group of Store Managers and District Managers who had gone through LIFO® training were invited to serve as members of an advisory committee for the project. They represented all types of stores (low to high sales volumes) and varied environments (inner city, suburban, small town, and rural locations). In advance of the first meeting, they were asked to rate each LIFO® strength in relation to its importance in the CSR role. From their ratings, a "strawman ideal strength profile" was developed.

In the first meeting, behavioral style concepts were reviewed so that everyone would be at the same level of understanding. A typical CSR job description was then reviewed and all tasks identified. The straw man strength profile was adjusted based on discussions of what strengths were most essential (or inappropriate) for each task.

To test the model profile, staff in the 15 stores that were managed by the committee members were asked to complete a LIFO® survey. In return, they would be provided with a full report based on their results, and would have an opportunity to learn more about behavioral theory and their own profiles. They were promised that all results would be consolidated to ensure anonymity and that no one within TBS would see the individual profiles unless they wanted to share their profiles with others.

In the CSR meeting, not only were participants debriefed on the interpretation of their reports, but they also were asked to provide ideas on what they felt constituted "fit."

Store Managers and District Managers were asked to provide performance ratings on all of their own staff who completed the survey. A 4-point scale from ++ (the best) to — — (the weakest) was used for performance on the specific tasks of the job. They also were asked to assess each participant's LIFO® strengths.

While it was useful to have the Store Managers' and District Mangers' opinions on the strengths needed to do the job well, we also asked those CSRs who were seen as being top performers for their opinions. They were the ones who did the job well, knew their own strengths, and also knew what was and was not important or appropriate in others. Only those CSRs who were rated as ++ and + were asked to provide this. The ideal profile was further refined from what they reported.

With no names attached, the profiles of all those who completed the survey, along with their performance ratings, were used to analyze the data. Only total results under favorable conditions were used since it was assumed from discussions with the CSRs that this would most accurately reflect the work environment.

A statistician analyzed the data, but due to the small sample size and narrow range of potential LIFO® style results (from 9-36, using the traditional statistical measures), no significant differences were found based on style. However, when a manual scatter analysis was performed plotting each CSR's result by behavioral style, coupled with their performance rating, clear differentiations emerged between the better and the poorer performers. This enabled the development of guideline ranges for the ideal fit in the CSR role.

It was recognized that guideline ranges were useful for helping select the "typical" CSR. However, some slight modifications to the ranges would help to accommodate variations in the stores, e.g., higher Controlling-Taking could be more appropriate for very small stores where CSRs would have more responsibility and need to take more initiative, and higher Adaptive-Dealing could be beneficial in those locations where there could be potential for more conflict.

For the committee, style-specific behavioral questions were developed, based on the actual tasks of the role, to determine if the person was a suitable fit for the job. These were tested within the committee and refined to even more closely fit the job.

Procedures were developed for Store Managers so that they could easily and successfully use the new hiring tools. Before rolling out the new procedures, all Store Managers received training on how to use them. In addition, whether they had previously been trained in The LIFO® Method or not, they were given a short training program on it. This included completing a survey so they would understand themselves better and have a point of reference for using the guidelines.

THE PROCEDURES

The procedures were designed to:

- Minimize Store Managers' time spent in hiring while still giving them the final choice in who would work in their location.

- Provide consistent hiring criteria and processes for better candidate selection.
- Minimize opportunities for possible discrimination in the initial steps.

To minimize Store Managers' time, TBS's online application system, which is managed from the Head Office, was adapted to the new hiring procedures. Applicants are encouraged to use it. However, those who do not have computer access are still able to apply in person at their local TBS store. Whether applying online or in person, the hiring processes are the same, except that, if not online, the Store Manager does all steps in the store.

The steps are:

1. *Initial Screening Questionnaire.* Completed by applicants, this determines some very basic rationale for either accepting the applicant into the potential hiring pool or rejecting them. It is comprised of items critical to the role and the company, such as whether the person is legally able to work in the country, willing to accept part-time work, able to stand on their feet for an extended period of time, able to get to the store, able to carry a certain amount of weight, and willing to work evenings and weekends. Once scored, those who are acceptable are put into a pool of potential candidates for hiring as needed by specific store locations.

2. *Review of applications.* When a Store Manager needs to hire, he or she accesses approved applications from the pool and reviews the information about the candidate. Those who appear to have the skills and abilities that are needed for the job are selected; the others are returned to the bank.

3. *Telephone interview.* Store Managers call the applicant, and if the person is still interested in the position, the Store Manager uses a prepared script to very realistically describe

the responsibilities of the position. The Store Manager also asks a series of questions to determine if the applicant was willing and able to do the job. If so, the person is invited for a face-to-face interview and is asked if they is willing to complete a LIFO® survey in advance of the meeting.

4. *The LIFO® Survey.* The applicant is told that the survey will not be used to determine whether he/she is hired, but rather assist in helping the Store Manager understand the profile of the candidate and how he or she may best fit into the organization. It provides the Store Manager a better understanding in interviewing the person. The Manager then contacts the Head Office and asks that a survey be sent to the applicant.

Once the survey results have been received, the Head Office sends the applicant's total favorable results to the Store Manager in an interview booklet. Among other information, the interview booklet has a page that has a continuum with the range of possible results, i.e., 9-36 for each style. The ideal candidate profile is highlighted in each style's range, so it is simple to see where the applicant's result is in relation to the ideal.

To prevent the perception that the LIFO® survey has been used to make the hiring decision, all applicants who completed the survey had to be interviewed. Further, because the ideal candidate profile is a guideline, the survey simply helps the Store Manager identify areas to explore, particularly in those styles where the applicant's results are outside of the ideal profile.

5. *Face-to-face interview.* Each behavioral style has specific strengths associated with it that have been identified as being important for performing the CSR job well. Questions used in the face-to-face LIFO® portion of the interview are standardized for each style and are designed to determine if the

applicant is able to use the strengths of the style appropriately for the job. For each style there are several questions from which the Manager can select to use based on what they want to know about the applicant's use of their strengths.

The ideal profile is only a guideline for the Manager and is not to be used as a hard and fast determinant for hiring.

Applicants who do not fit within the ideal profile may be hired if they can exhibit in their responses to the questions that they have the appropriate strengths for the job. Also, based on the store's unique needs and demographics, ideal applicants may be needed who are either higher or lower in a style than the ideal profile. The applicant's answers are then scored using a standardized rating scale.

If the applicant does well on their responses to the questions, they will be asked to complete a Behavioral Descriptive Interview (BDI) and a math test based on actual functions a CSR will need to use in the job.

6. *Reference Checks.* For those applicants who have done well on all phases of the interview, the Store Manager will conduct reference checks. If the applicant is deemed to be acceptable based on the reference checks, that person will be offered a CSR position.

RESULTS

Within the first year of implementation, management at TBS reports that turnover was reduced by 3.4%. More importantly, they say that the process has enhanced the opportunity to identify "best fits" in the early stages of the hiring process, reducing the Store Managers' time spent on hiring, while still allowing them to be in control of those selected. Store Managers are now more comfortable with the hiring process because they have a structure and guidelines for carrying out this critical function of their roles.

These two articles each show very definitive LIFO® applications. However, the consultant may wonder if the survey has been used to predict success in other occupations. This could be done, if, prior to use, survey data could demonstrate statistically significant differences in results for those who possessed particular characteristics and those who did not. As yet, this has not been done.

Chapter 15

APPLICATIONS TO TEAM BUILDING: AN INTRODUCTION

In this chapter, we examine how The LIFO® Method contributes to team building with specific tools and a typical team-building workshop design. Then, an article by **Gerrit Knodt, PhD,** *A LIFO® Analysis of a Team,* presents a LIFO® analysis of a team with observations and recommendations.

WHAT IS A TEAM?

A team is a group whose output depends on the vision of a common goal, requiring cooperative interaction to organize and carry out needed tasks. It shares rewards for achievements and also accepts responsibility for failures.

In effective teams, members:

- Achieve recognition that all are needed to do the job.
- Know about the special skills and abilities that are available and who possesses them.
- Demonstrate appreciation and recognition when those skills are utilized, or offered for use.

- Have a process that guarantees hearing of views and ideas that are offered, opportunities to explore ideas before evaluating them.
- Have a feeling of oneness, speak in terms of "we," and feel both cohesive and coordinated.
- Have a methodology for resolving differences in views and conflicts without a win-lose focus.
- Are encouraged to express ideas fully and know that they will receive fair hearings.
- Establish an agreed upon criteria for evaluation of ideas.
- Reach consensus on final decisions, unless delegated to a smaller group or individual.
- Commit themselves to the final decision.

HOW THE LIFO® METHOD CONTRIBUTES TO TEAM BUILDING

The LIFO® Method Contributes to team building by providing:

- A way of describing the strengths that are available to do the job.
- Recognition of excesses that happen when overused.
- Means for monitoring excesses.
- Ways of finding needed strengths at the moment.
- Ways of communicating to assure understanding and acceptance procedures for follow-up evaluations, reinforcing strength use, and energizing work to resolve problems that occurred.

LIFO® SURVEYS AND TOOLS

Following is a list of LIFO® Surveys and Tools (see Chapter XI for detailed descriptions; not all tools are used in every team-building project):

- Life Orientation Survey
- Life Orientation Survey for Another Person
- Leadership Survey
- Leadership AP Survey
- Dialogue Sharing exercise
- Strength Management Feedback Chart
- Leadership Management Feedback Chart
- Teamwork exercises (most frequently used: Tinker Toy exercise, Zim Obelisk exercise, Selecting a President exercise.
- Strength Bombardment exercise

COMMON TEAM-BUILDING WORKSHOP DESIGN

The following design for a team-building workshop was used in several banking, electronics, and food industries:

Introduction. This involved determining reasons for team-building request, some brief report of background and experience, and discussion of the process that would be followed. All members of the team would be notified about the project, informed that the consultant(s) would be meeting with each member individually.

Team member interviews. Individually, members are asked to review their group meetings, identify problems, and describe issues that needed to be resolved for the team to increase its effectiveness. They are told that a composite report will be shared with the total group in the workshop, but that confidentiality would be preserved. They are asked to complete a survey that could provide both helpful information to the individual as well as to the group. They are also told that they would receive a personalized report at the meeting. It was emphasized that the report described how they tended to approach issues when things were going well and when they were not.

Team workshop design. The following program for a two-day workshop in team building is not intended as a mandatory method. Indeed, consultants will use part of the design and vary it because of their own experience, different theoretical biases, and other considerations. It is, however one that has been used and found to be valuable for a number of corporations.

TWO-DAY PROGRAM OUTLINE

Day 1, Morning
Since tensions are usually high at the outset of such a workshop, we began with an activity that looks different and has the possibilities for fun.

Team Exercise (Tinker Toys) – 1 hour. Tinker Toy parts are randomly distributed to each participant. The team is told they have twenty minutes to plan what they will do and 40 minutes to complete the building of something that best represented the typical interactions of an effective team.

Exercise Review Questions – 1 hour. Team members are asked to rate their experience in five categories on a scale of 1-10, where 1 is lowest and 10 is highest:

1. Rate the quality of the product produced.
2. Rate the process used to develop the plan and build the model.
3. Rate your own participation.
4. Rate the amount and kind of listening that was exhibited.
5. Rate the degree of similarity of the exercise behavior to everyday work-related team discussions.

If a videotape was made, an additional 30 minutes will be taken to show highlights and invite discussion.

Discussion of questions – 1 hour. Ratings were averaged and then displayed. After each categories' ratings appear, the group is asked to comment and provide examples they saw that influenced their ratings. Finally, the group was asked to make some decisions about how they would improve their group process for tackling other problem situations.

Day 1, Afternoon
Reports – 30 minutes. Individual LIFO® reports were distributed, and members invited to read them and make any changes they feel would be needed to ensure accuracy.

   Colleague Dialogue Exercise – 2 hours. Each member completed an incomplete sentence survey that relates to various behaviors in groups and in colleague work situations. Pairs were then assigned to work together to share information about their profiles and discuss why they had responded the way they did to each of the questionnaire items. It was suggested they pair with members whom they knew least.

   At the end of the exercise, each member was asked to share what he or she thought was most interesting about the pair partner.

   A Brief LIFO® Overview – 1 hour. An overview of The LIFO® Method is presented, covering the following:

   o The law of differences – understanding, valuing and accepting them
   o Description of major concepts, such as:

   ▪   The strength-weakness paradox
   ▪   Strength management
   ▪   LIFO® Golden Rule

   o Application to teams

Day 2, Morning
Strength Management Charts – 2 hours. Charts were posted on one wall of he room. Members were asked to go up to a chart, enter

their scores, and using black crayons place a check next to left-most squares that were next to the different behaviors indicated on the charts. Then other members went from one chart to the next and indicated, using a red crayon (for less) and a green one (for more) those behaviors they would like to see less of or more of. They were to do this, even if the person had not made a mark on his personal chart for the particular behavior they felt should be changed.

Then each individual stood before his chart and reviews what he understood and agreed to, inviting comments from the group if he couldn't comprehend what behavior they were referring to. They were asked to make a note of the next change they will try to implement when the group holds a team meeting.

Afterwards, the team analyzed itself, using the LIFO® profiles arrayed in group form, then identified its strengths, possible excesses, and recommended means of managing strengths most productively. Consultant(s) assisted as needed.

Solving real work problems – 1 hour. Problems cited by the team in individual interviews are cited. Each member is asked to identify the top six problems that need to be solved in order for them to do their work efficiently. The results are tallied and summarized. Then the group narrows down the list to three.

Day 2, Afternoon
Reports of Problem-solving groups – 1½ hours. The team is divided into three groups, each group to solve only one problem. The group is mixed so that they have representation of different styles, if possible. They work for 45 minutes, then report back to the total group for 15 minutes each.

Strength Bombardment Exercise – 1 hour. See previous discussion in Chapter IX for a description of this exercise. The team did this exercise for each team member and then to the team itself, by directing the exercise to an empty chair placed in the middle of the room to represent the team.

Commitment to follow-through reviews and changes needed. Schedules were established and monitors either designated (or consultants assigned) who would serve in that role, depending on budgetary considerations.

LIFO® GROUP ANALYSES

Analyses can be made from profiles, constructed out of the individual ones (see below) that lead to important insights for team members. This can be either provided by the consultant or from questions directed to the group as to the nature of group strengths, potential vulnerabilities, characteristic interactions, decision-making processes, and other aspects of team functioning.

Such questions might be:

- What do you see as the major strengths of the team?
- What are some of the possible excesses that could occur?
- What are possible vulnerabilities?
- What can you do to guard against the vulnerabilities?
- Where are the existing resources to do this? Are external ones needed?
- Where are conflicts likely to occur?
- How can conflicts be resolved so that team productivity is not affected?
- When can disagreements be helpful?
- How can we be assured that arguments can be fully heard before reacting in a judgmental mode?

Members of a team familiar with the LIFO® concepts can readily engage in discussions stimulated by such questions. However, in the following analysis, the material is presented as a diagnostic presentation to the group.

─❈─

A LIFO® Analysis of a Team
By Gerrit Knodt, PhD

LIFO® TEAM PROFILE OF TELCO INTERNATIONAL

	Fav. Conditions				Unfav. Conditions			
NAME	**SG**	**CT**	**CH**	**AD**	**SG**	**CT**	**CH**	**AD**
JAMES (LEADER)	17	**32**	15	**26**	22	20	19	**30**
AMELIE	23	**25**	17	**25**	22	20	**26**	22
HANNO	**25**	20	**22**	**23**	21	14	**32**	23
TRACEY	**25**	**28**	20	17	18	**28**	16	**28**
EMMA	20	**29**	20	21	**25**	18	**23**	**24**
DARIO	**30**	**24**	18	18	17	**23**	**26**	**24**
ALEX	21	**28**	**26**	15	15	**28**	**24**	23
Lucille	21	**29**	22	18	22	21	**27**	**20**

NOTES ABOUT THE GROUP:

Favorable Conditions. If you observe the number of underlined scores, you will see that the group's primary and backup styles are mainly centered in the CT area, backed-up by SG, with the least preferred style being CH.

Strengths: The group is likely to engage with a fair amount of participation, especially when decisions need to be made. The group has five members (most preferred CT) and three who have backups in that area as well. They are therefore likely to assert their opinions in a very strong manner. Decisions are likely to be made quickly and put into actions swiftly.

There are several people who can take charge and get things moving if needed in addition to the team leader. Backup styles suggest that there will be a fair amount of interest in establishing tactical goals and seeing them accomplished. In addition to willingness to offer ideas, there is a good deal of willingness to listen fairly to new ideas.

Least Preferred Styles (vulnerabilities). Generally, the group relies least on CH behavior. This means that it may function without spending a great deal of time planning what needs to be done, carefully spelling out responsibilities, schedules and budgets. They rely more on the confidence gained by their experience and may make assumptions about how informed subordinates and colleagues are about what they propose.

The main person who may feel frustrated by this approach is Alex. He is the one most likely to be able to function as a planner and coordinator, providing he is given such responsibilities by his role and the recognition of the group that his concerns are worth the attention of the group.

In addition, many of the group members use AD behaviors least. This means that the group may not provide enough recognition for ideas and behavior, may be inattentive to feelings, be occasionally tactless, and may lack the willingness to explore new ideas to their fullest extent. They tend to be more serious than playful, with the exception of Amelie, Hanno, and James.

UNFAVORABLE CONDITIONS

There is the danger that at times Tracey, Alex and Dario can engage in protracted disagreements if they have opposing views. This may stall action and decision-making since others will be uncomfortable with such a display, especially James.

Strengths. There does not seem to be any clearly dominant style. This allows for many possibilities for response during conflict or when experiencing stress. Hopefully, the group can recognize this and utilize the various resources to cope with the situations that arise.

When contention is high, rather than engaging in endless fights, the high presence of AD (underlined scores) would help to compromise on severe differences and find a win-win solution to which everyone could agree. Indeed, their investment in AD means they are least likely to be demeaning or disrespectful to others during disagreements and concerned about morale when under pressure.

When pressure is high, they combine analytic assessments of what is involved with action to meet emergency conditions.

Least Preferred Styles (vulnerabilities). There is the danger that disagreement among those most likely to express their disagreement in bold and direct terms (high CTs) could create an environment where people reach compromises too readily (AD), not providing sufficient time to really listen to the content of the disputed issues. They also may be too quick to be distracted and explore too many other possibilities, thus delaying decisions and actions.

The group seems least likely to engage in SG behavior (give in readily to others, acknowledge blame and responsibility). They are likely to conceal true feelings when pressured.

The least active person would be Hanno, albeit polite and reserved. Nevertheless, she is not likely to accept a dominant position if she disagreed strongly with what had been proposed, but the group may be unaware of her resistance. Therefore attention should be paid to soliciting her opinions, especially if she will be responsible for helping to carry out the decisions that are made.

SOME EXCEPTIONS

Alex appears to function differently than most; his preference is to disagree in a highly rational manner, basing positions on facts and accurate information. He would be willing to argue his points strongly but would not wish to antagonize anyone, so if it appeared that consensus was against him, he would accommodate to the major viewpoint. Alex, Dario, Emma, and Tracey are likely to be more serious in their general manner. Dario, Tracey and Hanna are more willing to follow others, prefer having a strong and ethical leader, and are most willing to cooperate with others.

LEADER BEHAVIOR

James is consistent in expressing opinions directly, trying to exert leadership under favorable conditions and keep things going at a lively pace. However, under stress, the relatively low CT may mean he fails to take control and help the group to focus on the more difficult decisions that need to be made.

In unfavorable conditions, he does show more evidence of being concerned about others, feeling empathy and being more flexible. Hopefully, this reflects his behavior while in a leadership mode.

OTHER OBSERVATIONS

Amelie would seem most likely to act in a cooperative, friendly, and concerned way normally, and could change if being forced to accept decisions which she feels are not in the best interests of the group or have been too aggressively thrust when presented. She may silently hold on to her resentments and concerns for some time. Therefore, she too, may have to be asked about her feelings, rather than accept passive compliance.

Emma seems like two different people when comparing her favorable condition responses to those she exhibits when under stress or conflict. She gives in more than she would like to, or she minimizes conflict and strives to achieve favorable responses when tension arises.

SOME RECOMMENDATIONS

1. Goal setting would be an activity readily engaged in by the team. However, the bias may be more long-term consideration than tactical. Therefore, a committee of Alex, Hanna, and Lucille (high in CH) could be responsible for ensuring that attention is devoted to practical issues and to the necessary planning required for achievement of goals.

2. Discussions may tend to get distracted by individuals. For this group, priorities need to be established and agreed to. Actions need to be related to those priorities. This is especially the case since the group may overconfidently assume much larger responsibilities and challenges than they can handle effectively.

3. The team is vulnerable in the CH area, perhaps lacking the detailed planning, concern for accuracy, and flow of process that is required to execute accurately. Preparing agendas for meetings, providing members with information relevant to discussions before meetings, and double-checking critical information are essential for making appropriate decisions, staying on track and enhancing the group's reputation when dealing with other parts of the organization. Reviews will be necessary to assure that those long-term objectives are indeed being pursued.

4. While there is a fair amount of polite and attentive listening when things are going well, it becomes less so under conflict and stress. The increase in CH scores suggests that people have to be encouraged to individually express their feelings and reasons, lest valuable inputs will not be provided during discussions at such times.

5. The group would be more responsive to decisions that are made by consensus rather than by fiat. While this may not be

the preference for the five high CT members, they will likely force attention to the importance of timeliness in decision-making. However, someone needs to remind them when they tend to overdo this.

THE PLACE OF SUCH ANALYSES IN TEAM-BUILDING

If such an analysis were done prior to the workshop for improving teamwork, the presentation would be discussed as to its accuracy, and members asked to express opinions and ideas about how it should be changed to reflect reality. They would also be asked for additional suggestions for dealing with team problems.

Chapter 16

TEAM DEVELOPMENT AND COACHING

In the following three articles, both the elements of team development and coaching are involved, although different techniques are employed.

The first article, ***The LIFO® Method and the Development of a Team* by Al De Leo**, relies more on the consultant functioning as a coach-arbiter for the group, utilizing conferences with members of the team in private, and also with permission of the people involved, revealing information that could be discussed by the whole team.

The second article, ***Selecting, Coaching, and Team Development: A LIFO® Method Case Study* by Willie Donald** relies more on the team process and discussion.

The third, ***Values Provided by Having a Mix of Styles in a Team* by Roger Harris** demonstrates one important use that can be made of LIFO® team training. Despite different consulting styles, consultants find ways to use The LIFO® Method effectively for enhancing teamwork.

Had these consulting efforts been followed by the later development of tools such as Strength Management charts, the feedback and resolution issues could have relied more on the team's analysis of the information and allowed them to contribute more directly to the final solutions.

⚌⚌

The LIFO® Method and the Development of a Team
by Al De Leo

DEVELOPMENT OF CLIENT-CONSULTANT RELATIONSHIP

It was several months after my retirement and my first real consulting job. The president of a large commercial bank called to ask me to meet with him in his office the following day. I had never had any dealings with this bank or this president. One of my pro-bono clients had recommended me to him.

I arrived early for the afternoon meeting and noticed that the president's office was wide open—indicating what many call an "open-door" form of management. However, when I met him for the first time, I found that this was purely an illusion. The gentleman was quite directive and controlling. There was no doubt who was in charge and that he had the objective of this meeting firmly understood in his own mind.

"Sit down, please," he commanded me. "I hear that you have had considerable experience in dealing with dysfunctional teams, and I wish to have you help me improve my team. Several of my board members do not get along with each other. Our meetings are a disaster and we must become more productive. I have a strategic plan in mind that will get us growing at a faster rate and with a better structured work force and I need your help." Certainly, in LIFO® language, this was Controlling-Taking (CT) behavior with some Supporting-Giving (SG) backup.

My first reaction was to make a fast escape. I do not enjoy working with those who are Controlling-Taking in their behavior, and this one apparently with such high scores. At least that was my first impression.

"Well Sir," I said, "I really do not think I can be of much help. You see, I have never worked with a banking institution, and I really do not know anything about banking."

"Look," he interrupted, "you don't need any banking experience. My management team is a disaster. They argue and fight over complex and simple things but mostly about their own ambitions. I really do not know what I can or should do. Individually they are very talented men. And I need them to be able to compete in this market and to become a larger and effective bank. We have a strategic plan to grow this bank from the current $700,000 in assets up to $2 billion. So please don't make any decision now. Come back tomorrow at noon and let's have lunch. By the way, this is what I have determined: you will be paid a weekly fee, and you can make out your work plan for any length of time you need. I will support any activity you devise fully and without reservations. Go home and think about it and have lunch with me tomorrow. What do you say?"

I did return for lunch the next day and planned our client-consultant relationship agreement, which included his responsibilities as well as what I would do. The plan included an three-day off-site meeting to complete the development of the strategic plan, as well as a vision to share with the other members of his senior staff.

The plan also included the need to interview each member of the board of directors. These interviews would help to determine for myself what really is transpiring in these board meetings and what the relationship issues between the members were. At the same time, I introduced the LIFO® survey to each member and was able to identify their styles (most preferred and secondary) for a better understanding as to how they liked to interact with others). The LIFO® Method became a critical tool throughout the consulting because it gave everyone a common language to talk about their behaviors.

The consultant agreement also outlined the vital steps that I would take with each board member, including the president: 1) the individual interviews of the board members would be held confidential and conducted in their respective offices; 2) the results of the LIFO® surveys completed by the board members would be considered confidential and only revealed at the off-site meeting if each member gave permission to do this; and 3) An off-site meeting of three days would be held a month later. Prior to this meeting, the consultant would have had an opportunity to discuss the results of the survey with each board member.

An outline of the details of the off-site meeting was presented to board members at a special meeting, and this agenda considered the following: 1) a review of their strategic plan and the development of an acceptable vision statement that would be communicated to the key staff members; 2) a discussion of the responses from individual interviews with guarantee of anonymity; 3) a discussion of the results of the LIFO® survey (the interpretation of their styles and their implications for the development of a productive team; 4) the development of a plan to monitor the implementation of the strategic plan and the communication of the vision (This would include the details of the growth plan and its possibilities of success); and 5) a plan to maintain constant monitoring of the improvement in the functioning of the board meetings and the behavioral styles of individual members (The monitoring would take place on a one-to-one basis and overall improvements reported to the board as a team).

USE OF THE LIFO® MODEL

Throughout the consulting period, The LIFO® Method became a critical element in the successful conclusion of the contract with my client. It enabled me to gauge and measure the preferred behavioral styles of each board member (to demonstrate the extent to which their behaviors during their interactions were contributing in a positive and productive way to the stated goals of the team). They had to keep in mind that their LIFO® styles were essential behaviors and to a great extent ameliorable to some alteration and change. This was especially true if the required changes were viewed by the individuals concerned as important for the successful conclusion of their team's goals to be their preferred manner of behavior, that is, the meaning of their individual LIFO® scores and providing a vision, so that each individual could understand how changes in their behavior would result in improving the possibility of achieving the team's success.

The first step in this direction was to ascertain the dominant LIFO® styles of each board member. The following are the two highest scores of each member of the board.

President: A combination of Controlling-Taking and Supporting-Giving behaviors (roughly, an individual who likes to initiate things and have his view prevail, yet is concerned about involving others, hearing their opinions, and desiring his staff to achieve consensus and act as a productive team).

Operations director: a combination of Controlling-Taking and Conserving-Holding behaviors (someone who emphasizes control, taking charge of what needs to be done in an organized way, respecting facts and realities about what affects the business).

Financial director: A combination of Conserving-Holding and Adapting-Dealing behaviors (someone who likes to proceed in an organized way, respects facts, procedures and structures, yet is attentive to how his remarks are accepted by people and tries to behave in a friendly and tactful way).

Human resources director: A combinations of Adapting-Dealing and Conserving-Holding Behaviors (similar to the above member).

Branch director: A combination of Adapting-Dealing and Controlling-Taking Behaviors (someone who is assertive yet flexible and tries to influence others by appealing to their needs; interested in providing direction that will be acceptable to others, concerned about gaining approval from team members).

Systems (IT) director: A combination of Supporting-Giving and Conserving-Holding behaviors (a person who is influenced by idealistic concerns, wants people to live up to their goals, likes to function in an organized way, pays detailed attention to facts, is somewhat of a perfectionist but needs to feel that people are behaving according to what is valued and established as important goals that will benefit everyone.

Each of these individuals was seen privately in his or her respective office. The consultant provided a one hour briefing about The LIFO® Method; how each of the styles were measured, and the distinction between primary and secondary preferences (that is, the major influence on one's behavior and how that is influenced by another dominant factor in one's profile). One of the main purposes of the meeting was also to gain concurrence that the scores essentially reflected what they believed was true about their preferred manner of behaving and how they interacted with other team members.

THE OFF-SITE BOARD MEETING

It became apparent during the first hour of the off-site board meeting that the branch director and the operations director were in a conflicting relationship. These were the two directors that were giving the president his headache. They were constantly disagreeing with each other's statements and views, with the financial director adding fuel to the fire by siding with the branch director whenever he had the chance to intercede. The branch director was doing all he could to discredit the Operations director who was considered by everyone to be the (unofficial) second in command. This behavioral pattern was what the president had described during our first meeting. To some extent, the branch director was acting in a Controlling-Taking mode, versus the same mode of the operations director (both wanted to influence the team heavily but disagreed about how it should be done). There was clearly evident a deep rivalry between the two, creating negative consequences for the team being able to achieve desired results.

The first day, I asked the two directors to meet with me for lunch. I called their attention to the conflicting behavior observed during the morning meeting and asked them for their views of what had happened. I took some notes and suggested that I would like to follow up on this incident and indicated that we could meet this evening. They agreed and this is what resulted from the evening meeting.

I requested their permission to discuss their LIFO® scores in depth because I felt that such a discussion could lead to some clarification as to the source of their apparent conflicts. I indicated that their conflicting stance was causing the rest of the team extreme discomfort. Other members decided not to give them any negative feedback because they did not want to cause more friction in the team. I told them that members of the team felt that the two seemed to be in a state of rivalry for second in command and did not regard this as healthy for the team's success.

However, four of the members were in favor of my providing this negative feedback to the two rivals, hoping that they would find a way to resolve this issue peacefully for the benefit of the team. They stated that they wanted a strategic plan and a vision to be developed, and were confident that the two conflicting members had the skills and talent to help everyone to accomplish these goals, providing they relinquished their rivalry.

I asked the two directors for their reactions, which at first appeared with some hesitation. However, they finally agreed that they concurred with the view of the team and indicated they would like my advice as to how they could alter their behavior pattern in a positive way without changing their LIFO® preferences. I pointed out they could lessen their Controlling-Taking behaviors and increase their Supporting-Giving ones (listen to and encourage others' views, collaborating with them to achieve what is of benefit for the total team—"considering possibilities"). I stressed that this is what the others would like to see happen and asked them to give it a chance, especially with the development of the new strategic plan and vision to become a $2 billion commercial bank.

I encouraged each director to explain his position, stressing the LIFO® strengths they were bringing to the team. The operations director expressed the fact the perhaps his desire "to tell people what to achieve" might be causing some stress. The branch director quickly agreed and indicated that the thing that really annoyed him was that the operations director did not ask for any suggestions from other directors. "He seemed to want to do it his way or no way." The operations director responded, "That is what annoys me about you (branch director). You are constantly trying to point out my failures instead of giving me support and ideas on how to make things work."

This interaction was a good beginning. It continued for some time before I suggested we meet again the next day so we could continue our discussion. I indicated that we planned to meet with the board again at 9 am, suggested that we breakfast at 7 am and continue the discussion. They agreed, but I suggested that they should also come with some positive solutions as to how to resolve their issues for the benefit of the team. They agreed to do so. I reminded them that the other members were really anxious that they agree to behave in a cooperative manner. They wanted to see this result as soon as possible. The two indicated that they would do so.

I reported briefly to my client, the president, that we were making some progress but still had more to develop. I told him we were meeting again in the morning.

At breakfast, after more discussion of their strengths and limitations of their styles, they wrote an agreement that they presented to the entire Board. This had a very salutary effect on the team and helped to unite them for the next two days of work.

On a different occasion, I met with the financial director. I discussed his scores and behavior, and it became clear to him that his interactions in the meeting, that is, favoring one director over another, was not a positive behavior pattern. He agreed to control that behavior and was willing to express his actions and behaviors to the team as a whole. This provided a positive strengthening of the team's efforts.

FINAL RESULTS

We left the three-day off-site meeting with a strong strategic plan and shared vision. It took the team two and a half years to achieve most of their goals. They finally reached their strategic market position and assets of over $2 billion, along with a work force committed to their vision, to become the largest commercial bank in its area dedicated to the financial needs of the people.

The six members of the team remained essentially intact until the president retired, bringing in a new president, appointed from a member of the ownership group.

─❈─

Selecting, Coaching, and Team Development
A LIFO® Method Case Study
By Willie Donald

BACKGROUND

My initial request was to support the board of trustees in selecting a new CEO for a high profile, non-profit organisation, operating nationally and internationally out of the UK. The board wanted to see

LIFO® profile reports completed on each of the 14 final candidates, along with a briefing regarding the implications of the reports for the CEO selection process. By consulting standards it appeared to be a relatively simple mandate, or so we thought.

How wrong we were! After an extraordinary 18 months, we are still working with the organisation and the case study. It turned into a project that required team development and executive coaching. The LIFO® Method is firmly embedded as an executive and management development tool, underpinning a number of coaching and team building interventions. It has also contributed significantly to the development of the executive team, helping to forge them into a sharper, more focused group. It has also helped the organisation deal with individual challenges arising in the senior management team. This article describes how such events came about.

Founded some 20 years earlier, the organisation was set up to provide charitable support for severely disabled young people. It has grown rapidly over the years and is represented nationally in the UK with a growing international presence. The organisation relies on funding from private donations as well as from the public sector. The latter utilises its services to provide community obligations in caring for the disabled. Over the years, staff turnover had been low. The original executive team had been in charge since the inception of the organisation. Promotions tended to come from internal candidates, but as the organisation grew, external appointments were often necessary at junior and middle management levels. Only in 2011, due to retirement, was the organisation faced with a significant organisational change challenge. It needed to recruit a new CEO for the first time in its history.

The board recognised that this would be a critical appointment for a host of reasons. Quite clearly, they had no experience in making such an appointment. They recognised that a new CEO would mean a new operating style at the top and the emergence of new interpersonal relationships, both internally and with external stakeholders.

They also realized that recruitment always carries some risk, since it is not a perfect science. This was occurring in an economic climate that had become less benign since 2008, causing funding challenges in both public sector donation areas, as well as in private and philanthropic donations. The challenge was to find someone with the maturity to recognise the organisational challenge his or her appointment would create. He would need to have a broad business perspective, possess the drive and capability to grow the organisation, and on a practical level, have experience of funding, specifically involving the public sector. An empathy with the plight of the disadvantaged would be a special asset.

The recruitment process involved placing a public advertisement in selected media. From the resulting applicant list, a short list was selected by the board. This final list of 14 candidates led to the next stage of interviewing and assessment. The board believed that an external objective assessment would also be useful and this is where The LIFO® Method was used. However, we positioned the LIFO® reports as only one component in the recruitment process. They were intended to give the board some guidance regarding the behavioural profiles of individual candidates, as well as to identify potential areas to investigate during interviews, such as pre-disposition to excessive or stress type behaviours. We could also "map" the job profile against candidates and look for high potential types. In this respect, we were not eliminating candidates based on their individual profiles, but rather giving the board data upon which to guide the interview and assessment process.

The 14 candidates varied considerably in their LIFO® profiles. We agreed with the board that before discussing the profiles we should create a job profile in LIFO® language. Because the organisation was looking for drive, competence, maturity and experience, they felt that a strong degree of controlling (CT) behaviour was required, and that this should be complemented by good people skills and a desire for excellence (AD and SG). Conserving (CH) behaviour was lower in the priority requirement since the organisation operated in a highly regulated environment, and high quality systems and procedures were already in place. In addition, there were strong safety-first preoccupations in the existing management team. We argued that the board should be mindful of very high scores and test for excessive behaviours during the interview process. Finally, we advised that care should be taken with candidates who exhibited significant deviations in congruence in the Intention-Behaviour-Impact scores, advising that the interview process should test for frustrations, lack of confidence, or other inconsistencies. Considering the purpose of the organization, we also considered the impact results in the (SG) dimension: excellence, service, and high ideals.

The trustees were so impressed with the data and briefing on each candidate made possible by the LIFO® profiles that the chairman asked us which candidate we would choose! Of course, we declined to make such a choice, pointing out that the data was only part of the decision, not the decision itself. Ultimately though, only four candidates appeared to pass the theoretical test presented by the LIFO® job profile, and the board now had a strategy for interview and observation during the candidate meetings and assessment centre.

All candidates were invited to contact us to receive a confidential feedback session regarding their profiles. We insisted on this in the belief that no one should be asked to complete a LIFO® profile without the support of a coaching meeting. This would allow them to fully understand the background of The LIFO® Method and its implications, as far as they were concerned. In retrospect, it came as no surprise to us that the first candidate to take up the offer of a feedback session and to follow it through with us energetically was the candidate who was ultimately appointed as the new CEO. Our job was done—or so we thought.

The successful candidate had performed well during the interview and assessment. His CV was exemplary and he demonstrated a great set of executive competencies, well matched to the role. However, the trustees reasoned that the organisational change demands would be so great that it might be worth supporting the new CEO during the settling-in process. His LIFO® profile, while excellent in terms of job match, did suggest some potential risks. As a result, we were asked to extend our involvement by delivering an executive coaching programme to support the new CEO, and help develop his self-awareness and deal with those risks. This, in effect became a team development project.

CEO LIFO® SCORES

	SG	CT	CH	AD
Favourable	24	27	20	19
Unfavourable	18	30	15	27

Our executive coaching programme utilises the *LIFO® Personal Style Resource Book* (UK publication) as the core curriculum, using the personal development exercises of *capitalising, augmenting, extending,* and *bridging*. These were designed to build self-awareness, and allow the coachee to investigate leadership and personal development style options. We then focused on the demanding territory of *managing excesses* and *managing others*.

The new CEO was a seasoned executive who, by his own admission, initially saw the board's requirement for LIFO® profiling as just part of the process. He thought behavioural or psychometric analysis to be "voodoo science" with little relevance to "real" management or leadership. After he received his results and first coaching session, however, he completely altered his view. Visibly shocked at the accuracy of the picture LIFO® painted of him, he subsequently threw himself into the programme. He not only used it as a personal development opportunity, but as a springboard into the job.

He also started to view the organisation and its people through the lens of behaviours as well as competencies, using the LIFO®

methodology to inform his thinking across a diverse range of topics, including strategy, organisational change, recruitment and training. Specifically, he recognised risks of excessive behaviours in himself, particularly in stressful situations. He set about managing his high *controlling* behaviours and introducing more *conserving* behaviour when pressurised, therefore regulating the risk to rush to judgment. His high *adapting* behaviour under pressure often manifested itself in an overly sociable, even jocular, style, and he recognised the need to control these behaviours in order to maintain his executive presence. This was a real strength in favourable conditions where we see a more balanced approach, evidenced by his LIFO® scores.

Again, we thought the job was done, but again, we were wrong. Of the 14 candidates who were short listed for the CEO position, two were existing executive board members, yet they did not get the top job. They had now become the new CEO's headache.

Disheartened by feelings of rejection, they were also feeling the strain of adjusting to the new man in charge. The CEO had also brought in a new director in charge of external relations, adding an additional change to the organisational structure and yet another new operating style.

Something had to be done, and the CEO acted decisively. All three of his executive team members would participate in the LIFO® coaching programme. Two members of the team, the finance director (FD) and the new external relations director (ERD) signed up immediately, but the operations director (OD) was hesitant. She had worked for the organisation for 20 years, growing up with it to become head of the largest division. Only a few years from retirement, she didn't see the need for leadership training. However, with the strong persuasion of the CEO on the basis that it would be "good for team" if everyone took part, she reluctantly agreed to go ahead.

LIFO® TEAM RESULTS

Position	Fav. Conditions				Unfav. Conditions			
	SG	CT	CH	AD	SG	CT	CH	AD
CEO	24	27	20	19	18	30	15	27
FIN DIR	30	26	22	12	22	20	23	25
OPS DIR	22	27	23	18	17	26	22	25
ERD DIR	21	30	11	28	13	29	18	30

FIN DIR = **Financial Director**
OPS DIR = **Operations Director**
ERD DIR = **External Relations Director**

The CEO's objective was to mould them into a highly motivated team possessing a common sense of mission and purpose, and a cohesive set of objectives. He understood the significant changes that had been thrust on the organisation by virtue of his appointment and his introduction of the new external relations director. He grasped that his role in achieving the objective was critical, and The LIFO® Method and coaching programme had helped him fine-tune his strengths. In parallel with the executive coaching programme, he launched a strategic review, held regular management meetings at all levels, and introduced a more open management style than had been the norm.

The LIFO® Method is a powerful tool, and the executive team quickly realized its significance. One of the great benefits of the model is that it is easy to grasp and most participants "get it" quickly. This is critical in overcoming cynicism, and we saw this in our work with the CEO.

We saw it again with the operations director. From starting with a negative attitude towards the programme, she saw in herself exactly what her LIFO® report described and quickly began to see the benefit of working through the coaching process. She recognised her high task orientation in favourable conditions, and coupled with her low AD inclination, realised that she could come across as cold. But she also recognised that when pressurised she demonstrated a strong AD orientation, using her social skills to finesse situations and help in preventing conflicts from escalating. Bringing those AD skills into favourable conditions was a key output of her coaching programme.

The financial director had a tendency to do things himself, believing he was the only person capable of achieving his own high standards. His high SG LIFO® score confirmed this tendency (only by reference to the standards that he used; it also suggests a cooperative and responsive orientation), and his low AD score in favourable conditions manifested itself in limited contributions at executive meetings, where he tended only to contribute when prompted. Like the operations director, his AD rose when in a pressure situation. Key outputs for coaching would be lifting his AD into favourable conditions and lowering his SG orientation, learning to allow others to take responsibility, rather than always doing things himself.

The new external relations director's profile indicated a very low preference for CH behaviour, and we saw this early in the process when it became clear that planning and reporting during the coaching process was weak. Coupled with the very high CT and AD scores, we were witnessing an executive who would make decisions on the run, whilst at the same time seeking to keep everyone happy and needing approval and recognition. Even early on, he seemed to be running ragged.

The programme of one-to-one coaching with the executive team was aimed at developing self-awareness, understanding and dealing with the risk of excessive behaviours, learning to introduce new or under-utilised behaviours, learning how to recognise preferred operating styles in others, and aligning behaviours to enhance communication between team members.

The team objective was to help create the highly motivated and focused unit that the CEO envisaged. During the programme, it became clear that whilst these objectives were being pursued on an individual basis, the question of team alignment repeatedly arose. They decided that a team-building workshop was required in order to flesh out together any communication roadblocks, to publicise and discuss each other's operating styles, and come to conclusions about how best to work together in order to achieve the organisation's objectives.

Our experience over the years has led us to believe that often strategy fails because of failures of implementation. In turn, failures of implementation often occur because the internal operating culture of an organisation is not fit for the organizational goals. The board and CEO were keen that we address the issue of culture, and formulate a plan to address any mismatch between strategy and cultural readiness

The individual coaching programmes were due to last six months. It was decided to run the team day four months into the process so that we would have time to reflect on the results of the workshop, and insofar as they affected individuals, blend them into the last two months of executive coaching.

It became clear that this would be a critical intervention. The executive team-building day followed our normal methodology. We started with a management game to plunge the participants into an unfamiliar task, creating a situation where operating styles and behaviours could be observed in action. The game was de-briefed and observed behaviours discussed in LIFO® terms. Productive behaviours were observed as well as excessive ones, as were opportunities where applying under utilised styles could have been helpful. These observations were mapped against the individual profiles and lessons designed regarding what worked and what could be improved.

We then looked at culture using the LIFO® Culture Model to build a picture of the preferred operating style of the team as a unit.

In the workplace, it appeared that dominant individuals tended to cut off open expression of those who were lower in magnitude, and the search for excellence led to a "blame culture" as well as a tendency to rush into action. Only when stress or conflict conditions arose were the other people noticed or even heard. Sometimes, they concluded, that can be too late.

This was observed in a management game when the team failed to complete the task in the allotted time and only succeeded when an extension was given. The overwhelming conclusion that the team reached was that a more facilitative approach to communication between them was required in order to become more productive and efficient. AD behaviours, from being seen as only relevant in unfavourable conditions, were seen as being very relevant all of the time. This would generate better and more open communication, since AD style users make it safer for people to interact by providing positive comments, as well as providing a willingness to listen to alternative approaches. Combined with the receptiveness indicated by their SG scores, such an approach would enable everyone's contributions to be heard, making for a more effective team and decision making process.

In addition, the strong CT preference for all members meant there could be a rush to judgment and decision-making that might prevent the group from considering all that was necessarily involved in making a decision. The group decided to utilize a checklist for decision-making to provide the needed CH element that was not being utilized.

Back in the workshop, tremendous progress was being observed. The board members were delighted with the CEO's positive impact on the business at all levels. The financial director and the operations director were making great efforts to re-align their operating styles with the cultural objective. But there was one exception. The new external relations director was struggling to contain his high CT and AD orientation. He continued to manifest excessive behaviours coupled with a very low preference for CH behaviours. Through the coaching process we observed him to be disorganised, unstructured, demanding and appeasing. These attributes were completely masking his CT and AD strengths. In short, he was not demonstrating leadership maturity or executive presence.

Out of the blue, the external relations director resigned. While regrettable, perhaps it was inevitable. On the face of it, his CT-AD preferences were in line with the cultural aspirations, but he was unable to come to terms with his excessive tendencies, nor build on his low CH style. He had been recruited without the benefit of a LIFO® profile being completed. The board then decided that given the success witnessed by LIFO®'s role in CEO recruitment, from then on, senior recruitment would always be supported in this manner. The organisation learned that it is worth investing in extra diligence up front when recruiting, so that it can maximise the chances of success. Job fit is critical.

By contrast, the operations director, who had commenced the process with a somewhat cynical viewpoint, had now come fully onboard. Not only was she working with her peer group positively, she had started to consider her direct reports from a LIFO® standpoint. Her team, the five operations managers, were a diverse group tasked with delivering services nationally through large teams of nurses, professional assistants, and volunteers. Delivering services to severely disabled youngsters is not easy. Stress levels can rise because of the nature of the work and, of course, the concerns of parents are ever present. Emotions can run high.

She decided to ask her team to complete LIFO® profiles so as to give her an insight into preferred operating styles. Her objective was to seek to find better ways to communicate with her team and build motivation levels. Meanwhile, the financial director did the same for the finance team and, having temporarily taken responsibility for external affairs, did the same with that team. We were then able to coach the executive team to use the LIFO® data to coach their teams. They were able to replicate the cultural aspirations of the executive team at the next level down, delivering a facilitative approach to communication, replacing what had been a traditional "command and control" culture. The strength management approach to personal and team development was becoming pervasive in the organisation, with the LIFO® behavioural style inventory underpinning the process.

In any organisation or team, the normal demands of daily life creates challenges to be overcome. These can vary from operational issues through customer complaints to interpersonal difficulties. The specific challenges in working with the disabled in a tightly regulated environment with highly dependent "customers" manifest themselves in long working hours and a requirement for total immersion in the role. Inevitably, difficulties arise, and it was no different here.

When the operations director and financial director started to work with their teams using the LIFO® approach to facilitate communication, three particular situations emerged where managers at the next level down were having specific difficulties with their teams. We were now asked by the board to consider remedial coaching, as distinct from development coaching. The objective would be to work with these managers on an individual basis to "fix" a particular problem. Here are their LIFO® profiles along with a brief description of the "problem."

Operations Manager 1 (OM1)

	SG	CT	CH	AD
Favourable	20	23	16	31
Unfavourable	16	29	19	26

Having been with the organisation 15 years, OM1 was a key player in the operations team with significant frontline experience. Although a lovely person and well liked, (probably due to the high AD scores), he had a tendency to flare up when faced with difficulty (CT under unfavourable conditions). His time management was virtually non-existent and he had difficulty completing projects. He took challenge personally and his confidence was at an all time low.

Operations Manager 2 (OM2)

	SG	CT	CH	AD
Favourable	28	23	22	17
Unfavourable	19	25	23	23

Having been with the organisation 22 years, OM2 had substantial frontline experience, having originally trained as a special needs nurse and worked her way up through the ranks to operations manager. One could also see that her high SG made it hard for her to assert herself and make her demands clear; also, there might be a tendency to be hypercritical when things don't meet her standards. Often such a manager has high expectations for staff members yet might not be explicit in making them clear before tasks are assigned). She was having difficulty with her team, and a formal complaint had been made against her management style. Again, confidence was at an all time low.

Marketing Manager (MM)

	SG	CT	CH	AD
Favourable	27	20	16	27
Unfavourable	27	25	16	22

Having been with the organisation three years, MM had been promoted six months earlier into this senior management role. She, in her own words, had endured a "horrific time" at her first leadership team meeting (where all senior mangers meet quarterly) when she found herself unable to articulate her departmental plan. She felt that from then on the organisation doubted her ability, and her confidence collapsed. She felt unable to command the respect of her team, and at times her style became irritable and defensive. (There was apparently a need for extending her CT style).

Our approach in any coaching situation is to gather data using the LIFO® profiling tool. The first step is then to validate the data in conversation with the coachee, using example behaviours to illustrate the numbers, and agree that the profile is an accurate reflection of how they behave. This is critical in the process so as to obtain buy-in from the coachee. It is from this platform of self awareness on the part of the coachee that we can identify coaching priorities, and in remedial coaching these priorities need to be sharply focused. In each of these examples, confidence had been shattered, and this is typical in remedial situations. So the objective of the programme had to be for the coachee to regain a robust level of confidence by applying successful management techniques that motivate their teams to achieve both their individual and organisation goals. The fall of confidence and management difficulties had, however, come from different personal challenges, and these are evidenced by the LIFO® profiles.

OM1's very high AD results meant for a very pleasant and sociable style, but the high score risked excessive behaviour. His excesses were over-socialising and interpreting any comment regarding his operation as personal criticism. He was easily distracted and lost time as a result. The combination of not having enough time leading to over work, coupled with his high social sensitivity often pushed him into stress responses where his very high CT kicked in and he became argumentative and disgruntled. He could see this in himself, and, of course, self-awareness is the first step in combating the difficulty.

OM2 on the other hand, showed a low AD preference in favourable conditions and coupled with her high task orientation meant that she demonstrated a "cold" management style, often using command and control as the managerial mechanism. When things didn't work, her stress response kicked in, and she became more AD—*too little, too late*, she agreed, and even then it wasn't coming from the heart. This may have been perceived as patronising.

MM agreed that her style was typically to "wing it" in management situations, using her intelligence and marketing experience to get by. The new CEO and leadership team approach was becoming more exacting, and she found that approach to be wanting. When challenged she became sharp and hostile, and the LIFO® profile evidences this in her high CT score in unfavourable conditions. In analysis we agreed that in favourable conditions, her high AD score coupled with her very low CH score manifested itself in her being poorly prepared for management events, preferring to rely on her natural charm and flexibility, a strategy that was failing.

So here we were, after an 18-month journey, starting with a relatively simple recruitment mandate, working in the guts of the organisation. We examined, in great detail, management responses in a host of conditions, working with these managers to help them solve their challenges and become better at what they do. The solutions would prove be different for all, but the core programme remained the same. The LIFO® profile underpinned the strength management programme, and we developed exercises for each of the managers to be practised over time, so that they became the normal response in managing and working with others.

With OM1, we agreed that he needed to recognise his tendency to over-socialise, be prepared to close situations, and move on. In addition, he needed to improve planning competency and structure in order to become more efficient in his use of time and resources.

For OM2, it was about recognising that the people were as important as the process. He had to work with them up front by adopting a more facilitative style of managing them and learning to trust their input.

MM agreed that it was critical for her to prepare for meetings or other management events more thoroughly, increasing her CH behaviour, relying less on her instinct and more on data and rational thinking. This would increase positive acceptance of her ideas by others.

In each of these examples we were seeking to minimise the risk of excessive behaviour, preventing, as far as possible, the ensuing risk of stress responses in unfavourable conditions. We were also trying to increase the use of and lift under-utilised styles so the manager became more proficient, practicing and developing a range of responses for different situations.

The LIFO® Method has proven to be a revelation for the organisation. It has given them a tool to collect data and use it in a variety of circumstances. Starting with recruitment, it has manifested itself as an executive development tool, used as a team-building tool and most recently a vehicle for remedial coaching for executives in crisis. The board reports its delight with the process, the CEO goes from strength to strength, and he reports that the leadership team members are working better as a unit and individually.

This case illustrates the power of the LIFO® tool with its multiple applications. It has also provided the organisation with a common language with which to discuss personal and team development issues.

Finally, you will recall that the external relations director resigned after a few months in the role. The new external relations director appointment was subject to the same process and criteria as the CEO, and after four months in the role, his is looking like a great appointment.

In a sense, we've come full circle. The LIFO® Method is firmly embedded as an executive and management development tool. This has supported a number of coaching and team building interventions. This has also contributed significantly to the personal development of the executive team, helping to forge them into a sharper, more focused group. In addition, it has helped the organisation deal with individual challenges arising in the senior management team.

Values Provided by Having a Mix of Styles in a Team
by Roger Harris

The material submitted in this document is based on an experience with an actual client and reflects my documented recollection of the events included.

BACKGROUND

The client is based in the Eastern U.S. and used The LIFO® Method for individual coaching, executive development, and team building. The emphasis in this case was on applications that would increase productivity. I had been working with the chief financial officer, as an executive, for a period of two years, when he suggested that he support an event that would involve his controller and the rest of his employees in a team-building event. He felt he personally had benefitted from his experience with The LIFO® Method. I suggested, and he agreed, that a LIFO® Method seminar for the 20 people in the organization would have value. He cited the relative newness of 6-7 people, the ongoing changes in the business model, the appointment of a new CEO, and a sense that the group productivity could improve if working relationships were strengthened.

We began with all group members completing the LIFO® Life Orientation Survey. I then conducted individual debriefings with all members, some in person, and some on the phone. It has become my standard practice to provide each participant in a team situation with an individualized session prior to the actual team event.

In the table presented below, the scores of all the team members are listed. Later, when I describe how people were selected for the exercise that provided the major results for this study, you will be able to refer to this table for the scores representing different individuals.

SURVEY GROUP RESULTS

	SG	CT	CH	AD	SG	CT	CH	AD
Gail	23	30	19	18	12	32	22	24
Lisa	28	15	17	30	19	16	23	22
Kellie	20	27	20	23	14	26	26	24
Lisa Z.	32	20	22	16	21	24	23	22
John	25	14	32	19	20	15	23	22
Allisa	26	20	18	26	22	24	20	24
Mari	30	18	18	24	21	19	22	28
Maureen	31	13	17	29	29	12	21	28
Robert	25	18	28	18	29	21	23	17
Dawn	26	23	20	21	24	12	27	27
Carrie	25	16	26	23	30	15	23	22
Robert2	19	35	18	18	10	34	25	21
Dawn2	28	19	17	26	17	22	31	20
Becca	30	16	24	20	23	16	21	30
Jill	24	17	18	31	24	14	21	31

What I discovered over time, is that this table generated more discussion during the seminar, reduced personal anxiety that sometimes occurs when personal data is presented in real time, and helped increase participation and learning as a team.

In addition, it also suggested the number of activities which reinforce The LIFO® Method learning, particularly in generating more complete discussion of Intention-Behavior-Impact increase and helping to develop team cohesion. Typically, the Team Profile was prepared ahead and presented during the morning portion of the full-day Productivity Seminar.

When we were discussing the viewing and moderating each others' excesses, there was a slowdown in the discussion, and fewer people seemed to want to participate. I determined that a major contributor to this dynamic was the makeup of the group, where people in manager-subordinate relationships were present. This dynamic had not come up earlier, but now as we were discussing and seeking to understand the impact of strong preferences on the management of the group, the less open behavior began to manifest itself. Again, it showed up as less discussion and fewer participants.

After we had taken a break, and I had given the situation some thought, I decided to do something to help with the learning process and perhaps free up energy in the group to get greater and more open participation. I chose to have the group organize into subgroups by most preferred style in unfavorable conditions. There were four teams of five people each. It worked out that there was one group where the preferences showed an almost equal distribution of preference.

The groups were all given the identical task (prioritized earlier after we brainstormed an issue the team wanted to address as part of the seminar). The task each team agreed to address was how to streamline and improve coordination of the preparation of the annual budget for the entire organization, one of their most important and visible tasks. My instruction was that they had one hour to organize themselves, prepare their proposal(s) after which each group would present their ideas. Those were the only instructions given.

The four groups of five each began their deliberations and interactions. I was both an observer and also there to answer questions or clarify language, terms, etc. We were at the place in the seminar when the focus was on moderating styles, and everyone had access to all individual preferred style information, as we had posted it earlier. I moved about the training room, observing small group behavior, reminding them occasionally of time available remaining, and generally staying out of the way.

At the end of the hour, we took a short break. We then reconvened, and the groups reported on the following:

- What have you accomplished relative to the task?
- How did you achieve the results?
- Provide a description of the group behavior overall
- What helped you achieve what you did?
- What may have gotten in the way of task performance or completion?
- What if anything, did you learn?

Some of the results are as follows:

- Not one of the groups completed the task.
- Time management overall was poor.
- Group collaboration was poor to non-existent.
- Some subgroups developed.

Here is what seemed to have happened in the subgroups, both from my observation and from their self-reporting:

- The SG group spent most of their time attempting to agree on a set of standards for improving the budget process revisions and a lot of time collecting input from everyone. They ran out of time before they could prepare a solution suitable to all.
- The CT group spent most of their time trying to figure who was/should be in charge of their group effort. They never did agree, and two people set up a subgroup, took another easel to work on their ideas, and never came back to work with the other three members.
- The CH group had a beginning by brainstorming and writing lists, forces and facts that affected the budgeting process. They started by doing this together, but drifted into working and refining their own individual lists, spending much time explaining to each other what the list was about.

At the end of the hour's discussion, they had five pages of items but had not consolidated or discussed similarities or differences.

- The AD team spent some of their time sharing information about what they liked and disliked about the budget process but drifted from topic to topic without writing much down. They spent the bulk of their time conversing about life outside of work and inquiring of others how their lives were going. When asked at the conclusion of the hour if they had a solution, they indicated they had not had enough time to get to that task, but had enjoyed their time together.

One could see that the behavior in each of the groups verified the LIFO® descriptions that would have been predicted for them. This demonstrated how too much of the same kind of behavior can be counterproductive when under stress or when severe conflicts and disagreements occur.

It was about 2:30 in the afternoon, with a couple of hours to go, and the most recent task was unfulfilled. People seemed surprised, even shocked at their lack of task completion. Their self-image, as stated earlier in the day was that they were among the top group of the company, if not the top performing one, with the most difficult work charter in the organization. We took a break, and I asked them to spend 30 minutes discussing what they thought had happened and what it might mean for the organization. They could use any resource available to them to help prepare the reports that would be shared with the group.

In their reports, each group indicated that they had quickly visited their own LIFO® results, the Slide-A-Style tool, and the definition of their most preferred style under unfavorable conditions.

Groups stated that they learned the following:

- Having only similar styles together created blind spots that decreased the possibility of resolving issues, and they suffered in those conditions.
- Working in groups of similar styles seemed to make people press even harder and deeper into that most preferred style.
- At a certain point, the CT group felt real anger with those who would not cooperate, because each person felt their solution was best.
- The AD team said that while they were sorry they did not provide the deliverable, they found the activity helped further working relationships and that would help them make more progress after the seminar.
- The SG team said they wished they had more time to polish their presentation because they had really made progress towards an almost ideal solution to the problem.
- The CH team said they recognized now that they had leaned so heavily on their group's most preferred style, that they probably would not have finished for a few more hours.

I followed the team reports with a full group discussion as to what they learned. They said the following:

- They repeated items 1 and 2 from above.
- They had a good discussion about their understanding of personal and team blind spots, and the impact of blind spots
- Having tools like the Slide-A-Style was helpful, and they planned to use them going forward.
- They had more belief that having a number of different styles available would more than likely improve both group functioning and performance on the task.
- They felt they had deeper understanding of their own preferred style now and of its impact on team mates.

- They were more interested in understanding how to leverage what other styles bring to the table.
- They would look into how to incorporate what they were learning into their core meetings and major business processes.

What started out as a spur of the moment idea turned into a decent learning experience. I learned a lot from trying it, and the group seemed to benefit from the experiment.

Chapter 17

IMPROVING TEAM COMMUNICATIONS

In this chapter, an article by **Betty Forbis** describes the Barnum Team Communications Tool and its applications

❧❧

LIFO® Online Tool For Team Communications
and Conflict Management
by **Betty Forbis**

INTRODUCTION

Though we all have the desire to effectively communicate with others in all walks of our lives, it is sometimes a challenge. When faced with working in a team with others who have different communication styles and needs than our own, we may find ourselves feeling misunderstood, or experiencing a lack of results.

The online Barnum Team Communications Tool (TCT) provides an understanding of a person's preferences and provides suggestions on how to communicate more effectively with each other. The TCT addresses the LIFO® Golden Rule: *Do unto others the way they want to be done unto.*

When using the tool, a click of the mouse provides information for each team member, often in tablet or graphic displays, including:

- Brief overview summary
- What to do and what not to do
- What the team member wants to know
- Potential challenges
- How you can help improve communications with the team member
- Contributions to a group
- Potential strengths when in stress or conflict
- Potential challenges when in stress or conflict
- How to help the team member when in stress or conflict.

Most team building falls into the category of: *It felt good while it lasted...but it didn't last.* Our approach to team building focuses on making it last. Team building is a process, not an event. Whether team building involves a short "wrap up" exercise or complete sessions, our goal is to give participants something they can apply immediately to improve the quality of their working relationships and use as an ongoing resource.

The Barnum Team Communications Tool (TCT):

- Provides suggestions for the user to apply immediately.
- Leverages team diversity through increased understanding of strengths
- Creates greater group transparency
- Provides conflict resolution resource
- Results in faster integration and transfer of learning into the group and the organization.

Team Building Workshop

We facilitated a highly successful team building workshop including feedback with the LIFO® Strength Feedback Charts. The results were greater trust, increased openness, and more spontaneous feedback. However, after a few weeks, team leader Carl noticed he did not hear much from one of the team members. Joan was quiet and appeared non responsive, even evasive when questioned on progress with a project.

Carl wanted to build on what they had learned about applying The LIFO® Method to increase effectiveness. He found the paper that had a team chart, and he saw that Joan's CH moved from a least preferred style in favorable conditions to a potential excess in unfavorable conditions.

Team Chart

Favorable Conditions:					Unfavorable Conditions:			
SG	CT	CH	AD		SG	CT	CH	AD
23	31	16	20	Carl	12	27	24	27
19	34	25	12	Frank	12	33	27	18
24	27	19	20	Joan	19	22	34	20
3	27	21	19	Jon	17	28	20	25
25	23	12	30	Kim	14	27	23	26
25	21	24	20	Marie	19	19	25	27

But...what did all this mean? How could he manage the situation? Carl remembered the online Team Coaching Tool (TCT), and with a quick click of the mouse he entered the team login-information and clicked on the Team Profile to see the following page:

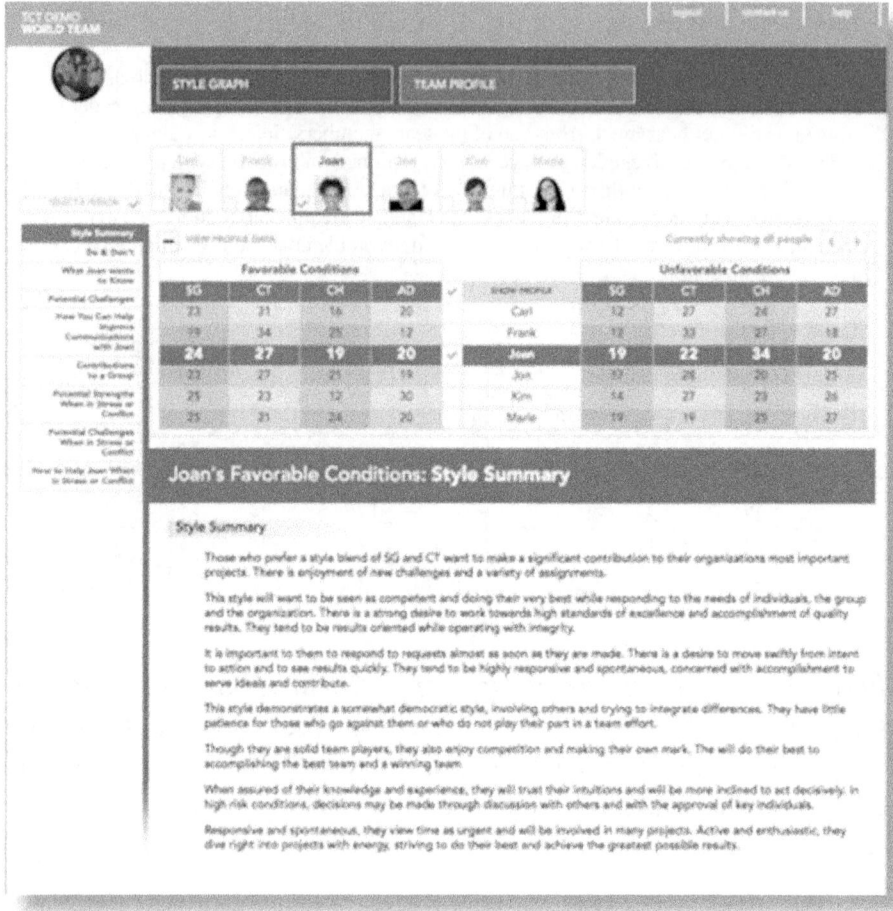

He clicked on Joan's photo, then quickly clicked through the *Style Summary*. Then he clicked on *What Joan Wants to Know*, *Potential Challenges*, *How You Can Help Improve Communications with Joan*, *Contributions to a Group*, *Potential Strengths in Stress or Conflict*, *Potential Challenges in Stress or Conflict*, and finally, *How to Help Joan When in Stress or Conflict*.

Carl knew Joan was very responsive, responsible, and committed to doing her best in all she committed to. When he read the description on the TCT of the SG and CT combination, he realized that her behavior could result in time management issues. She might have difficulty saying no in her desire to be helpful and responsive, and fail to notify him of how the request might influence her priorities.

In addition, he learned she could become critical of herself when she did not meet her own standards. She may be more results-oriented and not socialize as much as she should. This might result in less casual exchange that could cut off valuable resources and information.

The TCT charts also alerted him to problems that might be caused by her least preferred style, which was CH. This suggested that she might be less objective in her standards or expectations, which could result in feelings of embarrassment or inadequacy when unable to meet her expectations of herself or of others and the team.

Take a look at the style graph below:

TABLE 2 STYLE GRAPH OF UNFAVORABLE CONDITIONS:

Though Carl and Joan were pretty much aligned most of the time, and his profile became more CH in unfavorable conditions also. However, the style graph dramatically showed there was a significant shift to CH potential excess when Joan was stressed. Carl did not realize this was happening. *Now*, he wondered, *What should I do?*

He went back to the Team Profile page and clicked on *Potential Challenges When in Stress for Joan.*

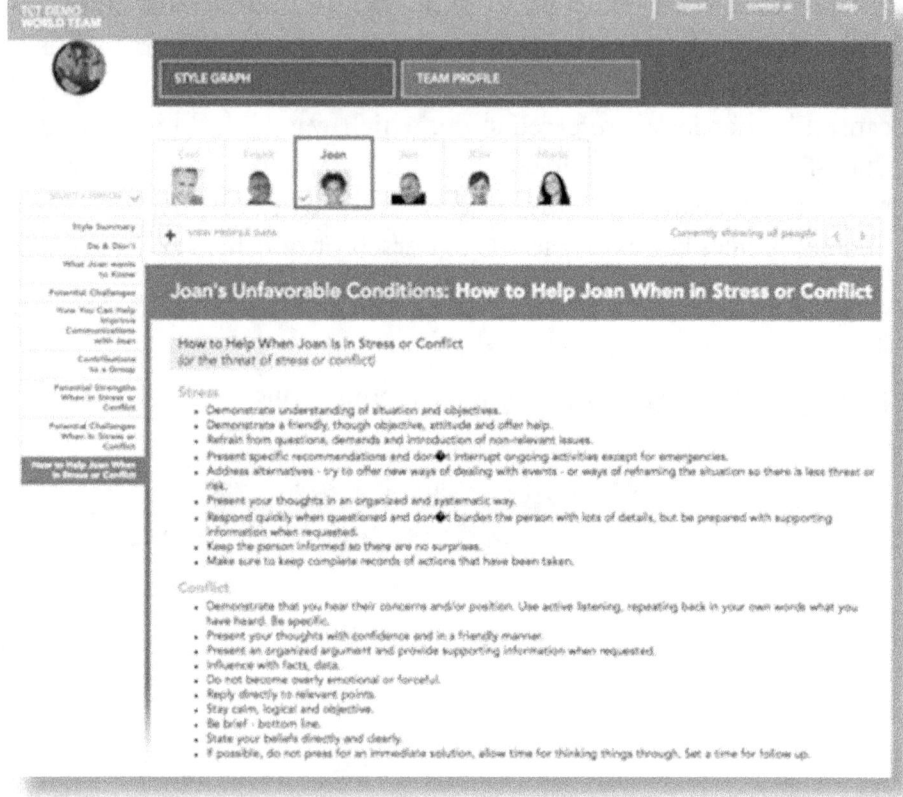

Her inability to say no resulted in her feeling overloaded, but she did not want to admit she could not handle everything she agreed to. Her cool, non-emotional attitude underplayed a sense of urgency from others, and she handled all the commitments in a timely manner. This caused her to shut down and stay quiet while continuing to try to balance priorities and responsibilities. In addition, she may not express her opinions until fully analyzed, which could impact others as her being disengaged or even unfriendly.

He learned Joan could be stuck in "analysis paralysis," which could slow down decision-making. Her concern about rules, policies, and systems limited her flexibility to explore options and innovative approaches to problem solving. She may even become somewhat stubborn and hold on to what has worked in the past.

Carl thought all that made a lot of sense, but how could he help manage the situation? He clicked on, *How to Help When Joan is in Stress*. See below:

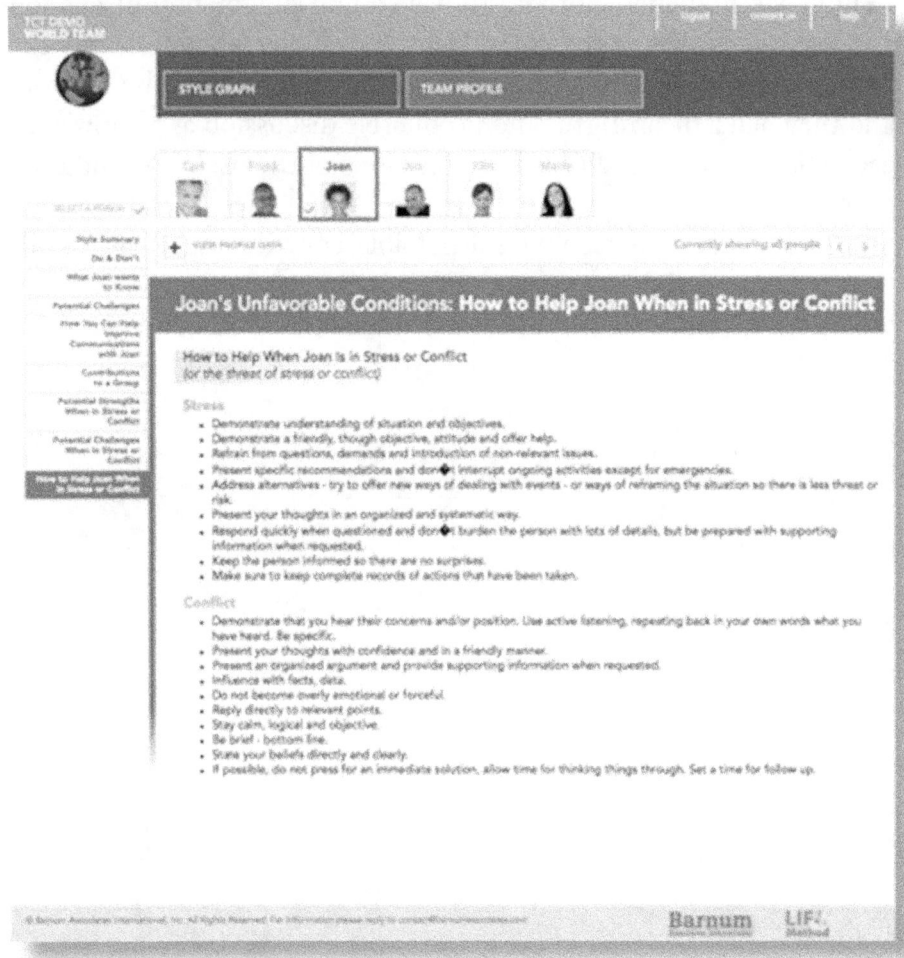

Carl recognized that he should not ask a lot of questions or make demands when dealing with Joan. He realized that he should empathically show an understanding of the situation, demonstrate a friendly, objective attitude, and offer help.

Carl also realized the most effective way to handle this was to be open, friendly, and objective. He sat with Joan, and they both looked at each other's profiles and discussed how they could both be more effective for each other and for the team in general. The LIFO® Method enabled them to have a non-judgmental discussion and they were even both able to laugh, especially when they saw the increase of CH on the graph of the TCT. This broke the tension, and they had a meaningful and productive discussion as to how they each could manage their own expectations of themselves—and each other.

Their success in resolving a possible conflict encouraged continued and ongoing use of the TCT within the team, which created lasting results and opportunities for individuals and the team to develop.

Chapter 18

LEADERSHIP AND ORGANIZATIONAL CHANGES

The following article by **Reiner Czichos** offers a detailed description of an application of The LIFO® Method in a German company. Some of the procedures described in the previous chapter are followed, but others are introduced that fit this consultant's style and experience. Note the amount of time spent to establish rapport and credibility with the client and his organization. In addition, there is an involvement of the top management in the actual teaching process that is rare and provides unique endorsement of the project that yields positive results.

Achieving Productive Changes in a German Company
By Reiner Czichos

INTRODUCTION

As a professional trainer with already 37 years experience by 2013, I have nourished a strong belief that it is not good enough to settle for only positive feedback to the trainer on what I call the "happiness sheet." What counts is the return on training, both for the company and managers, as well as for each individual participant.

To optimize the return on training, I strongly believe, that seminars should only be run after first conducting a proper needs analysis, followed by coaching. Furthermore, I believe that one should meet, if possible, all of the participants before the seminar for individual needs analyses and also to create many individualized training/coaching situations.

Finally I believe that participating in only one single daylong seminar (leadership, selling, communication, etc.) has limited value. A seminar has to be at least two days and preferably three or more days. The seminar experience itself should be divided into two parts. After the seminar(s), there should be at least an interim period of 8 to 12 weeks, to give participants time to transfer what they have learned, to try out new practices and ideas, and to report and build on their experiences in a follow-up seminar.

We focus on medium-sized companies, mainly production companies, for several reasons:

- In Germany, the majority of companies (thousands) are medium and small sized technical/production ones. They are mostly family owned, contributing much more to the gross domestic output than the few hundred big companies.
- Among those companies, the founding generation is now retiring, turning over the leadership to either sons and daughters or—most often—a hired manager. The new manager generations have many ideas about the re-orientations of their companies that sometimes are different than the owners.
- When working in seminars, coaching, or consulting in change projects for these medium sized companies, one can observe changes made by people and the company and

provide support and encouragement for them to continue making such changes.

- Running a leadership program in a particular company with all 100 managers, one gets to know every single individual. One can conduct research accompanying any programs that are involved.
- In addition, my team and I speak the language of these people: We felt accepted and listened to, although I, for one, have no technical background. All of this resulted in a relative high return on training for the customer.

My mission when using LIFO® methodology: I believe we can go even deeper and exploit the wealth of details in The LIFO® Method than simply using the method itself. This is what we managed to do in this project. We spent time probing the meaning of responses obtained, as well as using LIFO® Leadership Styles Surveys themselves.

THE PROJECT STORY

Here are some facts about the customer, a typical German Medium-Sized Company (GMSC):

- 1650 employees.
- Founded in the early 50s of the past century.
- Growth: In ten years (2002 to 1012) from 800 to 1650, including 160 trainees. 100 managers, from top-management down to the lowest team leader.
- Family owned.
- The family is deeply committed to the company and to their employees or, to use their words: to their people. The company philosophy is deeply value-oriented.
- Leadership by the founding owners and the first generation of employed managers was rather paternalistic

- In LIFO® terms, they seem to use heavily Supporting-Giving and Controlling-Taking ways: Command and protect people, take action, demand that people obey, leave them alone as long as everything is running well, intervene and even punish people when things are going wrong and give them another chance; feel responsible for people, give support even in private life.
- While still family owned, now run by employed managers.
- Leadership philosophy of the current management-team: SG. They call it a cooperative leadership style, which seemed to us more like a *laissez faire* style.
- Managers (and professionals) are developed in the company from trainee to professional and/or team leader and manager. Only a few came from outside and have experience in other companies.
- Products vary for different industries/customers: from traditional to high tech industries.
- Three plants in and around the hometown with only a few kilometres between them.

This article will show when and how we used The LIFO® Method. Some of the research and its results that occurred will also be described. In this project we used the LIFO® Leadership Styles Survey.

PHASE A: ACQUISITION

AN OVERVIEW

- Meeting with my sponsor: Needs analysis; Minutes and first concept
- Meeting with Task Force: Objectives, modules and process of project; Project plan

- Meeting with finance manager, administrative manager, and human resources manager: Negotiation and Budget

First Meeting. This project resulted from a cold call. We found this customer on the Internet. It seems we were lucky to be at the right time, since the customer, represented by the sales manager, was planning to conduct a leadership skills program.

When my colleague phoned the sales manager, he agreed to meet me. He was a tall, young man, and my first impression of him was as someone who used a lot of CT and SG behavior with some CH ones (idealistic, direct, open, neat and organized). Our style blends seemed complementary (my preference for AD behavior together with a bit less preferred CT style). If needed, I am able to activate some CH behavior (function in an organized and structured way).

In our first meeting, I talked briefly about myself. After a minute or two, I began to ask questions. I was curious. I took lots of detailed minutes in a "mind-mapping" way. I wanted to know in detail what was happening in the company. The sales manager was fast and precise in what he told me, and was also able to change subject within seconds. Since I understood him readily, this seemed to please him.

It seems he had previous experiences with external consultants who came in and started giving long sales pitches before they even asked any questions. Halfway through the meeting, I started to sketch ideas—not only verbally, but by drawing graphics on sheets of paper. These were ideas about what one could do to meet the needs expressed—trial balloons, if you like. I wanted to encourage him to be a partner in developing the ideas even further.

Of course, such a meeting is the first opportunity to convince customers of the value of The LIFO® Method. It takes a minute or two to draw up the four quadrants of the LIFO® grid and explain briefly the four styles in terms of pictures and behavioral cues. After I drew my style blend (AD-CT), I asked him to show how he would see his own profile. For this exercise, I asked him to only indicate his favourable styles.

However, before I let him draw his profile, I told him that I would draw his profile the way I see it on the back of a sheet, hidden from his eyes. When we compared the two profiles, we found a perfect match between the two.

This convinced him that The LIFO® Method could be a useful tool for leaders. I emphasized that people are different, have different strengths, and want to be addressed in different ways. In The LIFO® Method, there are no value statements made about behavior; it is simply a description of the person's behavior. The new generations of managers have many ideas about the re-orientations of companies that sometimes are different than the owners, in terms of how much behavior should be used and how much could be overused—also how much is uncovered and leaves one vulnerable.

In addition, a detailed description of the meaning of the LIFO® Leadership Surveys were provided to him, as well as to all participants in the study. The details of such an analysis are provided below. Naturally, this analysis often provoked questions and discussion of the material. Frequently, this led to insights about reasons for the person's behavior and exploration of how that person could change to be more effective.

LIFO® ANALYSIS OUTLINE:

Name: _____
- Your situation:

    - Your special leadership situation:
    - The challenges you see:
    - Your ideas for change:

- The requirements leaders/managers in GMSC should meet:
- Your strengths and weaknesses as described by yourself in the interview and in the seminar:
- What The LIFO® Leadership Survey reveals:

- Confirmation by manager:
- Some strategies for change:
- Your ideas for your own development:
- My suggestions for your development:

I emphasized that one can be successful with different leadership styles. In addition, I also stated that when applying leadership techniques, you have to see which style people use and try to make your communications match those of your people. It is very clear to everyone immediately for example that to motivate someone with a preferred CT style is quite a different ball game than motivating someone with a preferred CH style. This equally applies to delegation, feedback, and many other leadership behaviors.

We finished the meeting after one and a half hours, as planned. On the table were at least 15 pages with minutes and concept ideas. He said he would phone me after he had consulted his fellow managing directors. I promised to send him my minutes of our meeting, together with a very first concept idea.

He was positively surprised that he had my minutes and concept ideas for a Power Point presentation by 8 AM the next day, and he could use them when consulting with his fellow managing directors. I think that this was the final factor influencing his commitment: my matching his CT style and at the same time supporting him with structured minutes and concept ideas.

Second meeting: creating a high ranking task force. I called the Sales Manger the next day to ask if I had summarized the minutes correctly and to check if I had accurately understood the company needs that he had described. Three days later we completed the planning for the next meeting.

Experience tells me that a second meeting should include at least one more influential person. There were three more present: The human resources manager, the financial manager, and the manager of techniques and production. After the usual who-is-who introductions, the sales manager asked me to present my minutes and concept ideas.

In the first phase of this meeting, I had the impression that these four people complemented each other with their different profiles. The needs analysis was confirmed, and we went into more details and stories about how managers in the company were functioning—a very open discussion. The concept ideas from the first meeting were confirmed, appreciated, and developed further.

I also conducted a little "LIFO®-session" as I had previously with the sales manager. The managers were positively surprised that this was so. Their LIFO® results are shown below:

NAME	FAV. CONDITIONS				UNFAV. CONDITIONS			
	SG	CT	CH	AD	SG	CT	CH	AD
REINER	12	28	18	32	12	32	18	28
FINADM	24	18	28	20	24	19	25	22
SALES	25	30	17	18	25	27	20	18
PROD	21	31	26	21	11	32	26	21
HR	27	17	13	23	27	14	23	26

It turned out that these additional managers would be on the task force that would manage the whole program. This was proposed at this meeting, along with a description of my concept ideas. It seems that the task force members got the LIFO® message immediately.

Third meeting. In the third meeting, we wanted to obtain agreement on the whole project and its budget. I was confronted by the finance and administration manager, and also by the human resources manager. As might be expected, the financial manager took the role of the "bad guy" to negotiate a discount, leaving my sponsor, the sales manager, out—perhaps feeling he would have helped me too much.

However, the human resource manager extended warm support; he knew that I liked this project from the very beginning. He also knew that I would rather give some discount than not win this project. Finally, approval was granted.

PHASE B: BUY-IN

The members of the task force had been convinced in Phase A. Now in phase B, my team and I had to establish close cooperation with the task force, and help them understand and accept in detail all the modules we proposed. They needed to know this before the rest of the top management team learned about the modules in a workshop following this phase.

As we had done previously, we had members complete LIFO® Leadership Styles Surveys and followed the procedure used in the last two sessions. This group was also convinced of the value of The LIFO® Method, and we were able to demonstrate further how our trainer styles could complement their own styles.

The LIFO®-Profiles which I had constructed with the four task force members in the second meeting were confirmed by the surveys. We also wanted to let participants recognize the different strengths that existed and that we complemented each other as well; we wanted to give our participants a model of a team working together. The task force saw this, as did participants in the following seminars.

Here is a picture of our consulting team along with our three profiles:

NAMES	FAV. CONDITIONS:				UNFAV. CONDITIONS:			
	SG	CT	CH	AD	SG	CT	CH	AD
REINER	12	28	18	32	22	32	18	28
MARIE-THERES	28	26	28	16	24	30	30	16
STEFAN	26	28	20	16	22	26	24	18

Note: All of the dimensions are covered when the consulting team is considered as a whole.

Discovering GMSC's values in LIFO® terms. In addition to defining how the task force and trainers would be working together to prepare, conduct, and review all seminars and other actions, we also prepared a concept for the requirement profile for GMSC managers. Starting with their company philosophy, we derived through a brain storming session four major values: Inspire and develop people; ensure achievements; manage processes; and willingness to change. We then constructed a square containing those value dimensions.

SG	**AD**
Inspire and develop people	Willingness to adjust
Manage organization Processes	Lead to achieve goals
CH	**CT**

In summary, four titles emerged and mirrored, to a large extent, the four LIFO®-Styles. We placed the four GMSC leadership values in a grid, similar to the one we used to display the four LIFO® styles.

The individual LIFO® analysis as success factor. To anchor The LIFO® Method even further and get the members of the task force prepared to sell the program to the rest of the company (they were already willing to do so—not only to sell the project but also The LIFO® Method to the top management team), a LIFO® Analysis Report was prepared for each of the four, analysing their survey results. (I prefer individualized LIFO® reports, contrasted with computer-generated ones because they allow me to put my interpretation in the context of their individual situations).

Further, I could relate the interpretation to their situational requirements and support the interpretation with the observations made in interviews, meetings and workshops or seminars. This enabled people to really look into a report that mirrors themselves and their situations. In addition, some questions for their reflection and ideas for personal development were included.

The LIFO® Analysis as input for the needs analysis and to paint a picture of the company leadership culture. The Task Force members recognized that their managers would benefit from such an individual analysis-mirror. They especially liked the fact that there could be different profiles for favourable and unfavourable conditions. One of the problems/needs identified in the meetings before was that managers do not have a very thick skin and shy away from conflict.

They also realized that it made sense to analyse their intentions, behaviors and impacts:

- *Intentions*: Either one needs to question the intentions (Who tells you so? Why did you intend to do so? Etc.),
- *Behaviors*: One needs to discuss, in case of incongruencies, if people wish to learn new behaviors or modify old ones, and how they can best fulfil their intentions.
- *Impact* tells what managers assume their people would tell them about the effect their behavior has had on others: What is the picture people have of me? What did they understand— content, impressions? The younger managers, especially, do not have enough feedback from their people about their leadership style, and the older ones have not asked for feedback for a long time—if ever.

We had already discussed, at this early stage, that we could construct an overview of the LIFO® profiles of all of the people, and thus have a picture of the company leadership culture, its strengths and weaknesses, and areas that needed improvement. We emphasized that such an overview would help us further define the concrete needs of managers. Thus we would be able to prioritize the modules and work with individuals within the seminars.

PHASE C: ESTABLISHING COOPERATION WITH THE TOP MANAGEMENT

After the task force was convinced of the accuracy of our diagnosis, people realized that the whole project would only pay off and get the return on training in the long term if all managers of the top management team would not only buy into the proposed methods but also accept and commit to the roles as transfer-coaches. In addition, we wanted 12 top managers as co-trainers in the seminars. The four members of the task force were already committed; we needed eight more.

The task force and I chose the eight candidates after interviews with all of the top managers.

AN OVERVIEW

- Individual interviews with all top managers

    o Individual interview minutes
    o Summary of the interviews

- Briefing with task force: Preparation of workshop with top management team (2 days, 17 participants, 3 trainers)
- Needs analysis and project as proposed by the task force.
- Summary of the interviews
- Overview of all modules
- The LIFO® Method and LIFO® Survey
- Requirement profile and self-evaluation
- Role of the co-trainer
- Role of managers as transfer-coaches
- Briefing with task force: Preparation for train-the-trainer for co-trainers
- Train-the-trainer for co-trainers, (2 days, 10 co-trainers, 3 trainers)

Use of LIFO® Leadership Styles Profile in interviews with the top managers.

I had interviews (about 45 to 60 minutes) with each top manager. The interviews helped me to get to know each member of the top management personally and understand their views about GMSC's situation, as well as their needs for their own development and those of their people.

A key part in the interviews was a little LIFO® Session, conducted like ones done with other managers. They were quite open with their comments. They also seemed to be glad to finally have someone to talk to about themselves, their worries, and hopes.

Use of LIFO® Survey in workshop with the top managers. In the following workshop with the top management team (including the four task force members), the summary of these interviews was presented—of course, without breaking any confidences. This became the "ice breaker" in the workshop: to be able to see the strengths and weaknesses both of the company as an organization and of the people. The same positive reactions were expressed by the top management group, as those cited by the task force group.

We also asked participants to draw profiles of the other five people in their breakout groups. They were amazed about the feedback they received from their colleagues, even in those cases where their own perception of themselves was not the same as the perception of some colleagues. They recommended that we do the same exercise with their managers in the following seminars.

Co-trainers. After the workshop with the top management team, the task force was asked to identify the eight managers who would become co-trainers in the seminars. Why co-trainers?

- First, in our seminars we wanted to be as close to the real business life of our participants as possible. We felt that using managers as co-trainers could help us bridge this gap, translate and provide familiar examples.
- Second, these top managers are the superiors of the "normal" participants. We felt it would be a worthwhile objective to use seminars to help those managers improve their communication

and cooperation with higher levels of management. We also believed that those levels should be the "natural" transfer-coaches.

- Third, top managers do not tend to visit seminars. Taking a role as co-trainer is different, requiring them to take an active part in the training. We felt that as co-trainers, they would also learn better and more than as participants.

It turned out that lower level managers found it was great to have their bosses as co-trainers. This convinced them that their bosses were fully committed to the project and that they approved of all the skills that would be taught and trained. Almost all of them appreciated that they had the opportunity to meet, talk, and really get to know each other.

Set up of the seminars. To understand more about how we worked together with co-trainers and the role of the co-trainers in the seminars after each seminar, the structure of the first seminars will be described in detail.

We had planned to run about 83 managers through four seminars (two days each) with about 8 to 10 weeks in between to allow for transfer. The four seminar groups consisted of 21 participants each. The groups were a mix of people from different functions and locations. In the seminars we would have three learning groups of seven participants with one pair of trainers (one of the three professional trainers and one of the top managers in each group). These groups would stay together in all four seminars with the same pair of trainers. The co-trainers would then be transfer-coaches for the people in their learning group, in parallel to and in cooperation with, the regular superiors of the participants.

Our preference is for 21 students. We do not favor a one-way teaching methodology. Therefore, there is a change between input sessions (max. 30 minutes) in the big group and breakout sessions of the learning groups in their own break-out rooms (max. 75 minutes) in which the trainers can work intensively with their groups.

There were many personal encounters between people, the power of teams, some competition between teams on the one side and individual coaching on the other side - these were all part of the total learning experience. The use of The LIFO® Method helped participants observe other people and understand, by example, the various LIFO® insights that had been obtained previously with the task force and top management groups.

Train-the-trainer for co-trainers. To prepare our co-trainers, we ran a train-the-trainer workshop before the first seminar and had preparation meetings with them before each seminar.

Our co-trainers had already seen the modules of the seminars in the workshop with the top management team. Therefore, in the train-the-trainer workshop we could concentrate on discussing and agreeing how we would work together in the seminars, and how we would coach our learning groups. Each of us, Marie-Therese, Stefan, and I mutually decided with our co-trainers on our own way of cooperating. This, as you can imagine by now, depended on the mix of LIFO® profiles of trainer and co-trainer.

Have a look at my profile and the profiles of my four co-trainers:

NAME	FAV. CONDITIONS:				UNFAV. CONDITIONS:			
	SG	CT	CH	AD	SG	CT	CH	AD
AK	33	14	15	29	25	24	23	18
GT	29	25	31	15	24	21	33	12
HM	27	33	20	10	28	25	17	20
AM	26	24	20	20	28	30	20	12
RC	12	28	18	32	12	32	18	28

You can see very clearly that I (RC) had a real challenge because my CT was so dominant, compared to those of the other co-trainers, save for HM. With GT, I had to activate more CH behaviors. GT had to be encouraged to speak up, to leave the role as observer and listener. In working with AK, I had to help him focus and bring his ideas to a point;

time management was also a real challenge. However, he was very good at helping participants feel good and slowing me down from time to time. With HM and AM, because of HM'S high CT under Favorable Conditions and AM'S high CT under Unfavorable Conditions, I had to be stopped occasionally because they tended to answer questions before the participants could answer; they tended to dominate discussions.

I also had to step back myself from time to time to avoid competing with them. We discussed these aspects with our partners quite openly, laying our strengths and weaknesses on the table. From these discussions, they seemed to learn a lot about team building.

All input sessions were jointly prepared. I gave inputs in the big group, but there were always additional inputs from others in the small groups. We also provided a kind of "circuit training": a specific input-module was assigned to each pair of trainers who then prepared their training "booths." The three learning groups walked from one training booth to the next, following a given time schedule.

Since we use flipcharts and pin-boards for our input sessions, we had to prepare drawings for display. We very seldom used Power Point presentations for input because they are often boring and put people asleep, and, once you have finished a chart in Power Point, it's gone. Visual display charts are visible all the time.

Co-trainers as transfer-coaches. The co-trainers were each assigned to a learning group in the seminars. Thus, they worked with the same participants in all three seminars. Even further, they also served as transfer-coaches for their learning groups. After each seminar, they had at least one meeting (4 hours) with their learning group in which they discussed how the new skills were going to be transferred into their business practice. They reported that after the first seminar, they were openly sharing and discussing their written LIFO® Analyses.

Almost all participants said that they had taken an hour or two in drawing up the profiles of their co-workers; most of them shared these profile-pictures with colleagues and even with their superiors (members of the top management team).

PHASE D: DELIVERY

As you can see, preparation is key, especially if you have to involve three trainers, twelve top managers as co-trainers in the seminars and transfer-coaches, and an additional five managers as transfer-coaches.

AN OVERVIEW

- Individual interviews with all particpants

    - o Individual minutes of the interviews
    - o Summary of the interviews
    - o Briefing with task force

- Seminar 1: The LIFO® Method, LIFO® Survey, Communication techniques

    - o Individual transfer reports
    - o Summary of transfer reports
    - o Written individual LIFO® Analysis for all managers
    - o Briefing with task force

- Seminar 2: Leadership techniques

    - o Individual transfer reports
    - o Summary of transfer reports
    - o Briefing with task force

- Seminar 3: Conflict management, stress management, GMSC development review

    - o Individual transfer reports
    - o Summary of transfer reports

- o Summary of research findings and proposals for further change
- o Briefing with task force

- Workshop with top management team

  - o Review of seminars and transfer
  - o Research findings and proposals
  - o Leadership manual
  - o Action plan, further steps
  - o Briefing with task force

I really had to activate my CH behavior to design this plan and to keep on track. In addition, I had to manage the whole trainer-pool and also the task force. With my preferred style, the AD-style, I managed to get all people on board and to motivate them for their work on top of normal business. With my CT-style, I could drive things and people, get them to focus on the right things at the right time. Finally, with my CH style (which was getting stronger because I needed and wanted it to), I could keep the project on track.

I think that by using my CT behaviors (and with my CH ones), I was getting on the nerves of some people. However, they became and stayed motivated because Marie-Therese and Stefan, with their preferred SG-styles, patiently listened to people, explained my role and my intentions, and reported back to me about what was said and done. Only with the support of my colleagues was this possible. This was aided by the support of my sponsor and his belief that I would be able to handle everything, characteristic of his SG-CT style.

Individual interviews. Before we began the seminars, we had an individual interview with every participant (45 to 60 minutes). I interviewed 40 people. We used the same interview structure for the top managers. Here is what the minutes of the interviews looked like.

Name

Private info	39 years old married, 2 children (8, 5) high school 2 years with the army apprenticeship with GMSC production manager in plant A Hobbies: Engaged in church work Meet my many friends
Strengths of GMSC	Family owned ... visible, the live up to what they are telling us We are innovative
Weaknesses of GMSC	The „we-feeling" is weakening ... is the top management aware of this? We need to intensify our communication with our people ... most of us do not have/take the time for talking with their people
Requirements for managers at GMSC	Communicate openly Take decisions, also when they are negative Esteem people Cooperate in finding solutions Be open for innovation and change
Self evaluation	Strengths: Open for innovation and change I communicate proactively I do not worry people by talking about things which are still fuzzy Development needs: Fear from new situations Heart pounding
How do you see your profile in the LIFO®-Grid	

Self-evaluation in the LIFO® grid: Research Findings. We had 78 of 83 LIFO® self-valuations; five were mistakenly not recorded. Fifty-four of them were almost equal to the results of the LIFO® Survey. In 24 cases, there was no match; the difference was mainly in confusing the AD with the SG style. Given more time, it would have been interesting to analyse the biographical data and the strengths and weaknesses of GMSC that were seen by each style. My feeling was that there was a significant positive correlation.

The seminar modules. The general content has been outlined previously. In addition, we conducted similar discussions for our reviews of leadership techniques. Each time we asked participants to look at their people and ask: *Considering their different profiles, how would you give feedback to them?* There were then discussions of the various techniques that were mentioned.

SOME SPECIFIC FEATURES *IN* THE SEMINARS INCLUDED:

1. *Circuit Training.* As mentioned previously, we used circuit training in the seminars. People saw differences in the trainers' training styles. Some preferred Marie-Therese's style or Stefan's and some mine, depending on their own preferred styles. They saw and appreciated that each pair of trainers did a very good job in his or her own way. They were able to extend such consideration to their own teams.

Some people still had problems understanding how, with my flexible style (which those with preferred CH even described as "chaotic"), I finished these sessions always precisely on time, as agreed. I emphasized that people can employ some CH behaviors even though they have low scores in that dimension. Knowing what is required and needed for other styles can help people to extend their styles. People don't always have to exhibit behavior equal to their scores; they can manage to correct and manage behavior for different situations. This becomes easier to do after training and practice.

Considering the needs of this group, I always prepared a structure for my sessions, planned with some major milestones. I even showed students my structure with my milestones. In addition, I stuck to those procedures although some people feel that I let discussions get off-track, at times.

What has this to do with demonstrating the LIFO® Method? To have a preferred AD-CT profile does not mean that one does not use behaviors from other styles! You cannot stamp people with a label such as "XY type." This means that managers have to get to know and understand their people, discover their potentials and their vulnerabilities, and behave accordingly.

2. *Having fun and discovering it is fun to activate the AD-style.* We had discovered already in the interviews—and later proven by the results of the LIFO®-Surveys (see research finding below) — that the least preferred style of most GMCS people is the AD-style. Having fun, just having fun, for no obvious purpose is not really a habit of technically minded people. However, in the course of a creative outdoor-event, almost everybody enjoyed having fun. We saw even serious people "waking up," doing things they never thought they would do, the AD-style. We helped them to let out "their child." In addition, examining other possibilities and being flexible and open to exploration (other aspects of the AD orientation) provide opportunities for discovery that are also valuable to technically-oriented associates.

Listed below are some of the exercises we let them do in their learning groups (hopefully they realized that the exercises were models of leadership situations):

- Walking blindfold through a labyrinth while a coach outside of the labyrinth is giving walking instructions (coaching)

- Throwing with tennis balls at cans stapled on a table from 10 meters distance (coordinating a team)
- Putting three puzzles in a particular order, which we had mixed beforehand (help the team through frustrating situations)
- Holding 1 litre beer mugs in a special way (encourage, motivate)

SOME SPECIFIC FEATURES *AFTER* THE SEMINARS INCLUDED:

1. *Transfer questions.* We wanted to optimize transfer as much as possible. The co-trainers worked with their learning groups after the seminars and all the other top managers had individual transfer meetings with their direct reports after the seminars as well. However, we did even more to make sure people did transfer what they had learned in the seminars.

After each seminar everyone received an email requiring answers to the following questions:

a. What did I learn in the seminar?
b. What precisely am I implementing/trying out?
c. Feedback for the trainers and the seminars.

Although reminders had to be sent to send the answers, every single mail received was answered by our team, not only offering thanks for their participation but encouraging them to continue to use their newly learned knowledge and skills, sometimes giving specific hints that related to personal information obtained during the interviews, from LIFO® Survey results and observations.

2. *"Inaugural speech."* After the first seminar, we asked participants to write a draft for an "inaugural speech." To do this, we asked them to imagine that they had to give a presentation

to their people telling them about their own strengths and weaknesses as their manager. See the structure for the presentation below:

1. This is how we see our teams situation and my performance as a manager today:
2. These are the (negative) consequences resulting from the situation and from my behavior:
3. This is what I will do differently from now on (change my behavior):
4. This is what I demand of you to support me and all of us to make the necessary changes:
5. These are the benefits for you and for me from these behavioral changes:

Research findings: We received 57 (out of 83) inaugural speeches. There was no intention that they should actually make a real presentation to their people, but rather the activity was to make them think more in depth about their leadership situation, and think of and plan personal changes. Some of them told us that they did present this and that people were positively surprised.

However, they also tended to be concerned more about details and logic, trying to be calm under stress. (Data: The highest preference was for using the CH orientation under those conditions).

The above finding is specifically interesting in the light of GMSC's company culture: the strong value orientation that stressed concern for people that was espoused as the main company value. It is easy to act in such a way, when every thing runs well (favorable conditions). You trust people, believe that they will do the right things and also do these right things in the right way. In unfavorable conditions however, when it becomes urgent to solve problems, when they are experiencing stress, most technical managers become more cautious, and either become more CH in their mode of behavior, followed by taking-over from subordinates when necessary. The non-technical managers fell either into CH and/or AD behavior

Digging further: The GMSC management patterns in relation to value conflicts. We wanted to know more about how managers dealt with the conflict of expectations versus reality, in terms of potential innovators and in terms of process thinkers and planners

One of the most important success factors for the future success of GMSC is innovation. They are currently planning to establish a dedicated group of people whose mission will be to drive innovation, not only in products and services but also in the way they are for example managing finance or running projects internally and/or with customers—in effect, looking for people who rely more on CT and AD behaviors.

This is why the LIFO® Leadership Style Survey results were examined for statements directly related to "innovation." The items 32, 40, 52 and 68 seemed most related. A very simple pragmatic analysis was made by scanning all 100 LIFO® Surveys. The rankings which people gave to these statements varied from 4 to 16.

Although the differences may not be statistically significant, it appeared that people with "high" innovation-indicators (greater than 8), would have been listed by us as innovators, based on prior knowledge. We don't have any benchmarks from other companies. However, there seems to be quite a need to improve innovation in GMSC since most scores were in the low range. We felt that if the right people (those with more CT-AD patterns) were chosen for their planned innovation team, this might increase the chances for success.

As shown previously, a quite specific profile-pattern of managers was found in GMSC: High SG in favorable conditions, combined with CH. Often when there is such a pattern people tend to be somewhat perfectionistic, highly concerned about accuracy. This was followed by CT behavior. However, when it comes to crisis and/or conflict, managers tend to respond slowly after examining details closely, requiring additional information and therefore delaying or slowing the process.

Further findings. Seven statements related to process and structure were identified. Maximum points = 28. This is what was found:

The data showed that 9 of the respective 28 managers would be those who could best help GMSC to define reasonable processes and structures. However, innovative ideas would still be needed to define new processes and even avoiding decisions. Interviews and responses from the "inaugural speeches" revealed that the biggest problems of managers were "not well-defined processes and structure." As we have seen, their philosophy meant taking care of people and providing them the freedom to do what is right, trusting that they know what is right, and prescribing things as little as possible. GMSC actually has recognized that with their growth and diversification, as well with the younger replacements who were not "infected" by the founding "fathers," they need to define and prescribe common processes, and ensure clear organizational structures and follow-through with guided direction.

There did not seem to be a very high correlation between innovative and process thinking in GMSC, since more CT-AD behavior was needed. This represented a real challenge for GMSC. Eight managers with such patterns were not necessarily enough to make sure that GMSC could achieve innovation, clearer processes and structures. Alternatively, we recommended putting all 28 managers in a team-building program that could enhance the desired behavior, also allowing for different styles to complement each other.

The transfer questions and answers. In the section on Phase D (Delivery), it was mentioned that after each seminar people were asked to answer three questions. Given more time, it would have been interesting to relate answers to the three transfer-questions to preferred styles. The impression we had was that the feedback itself and the way they wrote the feedback (their writing style) correlated quite highly with their preferred styles.

Characteristic examples. Two managers commented on the first day of the second seminar. One with a strongly preferred CT style said that he felt a bit bored, that some discussions lasted too long and were going around in circles. The other manager with a strongly preferred SG style felt that we were moving too fast, that we should have gone into more of the background.

Other results were:

- People who used SG behaviors wrote lengthy paragraphs.
- Those with dominant CT behaviors kept texts short.
- People who emphasized CH behaviors in their styles tended to organize their responses better than others.
- People who used AD behaviors a lot tended to elaborate and illustrated their answers more.

PHASE F: FEEDBACK

When individual feedback was given to our participants, they were also asked for their feedback, not only at the end of the seminars, but also after answering the already above mentioned three transfer questions and further discussion.

The transfer-questions and answers. There was a lot of positive feedback. A few things are worth mentioning:

- People recognized and appreciated that the three trainers had different profiles and that they complemented each other. They enjoyed learning from trainers with different styles. They learned that every style has its strengths and weaknesses and that their reactions depended on their own profile.
- They liked the dynamic quality and variety of the sessions—the interaction, the changes from plenary sessions to

break-out sessions—in the seminars, and at the same time they stated that they liked the well-prepared structure. Some said that the seminars were very demanding, but because of that they were also very interesting. In addition, they commented that they learned a lot more than they had from other seminars that had been conduced in the company.

- They appreciated the individual feedback they received, believing it made them aware of their behavior potentials and how they could.

Transfer of the LIFO® Method. Before the third seminar, you may recall that participants were asked to send us a report on whether they did make any transfer of new skills and how they transferred them to their business lives. In addition, they were also asked whether they would use the new skills in the future as well as how they would be used. They were also furnished with a list of 20 skills and techniques which were taught in the first two seminars. The questions related to The LIFO® Method were detailed in four different items.

There were 78 reports submitted (out of 83). In addition, they were also asked to evaluate each module on a scale from 0 to 10, with 0 indicating that they didn't use a skill or technique at all and 10 indicating that they "always" used it.

N	Modules		0-3	4-7	8-10
17	Discover your own strengths, manage your strengths, use them.	Now	32	35	11
		Plan	12	32	27
18	Discover strengths of your people and use them accordingly.	Now	30	36	10
		Plan	12	41	30
19	Address your people in their preferred style.	Now	36	27	14
		Plan	12	32	28
20	Discover the different styles of people in your team and manage your team accordingly.	Now	40	26	10
		Plan	13	27	28

First line: Now (after seminar 2, before seminar 3)
Second line: Plan for further transfer

The numbers speak for themselves. The LIFO® Method was understood, accepted, and used in business life. After the third seminar, even the few skeptics said that they now could see how useful The LIFO® Method is for their leadership roles.

Almost a whole day was spent in conducting performance review meetings. The co-trainers played the role of employees for the participants, representing different LIFO® styles. This enabled participants to practice conducting such a review with people who have different styles. We also discussed how they would actually conduct a performance review with their people. (Remember: In the first and second seminar, we discussed a number of leadership techniques and how they applied to the different styles!)

Feedback/evaluation by the 17 top managers. After the three seminars, the top managers were asked for a specific report. They answered questions regarding identifying which changes they could observe in the leadership behavior of their direct reports, and what they were doing and planning to sustain these positive changes.

Here is their feedback:

	1	2	3	4	5
The three seminars	●●●●● ●●●	●●●●● ●●●●			
The coordination by the task force	●●●●● ●	●●●●● ●●●●●	●		
The probability for lasting transfer	●●●	●●●●● ●●●●●	●●●		

1 = very good; 2 = pretty good; 3 = good; 4 = not so good; 5 = awful

This was certainly a positive valuing of the experience.

We also feel that, because of the company's commitment to improving leadership and innovation, we will receive more requests for consultation in their future leadership development projects.

Chapter 19

PERSONAL COACHING

Moving Ahead with Personal Coaching
by Marijke Theunis

Coaching has become a hot item. Personal coaching as a field of developmental activity has grown enormously in the past 20 years and is still continuing to grow. There are coaches in business, life coaches, career coaches, coaches for politicians, etc. Wherever people strive to increase success and fulfillment, coaches are at work.

In my personal process of building a sound coaching practice, I have been constantly in search for the Holy Grail of coaching. What is it that makes a coach a professional coach? I found that in this matter, the LIFO® method could play an important role in facilitating the development of both parties involved, coach and coachee.

I'm often asked, *Why choose The LIFO® model for personal coaching?* In working with clients, I have found The LIFO® Method a valuable coaching tool because it provides the following:

- *The LIFO® Method creates a positive mood.* Discussing one's LIFO® profile is a safe and accessible opener, fostering self-reflection. Even in the setting of "need for improvement" in performance appraisals, the method always puts the person first in his or her natural strengths. It encourages trust and willingness of the coachee to learn about behavior and behavioral change.

- *The LIFO® Method serves as a guideline.* Analyzing and discussing one's LIFO® profile is only the beginning. Next, the LIFO® model offers practical, developmental strategies for how to behave more consciously and raise personal effectiveness. With the help of the bridging strategies, one learns to enjoy differences between people and to gain personal impact.

I would like to add a third element myself, which is that The LIFO® Method requires professionalism. As LIFO® licensees say, The LIFO® Method is not for wimps. The method is not just a tool; it's an integrative concept for development of people's actual and potential power. Consequently, as a LIFO® coach, you need to know what you are doing and to show in-depth mastery of skills.

With this article, I want to share my approach, experiences and effects with this method in personal coaching. I hope it may give insight and comfort to others who want to use The LIFO® method in their coaching practice.

THE LIFO® COACH AS A DIRECTOR OF GROWTH

Coaching is about creating a conscious path in different stages, from establishing the context and goals to completion and final appraisal. Coach and coachee are both putting things forward, but it's up to the coach to help the coachee to make the right connection between the subject matter and the overall developmental process for both of them. A master coach serves as a trustworthy guide in providing structure throughout the coaching process and is capable of managing the subtle interplay between directing coachees towards the desirable results and giving sufficient space for new learning.

The foundation for a progressive development process is made in the first session or intake session. Coach and coachee discuss the coaching framework by:

1. Establishing the context of coaching and creating a positive, mutual feeling.
2. Clarifying the expectations and focusing on the important development goals.
3. Providing development strategies in order to reach the coaching goals.
4. Drawing up the coaching plan on what coach and coachee have agreed upon.

In this early beginning stage, the coach will value various sources of input regarding the coachee and the coaching issues.

The LIFO® coach will utilize a highly client-centered approach. This begins with a thorough understanding of the coachee through the LIFO® profile and report review. While discussing the LIFO® profile, the coachee shows their sense of self. The LIFO® coach will spend as much time as necessary to make sure the coachee has an accurate interpretation of their LIFO® styles in both favorable and unfavorable conditions.

Then feedback is collected on how the coachee is seen by others with the help of the LIFO® Survey of Another Person. A 360° feedback delivers qualitative observations of strengths, the considered versatility in various interactions (for example, differences in observations by colleagues, manager, or customer) and possible excess of style behavior.

This is followed by a review and exploration of the current behavior in terms of intention, behavior and impact. Does the coachee believe they are getting what they want and do other people understand the motivation for coachee's behavior in the same way? Following this, the coachee's preferences in coaching and learning are identified. The LIFO® profile will provide the coach with this information and help grasp the positive and doubtful signs of engagement of the coachee. The LIFO® coach acknowledges differences in learning attitudes and behavior, and will be happy to adapt the coaching style or refer to a more suitable coach for the coachee.

The LIFO® framework ensures strength-based development of behavioral skills to help coachees identify their core performance issues, set goals for improvement, and determine the LIFO® development strategies—all aimed at combating the most usual enemies of personal productivity.

The framework also helps to align personal and professional growth by explicitly integrating individual goals for achievement in the coaching plan, as shown by the following example:

Alexander is an experienced manager of an engineering team that offers a solid range of products and services to its customers. However, for many years, the same range has been offered and the company wants to be more innovative in a competitive market. Alexander wants to improve his innovation skills through personal coaching. He will focus on expert management as part of a longer-term perspective of becoming "a fully-fledged leader for strategic development teams."

As for himself, Alexander chose an additional focus on learning and applying project manager skills. Alexander may be looking forward to a new role as a project manager in a next career step. This example shows how the company and the manager can find and mutually strengthen each other in their possible growth.

The LIFO® coaches will act in an appreciative way towards the coachee and their development. Then, coaches, such as Alexander, will be pleasantly surprised with the positive coaching climate, enabling them to achieve the outcome they really want to be in place.

During the intake session, the coach works toward the coaching plan as described through the processes of guided questioning and exploration of the coachee's answers. There are many different areas that are explored, including:

Fostering self-awareness:

- What is the feedback he gets from colleagues, subordinates, his manager?
- What does he describe for himself as his strengths and blind spots?
- When does he feel competent, what are difficult situations for him to manage?
- What is he aiming for, short term and longer term?
- What does he want to develop—for the organization, for himself?
- Identifying the focal point for the coaching process.
- Helping him to grasp the smart goals (desired output, new behavior) for the coaching.
- Helping him to clarify (questioning) the *what, by when,* criteria used for measuring success.
- Challenging and encouraging the coachee, being open for his communications and concerns.

Establishing a coaching strategy and tactics:

- Exploring the path towards the desired output: *How are we going to work on this together?*
- Scouting possible approaches (one-to-one sessions, field coaching, 360° feedback, other sources).
- Trying to find solutions to overcome obstacles and concerns of the coachee (e.g., lack of time, lack of support, confidentiality).
- Adapting to the coachee's learning style.

Working out the coaching plan:

- Setting the mutual agreements between coach and coachee.
- Establishing the agreements on what information will be shared with others (e.g., in order to monitor progress).
- Planning sessions and resources as well as drawing up the action plan(s).

Throughout the intake session, the client determines the pace in order to gain trust for the coaching and objectives. The client is regarded as the expert and must concur with any interpretations before proceeding.

GETTING THE BEST FROM YOUR COACHING STYLE

The LIFO® Method finds its origin in the idea that when we understand and build upon our natural strengths, we can reach optimal performance. This is applicable to the coachee, but also to the coach. With the LIFO® Coaching Styles Survey, coaches will be able to explore their favorite coaching approach and learn about how successful they are in coaching and mentoring others.

While self-awareness is the key, the LIFO® Coaching Styles Survey will help highlight the preferential approach related to six dimensions of the coaching process:

1. Establishing the development goals
2. Setting the context of the learning process
3. Asking typical questions
4. Dealing with failure or with lack of results
5. Dealing with resistance of the coachee
6. Providing personal appraisal for the coachee

Appendix A to this article gives an overview of how the behavior of the coach may slightly color these six dimensions, according to the preferred LIFO® coaching style.

The results of the LIFO® Coaching Styles Survey help coaches to manage their behavioral patterns in normal conditions and when stress levels become high or tensions occur. This sets opportunities for the coach to deal with three important challenges in professional growth:

1. Understanding and accepting differences in personal styles of coaching
2. Recognizing their personal strengths and vulnerabilities as a coach
3. Increasing versatility and re-focus to resolve excessive behavior

EXAMPLE:

Coach Marilyn has AD as her most preferred style and CH as her least preferred style. She has the reputation of being very easy in establishing rapport with the coachee and dealing with resistance. She is good at facilitating the process smoothly, fostering self-reflection and showing empathy for what happens with the coachee. This results in animated conversations and a huge appreciation for the coachee showing willingness, even if the desirable effects are still lacking.

In some coaching situations, Marilyn felt uncertain, especially when she was asked to specify the benefits of the coaching. Then she noticed that she had been reluctant in setting standards for success, and progress couldn't be traced. However, there is a strong intention from Marilyn's AD style to create consensus with all stakeholders on goals and success. To avoid the possible excess and show effectiveness, Marilyn benefited greatly from sticking to a coaching model

and using templates to make progress tangible. By committing her-
self to specifying the goals, to planning the learning resources, and to
systematically collecting feedback on the effects of the coaching in the
coachee's close circle, she increased the visibility of her coaching efforts.
Throughout her coaching experience, Marilyn learned to successfully
extend her behavior with best practices covering the overall process,
next to her natural strength of being in touch with the coachee.

As a coach, you can feel confident about your skills, but is this really true? Even an experienced coach can be tempted to overplay strengths or overlook the least used orientation. Here is a tip: take a look in the mirror and reflect at set times upon your coaching behavior to uncover any counterproductive use or blind spots. The LIFO® model helps reframing and provides additional paths for raising professional expertise. Peer-to-peer discussions are a very effective way of exploring and enhancing your coaching impact. They keep you on your toes!

MATCH OR MISMATCH WITH THE COACHEE

During the coaching process, coach and coachee are building rapport and creating relationship with each other. From the early start, their LIFO® styles instantly affect the mutual interaction. The coach will, in their preferred styles, assure that the coachee is interested, involved, and actively taking part in what is going on. On the other hand, the personal style of the coachee will determine the kind of engagement, the preferences in learning, and the perseverance to achieve fulfillment.

Whereas coaching is dealing with conscious learning, a certain amount of risk-taking behavior is involved. The coachee needs to change habits and go beyond boundaries towards the unknown world that might cause feelings of fear and uncertainty. The coach will encourage the coachee to overcome obstacles in building greater strength and confidence. To be able to do this in an effective way, the coach has to understand the needs, concerns, perceptions, and values of the coachee.

The LIFO® method provides a framework for understanding the attitude of the coachee and to "read" their coping and learning behavior. Taking into account this knowledge about the person, the method can be very useful for getting along in the coaching relationship and communicating more effectively in the sessions.

Reviewing the LIFO® profile is a good basis to get deeply involved with your coachee when you are involved in the coaching process. Observe the needs of your coachee, how they are communicating, reacting upon the style descriptions, open to learn or change their behavior. Don't forget that each person is unique and use your gift of active listening and make sure you grasp the specific situation, objectives, and requirements for the coaching. It will help you communicate in a style that matches the coachee's own style.

Although The LIFO® Method is very useful in understanding the coachee and adapting to their style, you are not using a magic wand. Bridging the gap to the coachee is not unlimited. At times, the style differences may be too huge, strongly affecting the coaching process. In some cases, coaching might not be a solution to the problem. Be aware of these restrictions and make sure that the right coachee gets the right coach or the right approach.

EXAMPLE:

Julie provides executive coaching and uses SG-AD as her preferred style combination. She is asked to coach Harry, logistics manager with a CT-CH style combination. Harry is very talented in project management and work flow organization, but his people management skills are poor. He treats his co-workers as he likes to be treated himself, which is by giving them a lot of autonomy and opportunities to challenge themselves. The co-workers, from their side, do not feel appreciated or supported in their efforts. Harry is also not aware of potential role conflicts within his team. His manager wants Harry to show empathy, to listen to people's needs, and to take initiative in resolving tension.

Harry complies with the coaching objectives, learns from his LIFO® profile, and translates his coaching needs in the developmental strategies, e.g. augmenting AD-SG behavior. Harry shows a quick understanding of the behavioral change with the complementary profile of Julie as a role model. But at the workplace, Harry is reluctant in developing AD behavior, as he keeps seeing it as counterproductive in his logistic setting. He starts postponing coaching sessions and doesn't commit to action items. Julie stays clear on the contract and confronts Harry with his responsibilities but without success. She eventually stops the coaching, as it is not the appropriate framework for Harry to make him change. Eventually, Harry's manager decides to redirect him towards a management role where he can focus on his CT-CH strengths.

In the example above, we learned about the boundaries of the coaching approach in attempting to change people's behavior. One can choose other solutions to make sure that everyone involved can use their strengths. (Appendix B to this article represents the style connections between coach and coachee, and gives guidelines in what helps to resolve differences and counter the coachee's feelings of fear and resistance.)

CONCLUSION

With the LIFO® model at hand, coaches are able to use a powerful tool to make the vague feeling of the developmental process tangible. The LIFO® coach will be able to establish awareness and change in behavioral patterns through a highly appreciative approach by:

- Starting with a profile review of the client focusing on strengths.
- Regarding the coachee as the expert of their own behavior.
- Aligning organizational purpose with the needs from the individual's viewpoint.
- Exploring incongruent behavior (intention-behavior-impact analysis).
- Translating behavioral change in simple but powerful development strategies: *confirming, moderating, extending, bridging*.
- Building consciousness of the coachee's own coaching profile and also what it means for the coach-coachee relationship.
- Adapting the coaching style to the preferences of the coachee.

Finally, it is my belief that not only the way of conducting a session makes a good coach. It's also about mindset, emotional intelligence, and creating the right chemistry between two people in order to reach the desired results.

	Supporting/Giving	Controlling/Taking	Conserving/Holding	Adapting/Dealing
Development goal	Optimal development for the coachee, making him/her aware of important values. Bringing hidden talents to the surface and developing them.	Developing required competencies, so as to achieve the business objectives effectively. Result-oriented coaching.	Listing and prioritising learning objectives. Making objectives measurable in the context of the learning plan. Providing step by step action plans.	Increasing the coachee's ability to enhance reputation. Creating advantage for all parties concerned. Learning in harmony with one another.
Context of the learning process	Supports, reassures and encourages. Relies on values. Very patient with slow progress. The coachee's request is the guiding theme. Creates the optimal, protected learning situation.	Creates opportunities and challenges. Action-oriented. Solution-oriented. Open and clear. Quickly assigns responsibility to the coachee. The coachee has to prove him/herself.	Provides structure to the learning process. A phased and logical approach. Expects the coachee to keep to procedures and agreements. Clear limits. Attaches importance to reporting.	Informal atmosphere with a high degree of consultation. Keeping the learning process enjoyable. Experimenting with new approaches. Dealing with the coachee's feelings sensitively. Enthusing and supporting.
Typical questions	Future questions. What do you want to achieve? What is the ideal situation? Why is this important? What could be better? How can I help?	Action questions. What are you going to do? When will it be ready? What do you want from me? How will this help? What is most effective?	Option questions. What possibilities can you see? What criteria will you apply? What risks are associated with the different options? Which options satisfy the requirements?	Perception questions What would you like best? How do you feel? What gives you energy? Who could be your ally? Who else is involved?
Dealing with failure	Provides understanding and	Immediate correction and	Slowing down the pace in	Understanding and

Appendix A: LIFO® Coaching Styles Dimensions

	Supporting/Giving	Controlling/Taking	Conserving/Holding	Adapting/Dealing
	acceptance of the behaviour but encourages exploration. Emphasises learning from mistakes. Critical but gentle. Is concerned and offers help.	rectification of the mistake. Allowing the consequences to be experienced. Reminding the coachee of his/her responsibility.	order to analyse how and where things went wrong. What are the obstacles? Measuring the mistake. Adjusting the plan.	empathy. Continues to emphasise the positive. Presents prospects optimistically and expresses confidence.
Dealing with resistance	Respects the resistance. Helps coachee examine possible negative consequences of behaviour. Convinces coachee of the importance of heading in the set direction with the coach.	Confronting the coachee, challenging him/her to maintain focus until the result has been achieved.	Incorporating breaks, leaving time for reflection. Detailed argumentation. Objectivising and channelling the resistance. Provide criteria for determining agreement.	Looks for a compromise. Allows feelings to be vented. Is able to see both sides of the disagreement.
Personal appraisal	Recognises the positive intention. Values commitment and personal input. Recognises contributions to group cohesion and the bigger picture.	Rewards the taking of risks and recording of results. Values speed and a responsible outlook.	On the basis of the agreed yardsticks. Assessment of progressive steps. Practicality and waste reduction.	Rewards creativity and enthusiasm. Appreciation of openness and mutual feedback. Assures the coachee of empathy.

Appendix B: LIFO® Style Connection between coach and coachee

	Supporting/Giving	Controlling/Taking	Conserving/Holding	Adapting/Dealing
Coachee's style – positive indications	Open to coaching and development Prepared to listen and receptive Does not interrupt Takes the learning process seriously Ethically interested Helpful	Asks direct questions Makes vague statements and ideas concrete Lively discussions May insist on speeding up the learning process Wants to demonstrate own competence Picks up ideas quickly and easily	Disciplined in agreements and procedures Very interested in details Notes down the different action steps Keeps going until the learning task is completed Wants to run a check or analysis with you Serious and businesslike learning approach	Aims for dialogue and consultation Enthusiastic about new approaches Enjoys sharing knowledge and experience with others Appreciates testimonials from popular people Is very flexible about behavioural change Seeks contact, open feedback, and communication
Coachee's style – negative indications	Does his/her best but becomes discouraged Does not respond confidently, becomes dependent Excessively critical or moralising	Is over-confident and takes control of the process Very impatient, addresses symptoms Gets into arguments and tries to browbeat	Picks up on details and raises them for discussion Spins out the analysis and delays taking action Always asks for more information	Beats around the bush and does not get serious Remains at the dialogue stage and does not reach any conclusion Makes concessions he/she is not happy with
In coaching it is advisable to...	Show personal interest Be guided by what the	Show expertise in the subject	Show expertise in the subject	Build a friendly relationship Explore needs in an

Supporting/Giving	Controlling/Taking	Conserving/Holding	Adapting/Dealing
coachee needs	Give direct suggestions about behaviour	Give direct suggestions about behaviour	unforced atmosphere
Act as a sounding-board, reassure and encourage	Work with short deadlines	Work with short deadlines	Be flexible about adapting arrangements
Refer to model behaviour	Make the coachee responsible for his/her own progress	Make the coachee responsible for his/her own progress	Give spontaneous positive feedback
Show that your own values coincide with the coachee's values	Check on progress	Check on progress	Remain diplomatic when discussing mistakes
Give expert advice	Give instant feedback	Give instant feedback	Encourage frequent contact

	Supporting/Giving	Controlling/Taking	Conserving/Holding	Adapting/Dealing
In coaching it is advisable not to …	Impose your own views Place too much stress on individual responsibility Only pay attention to the task Make personal criticisms Withdraw support	Set goals which are unclear or too vague Give endless explanations Take away resources Give too little responsibility Remove challenges	Be unclear about the steps, or changing them constantly Break agreements Get upset about mistakes Give feedback about progress Leave follow-up dates uncertain	Plan too tightly Take a detached and impersonal approach Judge mistakes critically or too seriously Have too little contact Fail to listen to personal concerns
Coachee's fear	<u>Fear</u> Not being genuine, authentic Not doing well enough <u>Signals</u> Critical about the situation Sceptical attitude Asking for advice and approval	<u>Fear</u> Losing an opportunity or benefits Taking the blame for other people's mistakes <u>Signals</u> Distancing him/herself from other people's problems Setting the boundaries of the learning process him/herself Being impatient, wanting	<u>Fear</u> Missing particular aspects of the learning process Finding him/herself in unexpected circumstances <u>Signals</u> Dwelling on details and points which still need to be learnt Asking for more time Asking for sources of information to rely on	<u>Fear</u> Loss of prestige and acceptance by others Becoming subject to strict controls <u>Signals</u> Diverting attention away from the obstacles in the learning process Going along with others' wishes Optimistic about the positive outcome of the

	Feeling discouraged, disillusioned	to make rapid progress Adopting an autonomous attitude		learning process
You can counter this fear by	Being as available as possible Showing understanding for emotional reactions Being reliable and remaining honest Ensuring confidentiality	Positioning yourself as an expert Keeping clear and brief, setting boundaries Giving opportunities for practice Giving tips which the coachee can use to improve his/her performance	Linking new things with existing things Structuring and regularly evaluating the steps Being generous with time and background information Providing a manual with possible problems and associated solutions	Becoming involved in the emotional process Coming up with comparable stories, examples which are appropriate to the context Helping the coachee look for positive anchors

Chapter 20

CULTURAL APPLICATIONS

The following articles, *Why Filipinos Are Known to Be Excellent in Service: What Their LIFO® Results Mean* by **Gem Brion Zabala**, and *Style Fit or Clash? How Generational & Ethnic Differences Affect Consultant-Client Success* by **Linda Wiens**, explore these applications of LIFO® theory.

⛐⛐

Why Filipinos Are Known to Be Excellent in Service: What Their LIFO® Results Mean
by Gem Brion Zabala

As stated elsewhere, LIFO® theory talks about the importance of "personal strengths" that each of us possess. The survey results describe our current strength usages, influenced by past circumstances and other factors that may affect present and future actions. The following article will show which LIFO® orientations Filipinos have that are contributory to organizations, as well as their society. These strengths have been influenced by our Filipino history and the way we were brought up, which helps us understand why and how we react the way we do in certain situations.

The LIFO® Method was introduced in the Philippines in 2004. We have been able to hold approximately 150 workshops representing different business sectors. The LIFO® Life Orientation Survey Version 2 has been given to more than 4,000 people. The use of this survey has given us a perspective on how Filipinos behave in favorable and unfavorable conditions. It also gave us a perspective on how Filipinos behave in favorable and unfavorable conditions. In addition, the results provided additional insights on how their behavioral orientations were influenced by their past experiences as a people - and how that may be changing because of the need to step up to the demands of globalization.

SURVEY RESULTS

The survey results reveal that the SG category was predominant as far as the main preferred style, and that the next highest, or backup style, appeared to be the CH style. The least preferred style seemed to be AD.

The picture changes when one considers their behavior under unfavorable or adverse conditions of stress and conflict). Here the CH and AD styles are the most prominent, and the other styles are less favored.

We will examine these results in the light of what we know as the Filipino culture.

FAVORABLE CONDITIONS

Supporting-Giving (SG) as Most Preferred Style. When using the SG style, the person's goal is to prove one's worth and be helpful. Filipinos' self-concepts and identities are strongly tied to their families. From birth to death, they see themselves in that context. For many, everything they do—or fail to do—will ultimately affect their family's reputation. This is because from childhood they have been trained to be accomplished and be the pride of the family. They are told that to do otherwise would shame the family. The Filipino family is a complex network of relatives tied together by blood and affinity. Affinity may come through marriage or religious rituals such as being a godparent of newly baptized children. It also includes parents and their children form the core family.

Filipinos' are also known for their "*bayanihan* spirit" in which they treat each other as one. The *bayanihan* spirit embodies the Filipino core principle reflective of the ancient Filipinos who had sailed together as one *balangay/barangay* (boat). Today's Filipino character is rooted in the prehistoric past, and second, it embodies the wisdom of our ancestors. Thus, the Filipinos' identity spirit lives on.

In the present context, the term *bayanihan* is now used to refer to teamwork, as acts of kindness and of humanity. Such acts are well practiced in the Philippines; Filipinos are kind-hearted beings who are always ready to extend their help, even when they know they are short-at-hand. They are very willing to share whatever they have, no matter how little they possess, just for them not to see their brothers and sisters suffer. In return, a warm smile will be given at the end of the day. (Driftwoodjourneys.com, September 13, 2012). This also supports the idea that the Philippine national culture is identified as a "collectivist" culture, indicated by their close family and community ties. Therefore, Filipino professionals can easily integrate and work together in groups (Fernandez, 2011).

Trust is also an important part of the manager-employee relationship in the Philippines. Managers typically have a patriarchal or matriarchal type of relationship with their staff. It's not unusual for managers to offer help and support when an employee must deal with a personal problem. In fact, managers know a great deal about their employee's personal lives, unlike in the US where involvement in employees' affairs is discouraged (perhaps not discouraged but often ignored), this is noted in *Manager-Subordinate Trust: A Global Perspective*, edited by Pablo Cardona and Michael Morley, indicating that employees give respect, gratitude, and obedience to managers who show strong interest in their personal and family welfare (Leviticus, 2014). To remain competitive, Filipino leaders and managers from all sectors must continue to build a workforce that is engaged and committed. (Ratanjee & Leong, 2014).

Conserving-Holding as Another Most Preferred Style. The Philippines was conquered by many cultures, including Spanish, American, and Japanese. This affected the Filipinos in a way that blends the behavior of all these cultural influences. The most influential in Filipino culture were the Spaniards. The Spaniards conquered the Philippines for a very long time, and as a result many values and beliefs are inculcated in our system. Filipinos were treated as "Indio" since the Spaniards were prejudiced against them. They became slaves that served higher-status Spanish people. Their way of living was to be subservient, and they didn't have any freedom to own anything. They just depended on the resources given to them by their masters. They were also not allowed to speak their thoughts because the Spaniards were in control. Hence, the Filipinos were trained to suppress their thoughts and actions in order to follow the Spanish master. In addition, with their freedom curtailed, they were trained to be cautious in their actions and to analyze everything before deciding what needed to be done.

In today's Filipino workforce, managers have traditionally been strong in giving direction and ensuring compliance with goals, but they must do much more (Ratanjee & Leong, 2014). This is a hierarchical culture where rank has its privileges. Decisions are reached at the top of the company, although a great deal of time is spent building consensus (SG) prior to reaching a decision. Managers are expected to provide their subordinates with detailed instructions that cover any eventuality (CT). Since they do not want to lose face (or have shame), many Filipinos are hesitant to ask for clarification if they are uncertain about a task (SG). Therefore, it is a good idea to use written instructions to supplement verbal communications whenever possible. (Intercultural Management, 2013).

UNFAVORABLE CONDITIONS

Conserving-Holding as Preferred Style. In times of conflict, Filipinos are very cautious and analyze all factors before they act, hence the CH style preference. As an example, the colonization of other countries led some Filipinos to revolt against them. But before they did that, they collated all of the information that was needed for the revolution. They took time to know the weaknesses of the other parties. Their style of revolution was through a secret agenda, like writing poetic materials and building alliances with other *barangays*. By this, the formation of Filipino values was set to be thinking first before acting. As a result, it took a long time before the Filipinos were able to gather enough will power to act on the situation and stage an armed revolt against the Spaniards.

Most Filipinos are shy and embarrassed easily (high SG-AD sensitivity). When they seem to disappear, it's not because they are lazy but because they are embarrassed to ask questions about the task for fear of how they will look to their superiors.. They either didn't understand or were not sure of the process. They are too shy to let you know that they are stuck on something. They don't want to disappoint you by letting you know that they are having a problem over the matter. The Philippines' intercultural adaptability and readiness for change is apparent, but because tradition is valued change is not readily embraced simply because it is new (Outsource Manager, 2013). Deadlines and timescales are fluid in the Philippines. Patience will play an essential part in successful cross cultural management.

Wait to be told where to sit. This dictum expresses the hierarchical Filipino culture; quite often seating conforms to the rank of the people involved. You may never actually meet with the decision-maker, or it may take several visits to do so. (CH)

Decisions are made at the top of the company (CT). Filipinos avoid confrontation if at all possible. It is difficult for them to say no (SG). Likewise, their yes may merely mean "perhaps" (AD). At each stage of the negotiation, it is necessary to get agreements in writing to avoid confusion or cross-cultural misinterpretation. Decisions are often reached on the basis of feelings rather than facts, which is why it is imperative to develop a broad network of personal relationships (Intercultural Management, 2013).

Filipino managers care not only about results, but also the processes that employees use to achieve those results (CT-CH). In other words, in the Philippines, the process is just as important as the results. Managers won't reward employees who take shortcuts or subvert the usual processes and procedures to get results. If the manager asks an employee to submit information or documentation to him using a form, an email containing the information might not be acceptable, even if it provides the information in a more timely manner (Leviticus, 2014).

Adapting Dealing as Most Preferred Style. Filipinos are resilient. Through times of adversity, they are flexible enough to cope with the situation. They try to see positivity in all situations, hence Filipinos are known as "happy" people. In building relationships, they are good in interacting with other people. Filipino festivities and other occasions are very common. That is why whatever happens, they still go along with life. This is very evident when some calamities occur in the country; Filipinos can still see humour. They mourn a bit but they do things in light manner.

Filipinos are also very flexible in learning new skills (AD) and learn fast, especially if these are demanded by the employer (Outsource Manager, 2013). If an employer is really interested in knowing the specific skills of the Filipino workers, being a member of online job-hunting sites is a good option. In these sites populated by Filipino jobseekers, employers can view their profiles, including optional resumes, which contain the work experiences of these individuals.

OTHER CULTURAL FACTORS

Actually, Filipinos are not very choosy about the type of work they will do. Most of them would say that the compensation is the most important factor to them. Let us not overlook the fact that all of them would love to have a job that is decent and safe, and will mold them into better workers and persons not only for themselves but also for their families and their country (SG) (Outsource Manager, 2013). Teamwork is becoming increasingly important in most organizations. The best ideas and solutions often come from having many people meet to discuss an issue.

The blend of CH and AD style Under Unfavorable Conditions has important implications. While timescales and deadlines need to be set well in advance and reiterated carefully, it should be understood that these will be viewed as flexible. Successful cross-cultural management may require some degree of patience (Intercultural Management, 2013).

Although Filipino culture is friendly and welcoming, formality is still very much the norm in businesses, particularly between supervisors and employees. Managers might expect to be called by formal titles, such as Mr., Miss, or Mrs., no matter how long they've known their employees. Respect is an important part of the Filipino culture, and those of higher rank or people who have advanced degrees are treated deferentially. It's not unusual for employees to show respect for their managers by addressing them as *Ma'am* or *Sir.* (Leviticus, 2014).

Most Filipinos are very emotional. They think everything is a big deal. You may not have recognized it, but deep inside they give more weight to your opinion than you ever imagined, whether it is positive or negative. How you give feedback really matters to them (Outsource Manager, 2013).

MORE SURVEY RESULTS: BACK UP BEHAVIOR STYLES

The LIFO® Survey Results also show that Filipino employees have Controlling-Taking/Adapting Dealing as back-ups under favorable conditions, and Supporting-Giving/Controlling Taking as back-ups under unfavorable conditions.

A recent study showed that about 35% of Filipino employees have been exposed to foreign cultures and management, such that self-expression and presentation of ideas have become easier and more comfortable for them. They have learned to adjust to the management of BPO companies that foster the qualities of confidence, competitiveness, persuasiveness, and even forcefulness. More and more Filipinos are also working abroad, so they have learned to adopt the culture and attitudes of the people they work with. Some have even married foreigners. This experience has a great influence on the upbringing of new Filipinos. This, in turn has contributed to a shift in behaviors.

Filipinos have seen the need to shift their attitudes with the demands of globalization. They have learned to adapt to the demands of work situations, and acknowledge the need to take on leader roles and become decision-makers. More Filipinos are also changing their attitudes towards entrepreneurship, becoming more risk-takers and owning their own business. This has led to a stronger economy, boasting a GDP of 7.2% for 2013. (Manila Bulletin, Jan. 31, 2014). (A critical question is, however, are they now being trained to extend their CT styles?)

Furthermore, the Philippines have produced a roster of great businessmen such as Henry Sy, Lucio Tan, Jaime Zobel Ayala, Andrew Tan, Jose Concepcion, John Gokongwei, Enrique Razon, and Tony Tan Caktiong, name a few who have made their mark not only locally but also internationally according to a Forbes list as of July 2013. These men exude confidence; strong will, and risk taking attitudes that have propelled them to the status they are in. For these men, their most preferred behaviour has been changed with the roles of their current position.

Having the strengths based on cultural aspects, there are other factors such as individual differences, socio-economic status, and education and training that can play a role in people's job commitment and performance. The experiences and situations that occur in the Filipino setting may differ in different countries. There is always a different story for how an individual should act in a situation. Based on the history of the Philippines, there are factors from the past that still manifest in a person's behavior in current situation. With intercultural management presence, the behavioral orientations of Filipinos are described as a blend of high standards and thoroughness. When the situation calls for it, Filipinos are also known as flexible with structure. They like to organize things out of chaos. It is best to keep in mind that national culture is not the only factor to consider in achieving the best performance from Filipino employees.

HOW CULTURAL KNOWLEDGE CAN INFLUENCE A CONSULTANT'S APPROACH

Respect for the CT style (from an SG point of view) means that efforts for change should have the endorsement of the highest group of managers. Communications of expectations should be in bold and colorful terms, highlighted by illustrations when possible (AD audience). Negative feelings, resentments, criticism, and suggestions for modifying the directives are not likely to be offered by the employees (SG emphasis). Therefore, it would be important to include some as part of planning committees—or to encourage discussions among employees about the issues involved and having a report that is based on "group" recommendations (to avoid SG fears about making any mistakes or offending anyone).

In a Japanese presentation, Katcher was surprised to find that no one would respond when he asked for questions. However, when discussion groups were formed around the room and groups were tasked with finding questions, many questions were reported in the name of the group. This allowed people to save face (extremely important in a culture that emphasizes SG and AD orientations).

When working with Filipino groups, periodic reporting of progress, with an emphasis on *we* would encourage identification with company efforts. This identification could also be reinforced, by showing pictures of outstanding achievers and groups (AD). It would be important to have well defined plans (CH appreciation) with clear expectations about the roles to be played by employees.

The consultant would be advised to spend a lot of time with the planning group, questioning them about their perceptions and desires for change, allowing suggestions for change to follow from the assessment of such discussions, and checking on the commitment. This will involve creating a climate where the expression of ideas is encouraged and not criticized—where value is provided by whatever ideas, criticisms, and suggestions are offered. This is influenced by the data on responses to unfavorable conditions (heavily CH and AD). The consultant may also have to bridge between the desires, ideas, and proposals of different groups, serving as a cultural translator for each group in stylistic terms appropriate for both groups.

Whereas action in as short a time as possible might be emphasized in the United States or other CT cultures, a more extended schedule would appear to be required for Filipinos, unless the proposed changes are a response to crises. Even in that case, time would have to be taken to assure that the people affected share the perception and see the need for prompter action. Slowness in response to new ideas, preoccupation with details of procedure and data gathering, as well as excessive avoidance of responsibility for failures, and providing pleasing and light comments to consultants should be warning signs that there are issues that need to be discussed. Observing this, the consultant can reframe programs or encourage expressions of feelings, doubts, and concerns to gather relevant data for changes that need to be made to original designs. Indeed, we have found that by obtaining LIFO® survey results of all affected groups, we can gain a cultural intelligence that enables us, as consultants, to frame our proposals in terms most acceptable to the groups we will be working with, thereby enabling consultants to achieve more with their interventions.

In facilitating change for more modern modes of functioning, managers may have to be trained in the importance of giving positive feedback for openness, innovation, exploration of all kinds of solutions, and even disagreement when they sense something isn't quite right or appropriate for the situation(s) encountered. This also should be reflected in choice of managers for promotion to higher levels.

⊰⊱

Style Fit or Clash?
How Generational & Ethnic Differences Affect
Consultant-Client Success
by Linda Wiens

Every LIFO® expert must thoroughly understand their own style and the way that style is likely to interplay with the other styles in a given group of clients. That is obvious, though it does not always happen!

What is less obvious is the way in which our ethnic and generational cultures shape the expression of the styles. This is important, too, since the consultant may misunderstand a style when it is expressed through language and gestures somewhat differently than what the consultant has learned and first experienced it. The consultant will be less effective and may even be rejected eventually, although by initial analysis the style of trainer and learners may have appeared quite compatible.

I think this is important to point out because we are often not aware of how quickly and significantly generational changes are now, and how rigid we tend to be in our own personal mannerisms and word/phrase use.

Here are three simple examples of cultural differences:

- Think of the changing use of hand and finger signals over time. Which ones are positive/negative? Which are new (high-five)? Which are unacceptable now but weren't in the past ("the finger")? Even facial expressions change meaning over time as well as between cultures. And these expressions are often associated with LIFO® styles!
- What does it mean to "piss"? (Not a nice word, right?) And what does it mean to "be pissed"? In the US, to be pissed means you are angry, and the word is now acceptable even on NPR radio. In Canada, to be pissed means you are dead drunk, and if someone else says it about you, it is highly derogatory. People over 65 in the US and Canada will probably not use either expression.
- Think about expressions like, *Whatever...* or *Just sayin'* or *I'm anal about that.* The first is a somewhat impolite way to dismiss something that may or may not be important. The second is a quick way to duck out after delivering a perceived criticism. The third is a way of making a CH excess statement (in favorable conditions) okay. These and many more are expressions of a younger generation that not only are foreign to an older one but are also often perceived quite negatively by those who don't use them.

The consultant may be put off by the "new" language and may not know quickly which style is most likely to fit with that expression—something the clients would surely want to know or think about. Furthermore, the consultant may use language to explain the styles that the clients or learners find outmoded and don't readily understand—and they probably won't say so.

In the LIFO®-based strength reports I provide to my clients, I have had to change language repeatedly to avoid misunderstanding – once from Canadian expressions to American ones, and more recently, to update for new expressions and for changes in meaning of old ones.

There are larger issues to consider. Changes in organization culture due to generational characteristics and new ethnic mixes can expand opportunities for consultants who take them into account. The awareness of and ability in working with changing organizational leadership can benefit consultants at any age and across industrial, business, and non-profit client organizations.

In the 1970s and '80s, I did a lot of work with industrial organizations in which the culture at the top was heavily CT-CH. SG tended to get lip service, and AD was considered "sissy" in quite a few industrial and business enterprises. *Shareholder value* reigned supreme. When *Excellence is Job #1* became the mantra, many company leaders had a hard time actually bringing it about. "Philosophy and Values" statements were prepared and languished on walls in many cases. Technical performance led directly to promotion to management—and often failure, since "soft skills" or "people skills" were considered HR responsibilities. Management-union conflicts often ended in strikes and lockouts as the AD element of sensitivity to groundswells, networking, and maintaining connections were largely lacking in top and middle ranks.

I was effective as a consultant, partly because I am CH-CT (thoroughly prepared), and, like my clients at the time, low in AD. As a female, I did not act feminine but was accepted as business-like and sensible. My only personal difficulty was that the leaders generally did not want to do the right thing because it was right (SG), but only if it also led to more profitable business.

At that time, I also worked with large hospitals. The nuns who operated them were just about as controlling, hierarchically oriented, and insistent on performance as the industrial soldiers.

Also in the '80s, one of my client companies was in the steel business. They thought their market was the Midwest US. When we, the consultants, asked who their competition was, they named Nippon Steel (in Japan). Suddenly their lights went on about the market! Some time later, they made an alliance and operated a joint steel company. It didn't work out well, due to the vast difference in cultures. That was apparent in the LIFO® styles of the leadership, as well, which were:

- Short-term perspective and planning (US: CT) vs. long term (Japan: CH-SG)
- Clear, reasoned, top-down decisions (US: CT-CH) vs. drawn-out discussions involving many levels and departments (Japan: AD-CH)
- Emphasis on production (U: CT) vs. emphasis on orderliness and cleanliness (Japan: CH).

Knowing the cultural differences, we predicted correctly that the alliance would not work. But things have changed in Japan, too!

These days, the alliances whose success is questionable are more likely with the Chinese. However, all over the world, large conglomerate organizations find new ways to work together. Client groups are increasingly diverse even for consultants limiting themselves to one type of business.

I am still consulting. I am still low in AD, though I think I now have added life experience, wisdom, and sensitivity. Without those qualities, I would have a hard time indeed, especially in understanding 30-year-olds: Most are completely comfortable with social media and manipulating many technologies but much less so with personal interactions. They loathe to learn things in depth, knowing they can always retrieve facts from their I-Phone. At 71, I might also have a harder time working well with Boomers (ages 50-60), many of whom have had an easy life growing up and take things for granted that I don't.

Given my life orientation and life experience, my likely problems would be impatience, a feeling of resentment that they don't take things seriously, and criticism of apparent low effort. Younger people, in turn, might easily regard me as much too "intense," demanding, serious, and "not with it."

I believe our differential life experience shows in the way we express our life orientations, as well as in what orientations are considered appropriate for and represented in different types of organizations.

There are far more non-profits through which society's work gets done now than there were in the '80s or even '90s. One might expect that the SG style is more strongly represented there than in business or industry. But is that true? The competition for the resources non-profits need has stressed the requirement to be business-like and to market themselves; and financial scandals in the business world have touched them, as well. It is worth a consultant's serious consideration and observation, in order to work well with any particular group.

Networking, *development* and *reaching out* are important buzz-words these days. Do these expressions suggest AD? I think so. But those expressions are also endorsed by leaders of other styles, who see their long-term value if done well, even if the leaders personally are not good at these activities.

I have repeatedly advised a very intelligent, achievement-oriented client in the hiring process. In the last ten+ years he has not (nor have I) found people who were even nearly as CT as he is. He is always seriously worried about whether they are "strong enough leaders."

Initially, I was equally concerned. I have watched and worked with some of these 35 to 55-year-olds who were hired, though their LIFO® profile did not fit their employer's (nor my) expectations.

As any LIFO® expert will know, people of other styles exercise leadership differently—it's not the prerogative of CT! But there is more to it than that. Except in some cases (Steve Jobs, Conrad Black), individual expressions of CT now are often softened, not initially by the person's own modifying style, but rather by the responses of co-workers and the team culture.

I suggest that changes in the way CT and CH are expressed at work are at least partly due to the fact that many people "in the ranks" are expert at their specific job, while their supervisors are not and never were. This fact makes hierarchy redundant and teamwork necessary.

Teamwork includes consideration of others rather than high persistence in one's own path or tendencies. Even though The LIFO® Method demonstrates that people of different styles can complement each other for greater synergy, it also points out that in excess—too much, too strongly put forth—each style can provoke others to excess rather quickly.

All of this is intended to help LIFO® consultants go beyond considering how their own style is likely to affect the quality and effectiveness of their work, given the styles of the client group. It has become increasingly important to assess the audience or client group for how the styles may be expressed differently and then interact differently, due to the increasingly rapid and major changes in generational experience and ethnic make-up.

Young consultants working with older clients will need to consider these differences just as much as the reverse. Furthermore, I believe generational and ethnic-mix differences are issues of escalating importance as our world becomes still more digital, virtual, and global.

Chapter 21

LEARNING AND TEACHING STYLE APPLICATIONS

Two of the overlooked applications of The LIFO® Method are those of learning and teaching styles. Nevertheless, the potential market is enormous. It includes all kinds of schools and universities, corporate training activities, as well as individual learners. Therefore, it seems only appropriate to include something about the subject in this book.

By now, you should be familiar with the fact that people have habits and preferences in all kinds of activities, even in learning and teaching roles. Perhaps you are a person who can only learn well when a teacher provides highly structured, clear and well-organized presentations. Others may prefer teachers who provide broad backgrounds, stress fundamental concepts, and allow for wide exploration of the implications of ideas. Some of you may prefer teachers who told you exactly what they wanted you to learn and insisted that you follow the paths that they described. Still others my have preferred learning from those who invited discussion and participation, illustrated concepts with familiar experiences and knowledge, and treated all learners with respect.

Imagine if you preferred the last mode and were faced with an instructor who favored the first mode. You might experience difficulties or find you lose interest in what is being taught. We believe that this does occur, and may account for major failures and lower grades when discrepancies between learning and teaching styles take place.

POSSIBLE RESEARCH AND APPLICATIONS

There are many possible areas to be researched in applying The LIFO® Method to teaching and learning, including:

- Identifying the prevailing learning styles and the distribution of styles from early school experiences to the highest levels of education.
- Identifying the prevailing teaching styles and examining changes as one proceeds from lowest to highest levels of education
- Studying the learning styles of students who are failing to learn and correlating those with the teaching styles of their instructors.
- Seeing the effects of providing instructors who can match their teaching styles to the failed students' learning styles
- Identifying the learning styles of students at the outset and, if mixed, either selecting subgroups of students who have similar styles and then providing appropriate teaching style instructors, or having two or more instructors of different teaching styles assigned to each class or group
- In training programs, using the above factors in the selection of instructors or students
- Modifying training materials so that all students can benefit from their training and educational experiences, especially valuable for on-line courses. Descriptions of such designs can be found in *Learning Dynamics* by Katcher and Czichos.

LEARNING STYLES

The four basic LIFO® styles that underlie all of the applications that have been described are equally valid for understanding learning and teaching. (For detailed descriptions of those styles see the above cited book on Learning Dynamics.) Below are some characteristic highlights.

LEARNING STYLES

Supporting-Giving (SG)
Strengths:
Careful
Receptive
Follows instructions
Thoughtful
Weaknesses:
Little spontaneity
Slow to reach decisions
Dependent when experiencing difficulties
Cautious, low risk-taking

Adapting-Dealing (AD)
Strengths:
Flexible and open
Enjoys novelty
Optimistic
Experimental
Weaknesses:
Acts without thinking
Takes unnecessary risks
Hogs the limelight
Gets bored by repetition

Conserving-Holding (CH)
Strengths:
Logical vertical thinkers
Rational and objective
Seeks practical applications

Questions when
needing clarification
Weaknesses:
Restricted lateral thinking

Controlling-Taking (CT)
Strengths:
Likes explanations brief
and to the point
Desires learning at own pace

Keen to test things out
Weaknesses:
Tendency to reject impractical things

Low tolerance for ambiguity, disorder,	Resists and resents criticism
uncertainty	Less interested in back-ground
Asks questions when fails to understand	Impatient with waffling
Pays attention to facts and details	

LEARNING STYLES SURVEY

A special survey provides information about how an individual prefers to learn. As an example, we will show how information provided by the learning styles survey can reveal valuable information about how a person learns.

JOE LEARNER'S LIFO® RESULTS

Favorable Conditions:				Unfavorable Conditions:			
SG	**CT**	**CH**	**AD**	**SG**	**CT**	**CH**	**AD**
24	20	28	18	30	14	26	20

From theses results, we can see that when in learning situations, it is most important for Joe Learner to:

- have a patient teacher.
- feel things are under control.
- receive clear and exact instructions about what needs to be done.
- have material presented in a systematic and organized way.
- have the teacher provide examples.
- have time to question, study and practice to achieve success before proceeding to the next step.
- have reasons for doing things.
- have routines that are consistent.

When things are not going well, Joe would like to have:

- a teacher who is willing to help in a pleasant way.
- specific information about what needs to be done.
- reassurance about capability.
- tools to analyze problems along with specific steps to take to solve them.
- time to get reorganized, review, and complete the task.
- distractions kept to a minimum and focus maintained.
- have teachers recognize that he feels badly about his mistakes and wants them to realize he is trying his best.

The worst kind of teacher for Joe to have is one who:

- is impatient and wants to hurry students along.
- skips from place to place.
- makes heavy demands and sets short time limits.
- shames students and criticizes negatively when they can't seem to learn.
- is disorganized.
- fails to provide detailed instructions.
- is not interested in helping.
- gets angry and demeaning when errors are made.

To improve his learning ability, Joe needs to:

- develop more confidence about his own ability to learn.
- let teachers know what they can do to help him.
- practice working at a faster pace.
- be less serious about everything that's being done.
- value his penchant for doing things thoroughly, for paying attention to details.
- explore more with ideas, to extend beyond what is known.

- learn to be more proactive in learning situations—to ask questions and probe issues.

You may want to review your own learning history and fill in the answers to the above categories to appreciate the information revealed by using the learning styles survey. Think about your learning experiences and relate them to the styles of your favorite and least favorite teachers. In courses where you were experiencing difficulty, what kind of teaching approach helped you most?

TEACHING STYLES

The LIFO® Teaching Styles Survey provides style information about how a teacher teaches. It uses the same four categories in the description of teaching behavior. Similarly, the four LIFO® orientations are used to describe how instructors teach their classes. Below, we have provided a brief description of teaching styles. Remember, too, that there are many combinations of these styles leading to modified descriptions to make them unique. We are simply providing a brief outline of the four major orientations.

TEACHING STYLES

Supporting-Giving (SG)
Strengths:
Provides background
information
Listens carefully to students
Invites participation
High standards
Weaknesses:
Lengthy and elaborate
presentations

Adapting-Dealing (AD)
Strengths:
Makes learning fun
Relates learning to
student experience
Encourages alternative
explorations Praises often
Weaknesses:
May minimize serious
side of learning

Overly critical
Loses time by attending
to individual students
and excessive group
discussions

May fail to correct
errors and mistakes
May sidetrack learning
by explorations
May not fully test what has
been learned

Conserving-Holding (CH)
Strengths:
Highly organized
Factual and detail emphasis
Logical and rational thinking
stressed
Provides clear and objective

Controlling-Taking (CT)
Strengths:
Makes major points clear
Emphasizes practicality
Is direct and does not
get distracted
Emphasizes his/her own
views explanations

Weaknesses:
Sometimes loses the forest

in the details

Fails to attend to feelings
Discourages intuitive thinking

Discourages lateral thinking

Weaknesses:
May be too brief in
explanations
Fails to relate material to
history
and alternate thinking
Focuses too much on practical,
too little on theoretical

While all four styles and their mixtures can be found, a study by Czichos revealed that there is a large prevalence of Controlling-Taking and Conserving-Holding styles that are used in schools and universities. Taking charge of what is happening, having an organized flow of topics and subject matter, testing for memory of details and recognition of key ideas, and emphasizing reasoning and logic tend to prevail, although there is more evidence of SG and AD styles (group discussion, role playing, and using metaphors and associations) increasing, the predominant emphasis is the use of CT and CH teaching styles.

It is interesting to note that while there is an expressed interest in developing more ingenuity and creativity teaching styles generally minimize usage of the AD style. Actually, in this book, we have fallen into an emphasis of SG and CH styles. This way of presenting information, may cause some consultants to lose interest.

In Chapter 6 of *Learning Dynamics*, Reiner Czichos describes what he calls "entertrainment," which is getting students involved by addressing all four learning styles. He provides a rich illustration of how teachers can extend their styles and have greater impacts if their teaching designs incorporate modules that provide attractive features for all of the styles. While we have described learning and teaching styles in ways that make them seem very different, they represent many underlying needs that are common to all, albeit in varying degrees.

Learning and Teaching Style Surveys thus have immediate practical application for all kinds of business and government training activities as well as educational institutions.

However, in companies where we have consulted, human resource and training departments have generally been concerned about the effectiveness of their programs, not only in terms of personal satisfaction and enjoyment but also in terms of specific knowledge, attitudes, and problem-solving skills that have improved as a result of attendance in the programs they offer. It would be worthwhile to study how different teaching styles affect participants in all of these aspects. It would also be valuable to load classes with one type of learning style, and compare the relative effectiveness of consultants and trainers with different styles. If, as often happens, companies tend to select people who "fit" their desired style, identifying that style in learning terms might make the selection of an instructor more appropriate for the group.

However, since learners may face teachers with less compatible styles, it is essential for them to be able to learn from every style. How can we prepare learners to extend and broaden their abilities to do that?

One possibility would be to train learners to identify the teaching style of their instructors, recognize what is likely to be emphasized and valued, and practice learning in all modes so they can benefit from every style. In our schools of education, we spend considerable time on teaching techniques but relatively little time on learning techniques! In addition, we spend more time on Controlling-Taking and Conserving-Holding teaching styles than on the other two styles.

In describing the benefit for a company that identifies the predominant learning style and emphasizing that one only, we may further increase a bias for a particular mode that can cause the company to lose sight of the value of other kinds of learning. Creative groups do tend to have a variety of learning styles in their composition. Providing different modes of input may also enable a group to extend its ability to learn—to think in different ways. There is a danger in homogeneity of staffing, as we pointed out in the chapter on selection applications.

Chapter 22

SALESPERSON-CUSTOMER STYLE APPLICATIONS

While the surveys for selling and customer styles can be generally applied to any situation, they are more geared to those where the interest is in acquiring clients rather than only for an immediate sale. In this chapter, we will be using LIFO® knowledge about customer reactions to sales and selling situations to selling approaches as the main focus of our efforts.

SALES AS THE ENGINE FOR GROWTH

In any business desirous of growth, sales is the driving force of the company. The best product engineering, and the most sophisticated manufacturing technology and fast delivery and customer service quality is not sufficient unless it translates into higher sales volumes. It is for this reason that sales recruitment, sales training, marketing, and customer service become key features of the drive for growth. While growth can be a function of direct sales, the retention of customers also becomes a prime objective. We will look first at how relationships are built that will lead to repetitive business from clients.

LIFO® SELLING STYLES AND CUSTOMER RETENTION

We will first highlight the different orientations, keeping in mind that a salesperson's selling profile is likely to be a mixture of these four orientations.

Supporting-Giving Selling Style. Underlying the focus of this style is the goal of making the customer feel attention will be paid to needs, feelings and concerns. Consequently, there will be such factors as listening carefully to what the customer indicates about preferences, determining attitudes toward sales approaches and company practices, previous experiences with salespeople, personal values, and interest in follow-up services. This approach will be stated in terms of reassurances to customers about their concerns, mode of dealing with customer problems and guarantees.

Controlling-Taking Selling Style. This emphasis is on behaviors that control the flow of the discussion. The salesman takes the initiative in greeting customers, asking questions about information needed to make the sale, showing product features, getting a decision, and commitment to the price of products and/or services. There is emphasis on quickly getting to the decision and finishing the final details of the sale.

Conserving-Holding Selling Style. There are two major concerns: 1) following a systematic approach to the situation and 2) emphasis on information. Such a person will not want to be interrupted to answer a question, if the question does not relate to the sequence that is being followed. Details of products and services are highlighted to an extensive degree. Such a salesperson believes that information should be the basis for convincing people to make a purchase.

Adapting-Dealing Selling Style. Here the emphasis is on building a relationship with the customer, trying to understand his perceptions of the situation, feelings and attitudes. There is an emphasis on convincing customers that the sales person is like a friend, desiring to provide a product or services that will bind the relationship and make for further contact in the future.

SALESPERSON'S STYLE RESPONSES TO CRITICISMS, COMPLAINTS, EFFORTS TO NEGOTIATE (UNFAVORABLE CONDITIONS)

Supporting-Giving Selling Style. There is a reluctance to get into a disagreement. Whenever possible, the sales person tries to give the customer what is desired. Guilt and discomfort will be experienced when sales are unsuccessful, and the salesperson will indulge in self-blame for the situation.

Controlling-Taking Selling Style. There is ready engagement with strong emphasis on what the salesmen believes is best for his or her cause. Pressure is exerted to convince the customer that the sales-person is correct. When there are signs of hesitancy, there will be pressure exerted to make the sale quickly. There will be little will-ingness to lower prices.

Conserving-Holding Selling Style. The salesperson does their best to remain calm, study what the customer says, and then try to logi-cally justify the sales position. There is considerable discomfort experienced when the customer becomes angry or expresses dis-approval and complaints. Reason and objectivity will be the major mode emphasized. If the situation becomes highly emotional, the salesmen may try to terminate the situation quickly or refer the cus-tomer to someone else.

Adapting-Dealing Selling Style. Every effort will be made to di-minish the tension, using humor or comments that show the cus-tomer that the salesperson understands what is being said and felt. There will be effort made to negotiate prices and to find some solu-tion that compromises any major differences. The salesperson wants to be sure that the customer leaves the situation feeling good about the seller, willing to return for future purchases, and willing to rec-ommend the salesperson to others.

COMBINATIONS OF SELLING STYLES

Of course, many salespeople may have combinations of styles that they emphasize in their approach, or know something about their own successes and limitations to know how to use strength management strategies to achieve successful outcomes, It would be extremely helpful if the salesperson had a main or backup style in the adapting-dealing area, so that if the non-AD style was not working, there would be the flexibility to shift to an alternate mode, depending on what is sensed about the customer.

By now, you should be aware to the fact that some one may purchase something from any one of these selling styles, depending upon the customer's own buying style. To predict an outcome depends upon finding a suitable match between selling and customer styles, other things being equal.

SOME PRODUCTIVE ASPECTS

- Establishing contact and friendly approach – AD
- Looking for customer concerns and needs – SG
- Knowledge of products and services – CH
- Being in control of the sales situation – CT
- Providing background and contexts – SG and CH
- Providing logical and rational bases for recommendations – CH
- Giving the customer what he wants quickly – CT
- Making the customer feel special and interesting them for future sales – AD
- Introducing customer to service manager – AD
- Providing assistance when sales presentations seems to be failing SG, CT, AD
- Following an organized sales flow – CH
- Handling customer complaints – AD, SG, CT
- Paying special attention to important customer life events – AD

SELLING PROBLEMS DUE TO STYLE EXCESSES

- Talking about self or company too much – SG and AD excesses.
- Talking about product features without attention to customer queries – SG and CH excesses.
- Striving for a quick sale, trying to close too quickly – CT excesses
- Failing to close the sale – SG and AD, to a lesser extent, CH
- Ignoring customer preferences – CT and CH
- Arguing forcefully to change customer's buying choice – CT, CH excesses
- "Buying the sale back" – result of overly focusing on all the features and failing to notice customer hesitation – SG and CH excesses

CUSTOMER STYLES

Supporting-Giving Customer Style. The customer wants someone to take care of him, to make it easy to connect. He hopes that the salesperson will be patient and willing to pay attention to his needs and concerns. There may be less certainty about making the decision to buy, so the customer will appreciate it if the salesperson will encourage the presence of an advisor or be willing to delay the final decision until the advisor has concurred. There is responsiveness to learning about product and service features. Guarantees and warrantees are seen as signs of trustworthiness, reinforcing the decision to buy. The customer would prefer a fair price, dislikes negotiating. Special discounts will be appreciated but not demanded.

Controlling-Taking Customer Style. The customer knows what he wants and desires prompt attention. There will be a tendency to resist different opinions unless presented confidently and with information that the customer didn't possess. The customer wants to feel that they are in charge of the process. There will be little patience with lengthy and exhaustive explanations; headlining and keeping things direct is what is desired. The customer may terminate sale if they get bored or feels time is being wasted, or may enjoy negotiating as long as there is the possibility of winning.

Conserving-Holding Customer Style. The customer is not likely to express emotion or feelings. He or she prefers an organized sales approach, loaded with relevant information. There is every expectation that the salesperson knows the features and specifications of products and services. The customer may comparison shop and raise questions about features and prices offered by competition. They will want to know details of guarantees and warrantees. If encountering difficulties or in conflict, customer may become silent or break off the sale process. There will be a determination of what price the customer is willing to pay and reluctance to move from that position unless a rational and objective answer is provided. Negotiating a price may be more the stubborn refusal to give in at all.

Adapting-Dealing Customer Style. Appearance and displays will be important, especially if they indicate success—the kind of place important people would feel comfortable shopping at.

This customer responds well when greeted promptly by a salesperson who desires to get to know the customer. The customer will respond by talking about self, interests and desires. There will be enjoyment of humor and responsiveness to salesman's conversation. Courteous attention will be paid to presentations. There may be some attempts at negotiation, but the customer feels satisfied when some kind of compromise can be reached. The customer may like being introduced to other parties, such as the office manager, service manager, etc., but will want to feel the same closure is made with the salesperson. It is almost as if the customer would like to feel they are dealing with a friend. There will be appreciation of follow-up calls to ascertain satisfaction with purchase and to identify any problems that may be experienced. Personal touches such as birthday cards and periodic contact will influence desire to return for future purchases.

COMMON PROBLEMS FOR PARTICULAR CUSTOMER STYLES

- Failure to greet customer and try to get acquainted (AD)
- Failing to attend promptly to customer or explain reason for slow service (SG, CT)
- No exploration of customer needs (SG)
- Taking too little time (SG and CH)
- Wasting time with lengthy explanations (CT)
- Trying to change customer opinion or desire (CT, CH)
- Being unwilling to negotiate (AD)
- Not paying attention to customer (CT, SG, AD)
- Lack of knowledge about product features (CH, CT)
- Deprecating comments about customer opinions (SG, AD)
- Failure to answer questions (CH, CT)
- Failure to reassure customer about wisdom of purchase (SG, AD)
- Arguing forcefully with customer (CT, AD)
- Unwillingness to negotiate (AD, CT)

SOLUTIONS TO PROBLEMS

- Providing framework for selling—training
- Emphasizing paying attention to you, to make salesperson pay attention to the customer, needs, interests, concerns and feelings
- Making customer feel welcomed
- Finding out about customer's buying interests and habits
- Observing and exploring concerns and questions

- Providing relevant information and demonstrations or illustrations of product use and service
- Discussing warrantees and guarantees
- Closing the sale, checking on hesitancies or resistance and arranging for payment
- Making customer feel appreciated for the sale
- Arranging for future contacts: service reminders, sales, checking on customer satisfaction about product or service.
- Having sales people understand strengths and limitations
- Knowing and learning to manage personal excesses
- Extending the practice of least used styles
- Where some limitations are strong, arranging for a sales team or pair to relate to the customer
- With customer approval, having event recorded, later reviewed by salesperson and coach so strengths and weaknesses of sales approach can be addressed, and training plans made for improving future sales.

OPTIMAL COMPATIBILITY OF STYLES

- SG sales style with SG customer style: AD and CT
- CT sales style with CT customer style: CT and lesser AD
- CH sales style with CH customer style: CH and some AD
- AD sales style with AD customer style: AD and some CT

STUDIES ON APPROACHES

Studies have been performed on recruitment of salespeople for retail positions in a department store. In one instance, the AD approach seemed to be most successful, and a selection program was initiated to select additional staff with high AD strengths, resulting in sales increases. However, one can imagine certain types of product sales where other styles would be more appropriate. AD types of behavior might be helpful, but high CH knowledge would be expected in selling computers, for example.

To use such findings for recruitment, it would first be necessary to ascertain whether different style salespeople do make a difference in sales, and whether a particular pattern has been most successful in that sales situation (federally required in the U.S. and this would be really needed, anyway, to justify use as a selection tool). It would also be valuable for consultants to see whether training could help those who were not using the "successful" styled behavior as much as might be required to achieve more successful outcomes.

SALES TRAINING

Katcher, Knodt and others have found the LIFO® tools and concepts helpful in sales training. Even experienced sales people have found it useful to identify areas they may have overlooked, despite their successes. In their training and those recommended for other trainers, extensive use of role playing activities is utilized, where salesmen play the roles of customers with different styles being treated by other role players who demonstrate various salesperson styles. Videotapes have been especially valuable in highlighting non-verbal cues as well as direct behavior.

In addition, some emphasis is placed on the use of advertising to focus on the role of how communication styles can influence different customer response styles.

APPENDIX

Appendix A

AUTHORS' BIOGRAPHIES

 **RENÉ BERGERMAIER, Ph.D.,** was founder and managing director of LPC. He holds degrees in industrial and organizational psychology from the University of Munich, and also holds industrial engineering and electronic engineering degrees from the Munich University of Applied Sciences. He has been a Fulbright Scholar at the University of Tennessee and a Summer Fellow at the Center for Creative Leadership.

René Bergermaier has more than 30 years of human resource experience, mainly with IT utilities and automotive companies. Before LPC, he founded HRC together with Dr. Ingwer Borg, and has worked extensively with HRC in all aspects of organizational surveys, as well as having personally handled major accounts for the firm. Before that, he worked at Digital Equipment for seven years as head of the human resource department at Motorola.

REINER CZICHO, Ph.D., holds degrees as a social scientist and as an economist. He received his doctorate in Munich at Ludwig-Maximillian University; his dissertation was about conflicts and conflict-management of managers. He has been a trainer, coach, consultant, facilitator, speaker and author for 37 years. He held the position of European organisation and people development manager with Digital Equipment Corporation until 1986. Since then, he has been an independent consultant. His competencies are focussed on change management and change leadership as well as on strategic selling. He is an NLP-practitioner and LIFO® master trainer

Reiner has been actively involved as trainer, coach, consultant and/or facilitator in more than 50 change projects, for example, with SAP or Deutsche Bank, as well as with dozens of medium-sized international companies, mainly in three industries: IT, finance, and investment goods.

Reiner is the author of eight books and of more than 60 articles, which are written in practical terms for managers and professionals concerning the whole range of theories and tools for managing and leading in change (change management, coaching, creativity and chaos management, account management, train-the-trainer, self-management, learning). Currently he is preparing his second book on change management, in which he will assemble his experiences and ideas from the past 37 years.

ALFRED V. DE LEO attended the University of Maryland and the University of Virginia in the fields of foreign affairs, economics and statistics. His professional experience includes overseas assignments at the U.S. Embassy in Chile and Argentina, and instructor posts at the University of Virginia, Duquesne University, and Andres Bello Catholic University in Venezuela. Until his retirement in 1986, he was at Exxon Corporation where his functions included strategic planning coordinator, manager of organization development, and senior advisor for training and development

Alfred's major consulting clients have included: Exxon Mobile's Latin America division, where he conducted workshops on leadership, idea generation, management skill training, executive coaching; financial institutions in Florida dealing with the development of their top executives and their strategic planning and direction; a top level Asian electronic corporation coaching and developing leaders and managers throughout their Latin-American operations. Presently, he deals with executive coaching, organizational team building, and the development of specific plans to achieve a competitive advantage in a client's market place, including its strategic position and brand development.

WILLIE DONALD spent over 20 years in a variety of management positions at Citibank, Scottish Widows and Bank of Scotland, where he was appointed to General Management and chaired a number of subsidiary boards. Afterwards, he joined Belgian investment bank Petercam SA in 2000 with whom he co-founded their UK subsidiary Financial Freedom

(Europe) Ltd., a corporate advisory and consulting firm specialising in product and funding development for financial retailers.

Prior to this, as head of eCommerce, Willy was responsible for setting up Bank of Scotland's online European business in The Netherlands, having previously headed up the mortgage business development operation in the UK. During the 1990s, he was responsible for developing leading product innovations including cheque book mortgages, equity release loans and the online savings account, iSave. He led Bank of Scotland's first ever securitisation programme, raising over £1 billion in the bond markets to finance specialist lending. As Sales Director, he led a 5 old increase in new business.

During his time at Citibank, Willy spent time in training and management development. He became an accredited LIFO® analyst in 1986, having been trained by Allan Katcher. This commenced a life long passion for managing individuals and teams to out-perform the norm. During 2007 he founded his specialist-consulting firm, Expico, to focus on executive performance improvement.

His clients represent a range of sectors including the oil & gas industry, financial services, professional services, manufacturing, FMCG, national sporting bodies and a charity. His principle activities include organisational development, executive coaching for individuals and teams, leadership and career development as well as sales and business development training.

He holds a degree in mathematics from the University of Aberdeen where he still enjoys a strong relationship, mentoring senior undergraduates and delivering workshops in positive communication for the Graduate Alumnus Association. He chairs the Mentoring Advisory Board at the University, a key strategic initiative aimed at delivering world class career mentoring to senior undergraduates through a global panel of over 100 mentors.

BETTY FORBIS has served as CEO of Barnum Associates International, Inc. since 1988. Prior to joining Barnum, Betty held various positions in several industries and managed her own business. Barnum Associates International Associates. She has a long history of leadership and organizational development that spans 55 years, working with major corporations in the United States and globally. It has a continuous record of success for over 45 years in Norway alone. A proprietary offering of BAI has been the Experience Compression Laboratory™ (ECL™), a leadership development process.

As CEO of BAI, Betty has expanded its consulting practice internationally and its leadership development workshops as well as the cornerstone program, ECL™. These Barnum processes have been experienced by hundreds of executives from all over the world.

Betty has considerable skill in utilizing various assessment techniques, especially the Barnum Proprietary 360 Leadership Assessment and the LIFO® Leadership Strength Management tools. She has designed, developed and implemented processes and programs for team development and strategy implementation. Her experience includes executive coaching, management training, and leadership development for both domestic (U.S.) and global corporations. Some of her outstanding creations are The LIFO® Team Coaching tool (TCT), the LIFO® Team Resource Workbook, and Barnum's proprietary personal coaching and counseling process, Inner*Vention

Betty received her education in psychology and anthropology at the University of Massachusetts and the University of Alaska. She is certified in coaching and implementation of Values (Hall-Tonna and Richard Barrett's Cultural Transformation Tool, CTT). She has experience with The LIFO® Method since 1988 and is a Senior Master LIFO® Trainer. Barnum holds the LIFO® agency for Norway and Sweden.

ROGER HARRIS is an experienced management consultant who has had extensive business, management development, and human resources experience with senior executives of domestic, international and governmental organizations in transforming core strategic business processes. This involved training and development designs, group facilitation and project management. In the course of his consulting, he has significant customer contact and experience in training sales/marketing managers.

Roger has been a leader of organizational improvement activities that required changes in vision, values, culture and norms to address short and longer term business requirements. He has been an advisor to senior executives in the development and implementation of winning competitive strategies. In addition, his experience includes working as a manager, so he knows intimately what is required to manage effectively.

Currently, Roger is the founder and owner of TABIC (Talent Assessment and Business Improvement Consulting). Before building his independent consulting business, he served in a variety of positions at Digital Equipment Corporation, Deltapoint Corporation, and Quantum Corporation. These positions involved working as senior human resources manager/director for computer industry corporations; principal consultant for an international consulting firm working with top teams; external and internal consultant providing plans and solutions for executive/leadership development, business process improvement, and problem solving.

Roger holds a BA degree from Regis University and has completed course work for a Masters in business at the University of Nevada. He is a former adjunct professor of management at Golden Gate University Graduate School in San Francisco. He designed, developed and delivered three graduate level (MS) courses in organization development and leadership for Golden Gate University in San Francisco; attended a four-week executive seminar in marketing at Harvard University. Roger is a Certified LIFO® Master Trainer, licensed to administer 360 degree and job fit assessments.

 **ALLAN KATCHER, Ph.D.** has been a consultant to a number of the Fortune 500 companies regarding organizational and strategic business planning, management development, executive assessment, performance evaluation and team-building. His client list includes such major corporations as: Cisco Systems, Citibank, Exxon, General Foods Corporation, the Hong Kong Bank, Household International, ITT, Litton Industries, Seagram's, Shell Oil, U.S. Steel, and the Xerox Corporation.

Allan is a co-developer of The LIFO® Method and was responsible for extending its use to 26 countries. Over 10 million people have participated in LIFO® seminars and several thousand professionals have been licensed to use the Method. In addition, Dr. Katcher developed and co-developed most of the LIFO® surveys, including the Customer Style, Change Management Style, Learning Style, Leadership Style, Marriage Style, Parent Style, Selling Style, Team Style Surveys and accompanying materials.

Prior to his work on The LIFO® Method, Allan was manager of executive development at Douglas Aircraft Company, the head of management development at the System Development Corporation, and a human factors scientist at the RAND corporation.

Allan earned a doctorate in psychology at the University of California, Berkeley and has taught at Brooklyn College, the California Institute of Technology, UCLA ,and the University of Washington. Amongst his publications are books entitled: *Managing Your Strengths* (co-authored with Kenneth Pasternak, 2002) and another, translated into Portuguese, entitled *The Importance of Being*

Yourself. Together with Reiner Czichos, he also wrote a book on the use of learning and teaching style surveys entitled *Learning Dynamics.* His latest book, *If We Knew Then What We Know Now,* co-authored with Irving S. Newmark, helps people to cope with everyday life problems. Included in his articles are those on the effectiveness of the Japanese management style, coaching with The LIFO® Method, LIFO® consultant and coachee styles, and many on team-building. Major interests are self-concepts, increasing congruency in communications, managing accelerated change, cultural diversity, and team-building.

GERRIT KNODT, Ph.D. Prior to co-founding InterContext, an international consulting firm specializing in the facilitation of change in business and higher education, Gerrit worked as senior manager for organization and human resources development at Master Card Europe; as training manager for DHL Worldwide Express (Europe and Africa); as vice president and director of training and organizational development for Citicorp's Global Payment Products Division, and as senior internal organizational development consultant to Citibank's consumer businesses in Australia and Asia.

Gerrit also held positions as associate dean of executive development and continuing education, University of Tampa; and director of international conference centers, Temple University. As visiting professor, he taught in the MBA, EMBA and IMM programs of Illinois Benedictine University, the Estonian Business School, the Audencia School of Management, and at WHU/Kellogg. Educated in Germany and the United States, he holds a BA in history, an MA in counseling psychology and a PhD in human resources development.

Gerrit's interests focus on managerial responsibility, employee rights, learning transfer from the classroom to the job, the evaluation and measurement of human resources development, and organizational systems change. In 1990, he was the recipient of the State of Florida's Walter Clausen Award for contributions to public vocational education and was cited as "Human Resources Development Professional of the Year" by the American Society for Training and Development. He has been a licensed LIFO® Analyst since 1986.

SHIRLEY MURRAY has over 30 years of hands-on human resources experience, much of it at senior levels within a variety of organizations, and is experienced in all dimensions of human resources leadership and administration. Overall, her experience spans union and non-union environments, family-owned and publicly traded companies, and also government and non-government organizations. Prior to consulting, Shirley spent 15 years in the corporate world and her last position was vice president of human resources, Toys "R" Us (Canada).

Shirley is able to provide knowledgeable and useful insights into the whys of individual, team, and organizational behaviors, drawing upon her experience, her Masters degree in psychology, and her certification in The LIFO® Method. Her track record demonstrates that she can develop effective, productive solutions for problems in these areas.

In addition, Shirley has been in instructor at Ryerson University and the University of Toronto, both in the classroom and through distance learning. She is also a noted trainer and conference speaker, and has had numerous articles published on human resources topics.

MARIJKE THEUNIS is owner and managing director of Human Challenge. She has been a strategic partner at LIFO® Benelux since 2011.

Marijke's consulting services include training, team workshops, Camino training, coaching, and organization development. She is a cooperative partner for LIFO® Accreditation Training.

Working with people has been the core business in Marijke's career. While supporting her clients, she uses her strengths, such as mutual understanding, spontaneity, and building partnership. Clients and delegates in training and coaching appreciate her enthusiasm, and the ease of matching to different people and business contexts.

Marijke received her degree in educational sciences in 1982 from Catholic University of Louvain and has been a LIFO® licensee since 1997.

LINDA E. WIENS founded the Prairie Crossing Institute in Grayslake, Illinois, in 2001, and served as its executive director from 2003 until 2009. Since then the Institute is under the umbrella of the Liberty Prairie Foundation where she additionally serves as senior associate for special projects. Linda has over 35 years of successful experience in all aspects of organization effectiveness work, including designing and delivering workshops and conferences; facilitating meetings, team building, consultations, coaching and mentoring; and helping companies with start-ups, turn-arounds, transitions, and transformations through strategic planning and sound implementation of plans.

From 1958 to 2003, Linda worked at Quetico Centre, a non-profit adult education enterprise and conference/retreat center in Northwestern Ontario, Canada. Initially, she designed, organized, and managed innovative adult skill training courses. Later, she became a professional organization effectiveness consultant working with mining, forest products, steel, manufacturing, small business, social services, and health care organizations.

In the mid-1970s, Linda became a LIFO® consultant and agent, using The LIFO® Method in her work with many client companies. She has valued this particular framework in many applications and has written articles about those experiences. For her last 10 years before retiring from Quetico Centre, she served as its vice president-COO, and then president and CEO.

GEM BRION ZABALA is president and CEO of ACG Human Capital Solutions, Corp in Makati City, the Philippines. She was certified as a licensed agent in The LIFO® Method in Los Angeles in 2004.

In her position at ACG, she has strategized expansion plans for the Philippines and Southeast Asia for The LIFO® Method and its applications, driving the first licensing agency in the Philippines of The LIFO® Method. In addition, she established OD Systems and implementation/applications of LIFO® Method; co-authored research on comparative studies of the LIFO® Method as opposed to competitors; co-designed, authored, and innovated The LIFO® Method Style Dimensional Tool, originally used in the U.S.; and expanded application of The LIFO® Method programs from core applications to advanced applications.

Prior to ACG, Gem was vice president at Ingenium Executive Search in the Philippines, and an active corporate member of People

Management of the Philippines. Her extended background includes being a practice consultant at Kepner-Tregoe Philippines (Manila Execon Group, Inc), where she served on the board of directors for the Philippine Society for Training and Development. She was head of the programs committee, responsible for coordinating initiatives for public programs for professional development.

Appendix B

LIFO® HISTORY

In 1967, the first LIFO® Survey (Life Orientations Survey) originated as a positive and structured tool to supplement organizational development efforts and group dynamics training. The LIFO® Survey helped people to understand their behavioral preferences, as well as how to improve themselves and their relationships by studying the interaction of each other's personal styles and strengths.

Responding to the feedback and research provided by groups, Stuart Atkins, principal author of The Life Orientations Survey, developed the instrument along with his business partner Allan Katcher and consultant Elias Porter. It was based on the work of Erich Fromm (including the concept of productive and unproductive character orientations, together with the concept that strengths can become weaknesses when overused), Carl Rogers (client-centered counseling; congruence between what people think, feel, say and do; which led to the LIFO® concept of congruence between intentions, behavior and impact), and Abraham Maslow (self-actualization theory and humanistic psychology).

People were fascinated with the non-threatening, easy-to-accept interpretations of their survey results and were delighted with the objective way they could now talk to each other about their strengths and behavioral styles, as well as to manage behavior more effectively.

After the positive experience of classifying their behavior, the respondents wanted to know what they could do with their new-found self-awareness and understanding. To answer these questions, Atkins created the Life Orientations Method to go beyond analysis of the LIFO® Life Orientations Survey results to include six developmental strategies: Confirming, Capitalizing, Moderating, Supplementing, Extending and Bridging. Atkins and Katcher also focused on the fit of the LIFO® Survey with other instruments, such as Hersey and Blanchard's Situational Leadership and W. Schutz's FIRO-B (now element B), which were other instruments used in the various programs of Atkins and Katcher.

To simplify and aid memory, the Life Orientations trademark was shortened to "LIFO® Method" using a contraction of Life Orientations. Atkins and Katcher soon found the demand for the initial LIFO® survey and The LIFO® Method outstripped their delivery capacity, so they started licensing organizational trainers in The LIFO® Method and developing workbooks to accelerate learning.

In 1977, Katcher began to focus his LIFO® practice internationally. Influenced by Peter Drucker (strength development and strength management), he expanded on the work, modifying the questions in The LIFO® Life Orientation Survey to tailor them to specific training topics, such as sales, leadership, executive coaching, teambuilding and organizational development applications. Today The LIFO® Method includes many topic-specific surveys, including: Leadership Styles, Change Management Styles, Coaching Styles, Customer Service Styles, Stress Management Styles, Learning Styles, Teaching Styles and Time Management Styles.

By appointing agents in many countries, Katcher spread The LIFO® Method to over 30 countries and had surveys translated into many different languages, creating a worldwide network of LIFO® practitioners and agents.

Atkins' LIFO® programs in the United States included Fortune 500 companies, small businesses, government agencies, religious organizations, universities, and hospitals. The programs emphasized the developmental strategies applied to management training, teamwork, individual productivity, and communications. He named this developmental emphasis LIFO® Training.

To date, over ten million people in 20,000 organizations have used the LIFO® Method and LIFO® Training worldwide. One of the earliest international agents, Business Consultants Inc. (BCon) grew to be among the largest consulting firms in Japan and also one of the largest users of LIFO® Training in the world. In 2001, Business Consultants Inc. purchased the two LIFO® companies, Allan Katcher International, Inc. and Stuart Atkins Inc., in order to integrate the worldwide reach and expertise of both companies. In 2009, BCon appointed The Schutz Company as the LIFO® agent for the management of the worldwide LIFO® business.

Appendix C

BIBLIOGRAPHY

Aronson, E. "The theory of cognitive dissonance: A current perspective." In L. Berkowitz (Ed.) *Advances in Experimental Social Psychology* (Vol. 4), Academic Press, 1969

Araujo, A. *Coach.* Marcondes y Associados, Sao Paulo, 1999

Atkins S. *The Name of Your Game.* Ellis & Stuart, 1981

Atkins, S. & Katcher, A. *Getting Your Team In Tune.* Nation's Business, March 1975

Bergermaier, R. & Czichos, R. *Die LIFO Methode.* In M. Schimmel Schloo, L. J. Sewart & H. Wagner (Hrsg), Personlichkeits-Modelle. Global Verlag, 2002

Brehm, J. W. & Cohen, A. R. *Explorations in Cognitive Dissonance.* Wiley, 1962.

Cotton, J. L. & Hieser, R. A. Selective exposure to information and cognitive dissonance. *J. Research in Personality.* 14, 518-527. 1980

Czichos, R. *Entertrainment Für Knowbodies, Train-the-Trainer einmal anders.* Reinhardt, 1999

Czichos, R. *Coaching – Lesitung durch Fuhring.* Reinhardt, 1991

Czichos, R. & Katcher, A. *Das lern ich nie*, Aachen, Shaker, Verlag Gmbh, 2012

_____ "Definitely Filipino: *Byanihan*" – post in *Driftwood: Journeys*.com, 2012

De Leo, A. V. *The Perils and Joys of Consulting: My Journey Through Corporate America and Beyond*, New York: Second City Books, 2011

Donnelly, J. H. & Ivancevich, J. M. Post-purchase reinforcement and back-out behavior. *J. of Marketing Research*, 7, 399-400, 1970

Drucker, P. *The Practice of Management.* Harper & Brothers Publishers, 1955

Festinger, L. *A Theory of Cognitive Dissonance.* Stanford University Press, 1957

Festinger, L. *Conflict, Decision, and Dissonance.* Stanford University Press, 1964

Festinger, L. & Carlsmith, J. M., Cognitive consequences of forced compliance. *J. of Abnormal and Social Psychology*, 58, 203-210

Fishbein, M. & Carlsmith, J. M. *Belief, Attitude, Intention and Behavior.* Addison Wesley, 1975

Freedman, J. L. Confidence, utility, and selective exposure: A partial replication. *J. of Personality and Social Psychology*, 2, 778-780, 1965

Fromm, E. *Man for Himself, An Inquiry into the Psychology of Ethics.* Rinehart & Winston, 1947

Heider, F. Attitudes and cognitive organization. *J. of Psychology*, 21, 107-112, 1946

Intercultural Management – Philippines – http://www.kwintessential.com.uk – June 15, 2014

Katcher, A. *A Importancia de ser Voce Mesmo.* Sao Paulo, Brasil. Atlas, 1984

Katcher, A. *I Am a Person: In Experiences in Being.* Wadsworth Publishing, 1991

Katcher, A. *Intention, Behavior and Impact.* Business Consultants Inc., 1989

Katcher, A. & Czichos, C. *Learning Dynamics.* New York, X-Libris, 2009

Katcher, A. & Pasternak, K. *Gerenciado Suas Forcas.* Rio de Janiero, Qualitymark Editora Ltda, 2005.

Kimsey-House, H., Kimsey-House, K., Sandahl, P. & Whitworth, L. *Co-Active Coaching: Changing Business, Transforming Lives.* Nicolas Brealy Publishing, 2011

Knodt, G. *Developing Excellent People Managers: A Road Less Traveled.* Xlibris, 2002

Knodt, G. "Do Your Homework...Don't Assume...And Use 'Fingerspitzengefuehl' or... How to Survive and Prosper as a Business Person in Another Culture." *Organization Development Journal,* 12, 2, Summer 1994

Knodt, G. *Effects of Feedback and Coaching on the Transfer of People Management Skills from the Cognitive to the Behavioral State.* Doctoral Dissertation, University Microfilms International, Ann Arbor, Michigan, 1991

Knodt, G. *Mitarbeiterfuehrung kann man lernen.* The Berater Guide, 2008, p. 94-97. Corps Verlag Gruppe Handelsblat

Leviticus, J. "Filipino Management Style in Business." http://everydaylife.globalpost.com/Filipino-management-style-business-41294.html, March, 2014

Olson, J. M. & Zanna, M. P. A new look at selective exposure. *J. of Experimental Social Psychology,* 15, 1-15, 1979

Osgood, C. E. & Tannenbaum, P. M. The principle of congruity in the prediction of attitude change. *Psychological Review,* 62, 42-55, 1955

Outsource Manager: "Tips on how to effectively manage your Filipino employees." htpp://outsourcemanager.net/tips-on-how-to-effectively-manage-your-Filipino-employees-part-2/. January 15, 2014

Porter, E. H. *The development and evaluation of a measure of counseling interview procedure.* Doctoral Dissertation, Ohio State University, 1941

Rapp, M. *Zur Wirksamkeit der Gesprechspsychotherapie in der stationaeren Alkoholentwohningsbehandlung.* Digital dissertation, Universitat Osnabruck, 2008

Ratanjee, V. & Tung, C. "During The Philippines, Next Phase of Growth." http:// businessjounal.gallup.com/content167096/ driving-philppines-next-phas-growth.aspx, Jan. 15, 2014

Rogers, C. R. *Counseling and Psychotherapy.* Houghton-Mifflin, 1992

Rogers, C. R. *Die Entwicklung der Personlichkeit.* Stuttgart: Klett-Cotts, 1991

Rogers, C. R. *Eine Theorie der Psychotherapie, der Personlichkeit and der zwicshenmenschlichen Beziehungen Entwickeit im Rahmen des Klientenzentrier Ansatzes.* Koln, GWG-Verlag, 1987

Rogers, C. R. *On Becoming a Person: A Therapist's View of Psychotherapy.* Houghton-Mifflin, 1961

Rogers, C. R. The necessary and sufficient conditions of therapeutic personality change.
J. of Consulting Psychology, 21: 95-103, 1957

Spierer, G. W. *Das differenzielle Inkongruenzmodell DIM –Handbuch der Gesprachspsychotherapie als Inkongruenz-behandlung.* Heidelberg: Asager, 1994

Starr, J. *The Coaching Manual: The Definite Process, Principles and Skills of Personal Coaching.* Pearson Education, Ltd., 2003

"The Philippines' 50 Richest," http://www.forbes.com/philippines-billionaire's/list/ March, 2014

White, G. L. & Gerard, H. S. Post-decision evaluation of choice alternatives as a function of valence of alternatives, choice and expected delay of choice consequences. *J. of Research in Personality,* 15, 371-382, 1981

Wicklund, R. A. & Brehm, J. W. *Perspectives on Cognitive Dissonance.* Erlbaum, 1976

www.ingramcontent.com/pod-product-compliance
Lightning Source LLC
Chambersburg PA
CBHW051851170526
45168CB00001B/68